Writer
~
Citizen

Catherine Houser
University of Massachusetts Dartmouth

Jeannette E. Riley
University of Massachusetts Dartmouth

Kathleen M. Torrens
University of Rhode Island

Kendall Hunt
publishing company

D1534655

Cover image © Shutterstock, Inc.

Kendall Hunt
publishing company

www.kendallhunt.com
Send all inquiries to:
4050 Westmark Drive
Dubuque, IA 52004-1840

*f*irst, this book would not be without my friends and co-authors Jen Riley and Kathleen Torrens. From the beginning, their total engagement and creative energy helped drive this project forward. When we finally made it to the red zone and I was in the hospital, Jen and Kathleen ran this into the end zone like the pros that they are. We began this project as friends and, I'm happy to say, four years and a few thousand pages later, we are still friends.

We've had a lot of help and encouragement along the way. Our friends and colleagues at the University of Massachusetts Dartmouth have been incredibly supportive. Nancy Benson, Susan Hagan, Elizabeth Lehr, Louise Nadler, Chris Peter, and Penny Piva classroom-tested *Writer/Citizen* in its various iterations. They each provided insightful and valuable feedback.

Personally, I'd like to acknowledge my family of friends. Susan and Arthur Ferrara provided moral support, countless steak dinners, and lots of champagne celebrations for this project over the years. My special thanks to Susan who never stopped believing. As always, Con Eschinger provided encouragement and genuine delight in every little success along the way. I've always felt my sister, Diane, and brothers Steve, John, and David have had my back, no matter what. Finally, I'd like to dedicate this book to my mom, Helen Elaine Asimakopoulos Houser Ray, who always kept the light shining on the path out.

Catherine Houser

Many thanks to Catherine Houser for starting the conversations that led to this project and her ongoing belief that we would finish and get this book out into the world. It's been a wonderful learning experience and journey, and I am grateful Catherine kick started this project that sent us down this road (despite all the work!).

For Kathleen Torrens, my thanks for her constant attention to the rhetorical tradition and her ability to share that tradition with students through this book. As the three of us believe, the effective use of rhetoric is at the heart of our democracy and how we each engage as citizens in the world. I am hopeful this book will energize students in the years to come.

My appreciation goes out to those who helped us review and fine tune the book along the way. Also, this book would not be possible without the inspiration of my students inside and outside the classroom who teach me as much as I teach them.

On a personal note, this book and the job I love to do each and everyday as a teacher would not be possible without the support of my parents, Dan and Liz Riley, who provided me with a world of opportunities, always stressed the importance of learning, and taught me that with hard work anything is possible. Thank you.

Jeannette E. Riley

This project came about because Catherine Houser said "yes" to a random inquiry. That word sparked four years of learning, writing, rewriting, and more learning – about writing, about friendship, about ourselves. For that journey, I thank her! The journey of *Writer/Citizen* has, among other things, re-energized my commitment to teaching and learning in tandem with a focus on citizenship in all of its forms. Our world needs people able to speak and write their consciences with clarity and purpose; I believe *Writer/Citizen* facilitates those skills.

I am also quite obviously grateful to Jen Riley for her energetic, organized, motivating, and always cheery co-authorship and management of our progress. Without her attention to detail, I fear Catherine and I would still be in the "big idea" stages of the project. Our partnership endures!

I must pay tribute to Phillip K. Tompkins, who many years ago told me I "have what it takes" to go to graduate school. Without that small push and his constant support and mentorship over the years, I would not be in the position to work with such great people, my commitment to social justice would not be as strong, and I certainly would not be able to quote Kenneth Burke at will.

Our families and friends surely wearied of asking about "the book." With their constant support and interest, people like Dan and Liz Riley, Karen Dolan, Lisa Evans, Laurie Herbst, and others all contributed to getting it done, even when they really weren't that interested. I hope the real thing makes it worthwhile.

Finally, my heartfelt thanks go out to all of the students who helped me think about teaching, communication, and citizenship, who offered me their words and thoughts as I wrote about rhetoric, and who were willing to learn.

Kathleen M. Torrens

Contents

*D*esigned as an introductory composition or freshman writing text, *Writer/Citizen* strives to engage citizens in their communities, locally and globally. Recognizing the importance of traditional writing theories, strategies, and concepts, the text reframes the standard writing text by focusing first on classical rhetorical precepts that underlay the democratic tradition. In other words, *Writer/Citizen* offers instruction in writing strategies and choices within the framework of "writing into citizenship." Students, addressed as contributors to and consumers of their culture, learn about the Western rhetorical tradition through history and recognize that writing, as a form of communication, significantly shapes their world. Through readings, a variety of writing assignments, and instruction, participation in a variety of public spheres is modeled for students as they are concurrently asked to learn, develop and practice the skills of rhetorical communication through writing.

Writer/Citizen highlights the decision-making opportunities faced by effective communicators. Rather than promoting standard modes-based essays, *Writer/Citizen* explores the rhetorical moment, complete with exigencies, audiences, varied purposes, and broad choices for appropriate, effective responses. Students learn that a standard academic essay may incorporate the strategies of narration, description, and persuasion, depending on their purpose, audience, and the communicative tools available to them. Students also learn that letters to the editor, blogs, and PowerPoint presentations may incorporate multiple strategies – all dependent on the requirements of the rhetorical situation.

Beginning with the history of the intertwining of rhetorical practices with the practices of democracy and citizenship in the Western tradition, *Writer/Citizen* frames the process of writing and communicating primarily as that of creating an effective argument. Students learn that the commencement of the writing process involves analysis of the rhetorical situation in order to determine their audience, purposes, and then to decide on types of evidence, strategies, and the ultimate shape of their message. Section One of *Writer/Citizen* focuses on the tools of the writing process, also characterized as the tools of democracy and citizenship. Analysis, decision-making, and strategizing effective communication are the overarching focal areas of this section. The writing instruction is embedded and integrated with the fundamental content dealing with rhetorical principles, the tools of democracy, and the decision-making tenets of the writing process, with the objective of presenting an holistic, almost organic approach to that process.

The case study, "Writing into Citizenship: The Environment," provides an important exemplar of citizen-focused issues that raise key questions of the modern rhetorical moment. The case study presents multiple viewpoints, multiple voices, and multiple writing strategies as models for student work and invitations for student engagement. For example, the reading contained in "The Environment" includes editorial cartoons as well as essays by conservative and liberal writers, including an excerpt from Michael Pollan's book *The Omnivore's Dilemma* and an op-ed piece from former Vice President Al Gore. These readings and examples are intended to demonstrate the various choices made by communicators in public forums as well as the strategies they employ to accomplish their varying purposes. By contextualizing and prefacing each set of readings, we challenge and encourage students to analyze the writing processes and decisions of each writer/communicator/citizen. Further, the readings are chosen with the hope of evoking student response – positive or negative – which can then be used recursively to generate productive writing assignments that serve to engage students in the ongoing conversations of these contemporary debates.

A key philosophical concern that drives *Writer/Citizen* is "it's all about decision-making." We feel that focusing developing writers on being in tune with, analytical of, and responsive to the challenges of the rhetorical situations surrounding them results in the citizen engagement critical to the contemporary moment. Rather than encouraging students to learn static responses to assignments "about" their world, we wish instead to model curiosity and engagement with, as well as responsibility to, that world. To that end, we present a potentially powerful array of situational factors and responses to those factors in an effort to introduce student writers to the multiplicity of opportunities and choices they have as writer citizens. ~

Writer Citizen

Chapter 1

Rhetoric in the Real World

*W*elcome to the world of rhetoric and public communication. What is rhetoric? We define **rhetoric** as the intentional use of language or symbols to accomplish a specific goal with a specific audience. Rhetoric is goal-oriented, audience-directed communication. Rhetoric is the foundation of public communication: it surrounds you all the time.

You have undoubtedly been rhetorical more than once in your life. If you have ever created a profile for a social networking site like MySpace or Facebook, made a public presentation, returned an item to a store, tried to persuade a friend to do something, or run for office at school or in your community, then you have used rhetoric. In fact, your application to college required you to use rhetoric if you were asked to explain why you should be accepted to the institution. Your application worked to persuade this institution to accept you. Whether we write or speak, rhetorical communication is something that we all do.

Rhetorical action surrounds us every day, whether we are at school, work, home, riding the bus or the train, or driving in our cars. We are bombarded with advertisements persuading us to buy something, people asking us to vote or believe a certain way, and TV programs or films portraying social problems or stereotypes. Your local newspaper presents information in such a way that you can find out more about your community and its concerns rather than a community in a different state. For example, a magazine designed to be purchased by teenage girls is likely to discuss such topics as makeup, dating, and school, so that the magazine's readers will enjoy the information and buy the magazine again. A magazine designed for young women ages 18–25 may include similar topics, but will present the information in a form tailored to that age group and its interests. In other words, we live in a world that shapes messages presented to us, regardless of whether we realize it.

Consider the social networking site Facebook. Mark Zuckerberg created Facebook to provide a place for students with classes and interests in common to connect outside of the classroom. Consequently, the site was not intended to build a community out of nothingness, but instead to foster greater community spirit and relationships based on shared experience, knowledge, and interests. Needless to say, Facebook as a tool of community building and networking has far exceeded its original purpose.

As you probably know, on Facebook people establish a profile, or online identity, containing information, photographs, videos, and other creative technological postings. People keep track of their schedules and of their friends' schedules. They invite people to events like parties or football games. They form groups that meet regularly in cyberspace and face to face. These communication practices have led to widespread growth in social networking sites—a success that is fueled by people's use of rhetoric to engage others. For example, your Facebook page may be designed to interest your friends with pictures and tales of your adventures. These bits of personal information keep your audience coming back. But if your audience was possibly a future employer, would you create the same sort of Facebook page with the same messages? Most likely not. Instead, you might turn to LinkedIn, another social network, which is intended for people who are interested in connecting professionally.

Facebook powerfully illustrates a contemporary communication event that has attracted thousands of people of all ages to communicate with each other on a variety of levels and issues. What's interesting is that through the use of rhetorical actions, Facebook—as well as other similar communication tools like LinkedIn, magazines, newspapers, and advertisements—are closely connected to how communities develop and how citizens establish and maintain a democracy. According to most scholars, democracy literally means 'rule by the *dēmos*,' that is, by the people or the many. Let's think this idea through:

- Democracy, in order to be effective, requires involvement and communication among citizens.
- Citizens need to be committed to something bigger than their own self-interests. As you will see in the next chapter, democracy thrives in cultural and symbolic environments in which most of the citizens are able to exercise their abilities to think, analyze, write, speak, and ultimately participate in public discussions and decision making.

Facebook, for example, exists because of communication and the freedom to participate. Even though Facebook requires membership and adherence to certain rules (and thus is not a completely free space), similar restrictions are imposed as a condition of membership in any community or democracy. Members must agree upon rules

REAL VOICES: "How Rhetoric Is Relevant to You"

Making Friends
- You can use rhetoric to communicate and share ideas. You can consider whom you are potentially meeting and shape your personality to better cater to their interests in order to find a common ground, although remaining true to your own ideas and beliefs.

Within the Classroom
- You can use rhetoric to aid your performance in the classroom. By testing ideas and participating in class, rhetoric allows you to discover facts, shape knowledge, and invite feedback from teachers and peers.

Planning Your Future
- You may come to college not knowing exactly what you want to do. You can use rhetoric to be true to yourself in order to figure out or pinpoint what you want to do based upon testing the water, acquiring the facts, and building a concrete plan of action.

Using Persuasion
- You can use rhetoric as persuasion in college for the following: applying for a job, internship, club, organization, or fraternity/sorority to convince others that you're the best candidate for the position and distribute confidence and power to yourself, so you get a step ahead of the competition.

—Greg and Derek

and practices in order to ensure the greatest good for the greatest number of community members.

In our world today, there are any number of examples in which such communication practices exist and flourish. They may not flourish for the greater good, and not all groups or communities are striving to make the world better, but democratic principles are nevertheless alive and well. Because we all engage in rhetoric by using it and consuming it, it is worthwhile to learn how to understand it. Rhetorical communication can change not just our personal interactions with our local community, but also the larger world around us. As such, *rhetoric is a tool*. However, it's important to recognize that rhetoric itself is neither good nor bad, but is instead an **amoral** tool—one that can be used for both good and evil purposes. It's all up to the user—and that's you.

As you work your way through this book, you will develop your rhetorical skills and interest in the communities you belong to and see around you. In addition, by developing your knowledge about rhetoric and building effective writing and speaking skills, your democratic skills are enhanced. When you observe or participate in weblogs, billboards, newspapers, TV news programs, campus meetings, political campaigns, or protests, you will know that there is rhetoric in action and that you are a vital contributor to democracy.

You begin your journey into the worlds of rhetoric and public communication by defining and exploring rhetoric in your everyday life. You will consider how it functions as a tool for communication and persuasion. By the end of this chapter, you will be able not only to define rhetoric, but also to identify rhetorical practices across a range of media that we encounter on a daily basis, to understand how rhetoric affects our daily lives, and to shape your own rhetorical acts.

Rhetoric as a Public Tool

Rhetoric is a form of communication that has been defined by many theorists. The basic definition noted earlier is just the beginning. Rhetoric has a long, rich history. Because rhetorical communication was first examined as a social practice in ancient Greece, let's first consider one of its best-known definitions from Aristotle. (We'll talk more about Aristotle's influence on rhetoric and public communication in Chapter 2.) Aristotle defined rhetoric as:

> The faculty of discovering, in the given case, all the available means of persuasion.

What does this statement mean?

- A **faculty** is an art or ability. So rhetoric involves some kind of ability to discover.
- **In the given case** simply means that one must look to the immediate situation. A given case, then, is the case or situation at hand.
- **All of the available means of persuasion** means that any person is going to have access to a variety of ways to accomplish a persuasive goal and must choose which persuasive (or rhetorical) tools to use.

Following Aristotle's lead, you can refine the definition of rhetoric to "the ability to analyze a situation and choose the appropriate tool for accomplishing a persuasive goal." For example, if you are campaigning for a seat in your student government, your communications will be focused on a particular audience and you will use certain strategies and tools in your messages. On the other hand, a letter to the editor of your town newspaper concerning the lack of recycling bins at the local supermarket will engage a different audience and use different tools.

Aristotle was extraordinarily wise to define rhetoric in this way because it requires people to think creatively and analytically about the situation they faced when trying to persuade people or make an effective argument. It is pretty basic thinking, but during Aristotle's time this strategy opened the door to new ideas about communicating orally and in writing.

You may be asking, "So, is everything rhetoric?" at this point. As you begin to understand the ways in which you can use and analyze rhetoric, knowing some concrete characteristics of rhetorical communication will be helpful. When you know what requirements must be fulfilled, you will know that you are definitely talking about rhetorical communication. Specifically, for communication to be rhetorical, it must:

- Be targeted toward an audience
- Have a purpose
- Respond to a situation

Rhetoric requires an audience. Rhetoric—because it is an instrumental, goal-oriented form of communication—must be directed at other people. Aristotle was concerned with the situation in which the communication was to occur. Part of that situation includes the audience for the letter, speech, or

> **Rhetoric...**
> - Requires an audience
> - Has a purpose
> - Responds to a situation

other communication event. This requirement effectively excludes self-oriented forms of communication, such as writing in your private journal or diary. The inherent social significance of rhetorical communication means that it is structured for an audience of decision makers or potential agents of change.

Rhetoric has a purpose. Rhetoric is concerned with society, social issues, and human matters. You could also say that the practice of rhetoric keeps democracy alive today. When people communicate about public concerns such as school prayer or the rising costs of higher education, their communication is a democratic practice; that is, people have a chance to express themselves on matters that concern them and, in doing so, have an opportunity to effect change. Speaking on topics that concern the larger society and how it functions is an important component of democracy and the act of citizenship. Although that claim is a big one—and one that you will see often in this book—it clearly points out that rhetorical communication is communication with a goal.

Simply passing time with your friends, whether in face-to-face communication, text messaging, or on the phone, is not necessarily communicating with a clear purpose in mind. Most of the time, you probably don't plan your casual conversation or instant message exchange. However, if you intend to motivate people to action or to change their beliefs in any way, such as through a letter to the editor of your town or campus newspaper, you will need to think through your goal carefully in order to figure out how to accomplish your goal. So, if your letter to the editor is an effort not only to express your opinion but to participate in a broader conversation about social change, it has fulfilled one of the key requirements of rhetoric.

Rhetoric is a response to a situation. Aristotle expressed strong concern regarding the analysis of the situation calling rhetoric into action. This concern remains true and important today. For example, imagine that your state legislature has determined that high school sports are too expensive, concluding that all high school sports programs should be eliminated. Imagine how upset people in your community would be at this prospect. What happens? Rhetoric. People in your community would call and write letters to their state legislators asking them to change their policies. People would form committees and brainstorm about how to convince the legislators to change their minds. Notice that regardless of how many people are involved, they have an audience (the legislators), have a purpose (to get them to change their minds), and are responding directly to a situation (the elimination of high school sports).

That rhetoric requires a situation to respond to may be a difficult concept to understand. However, if you think through all of the characteristics of rhetorical communication, it should eventually make more sense. In other words, there must be something going on that needs to change. You will find rhetorical communication at all levels of government, and more important, at all levels of community.

This textbook is a rhetorical document as well. Here's how:

- We have a specific audience: you.
- We have a specific purpose: to help to teach you about writing in a particular way.
- We are responding to a situation: we saw a need in college classrooms for a book that approaches writing as a rhetorical process.

Our response to that need, this textbook, is written and shaped according to our assessment of how best to accomplish the goal of helping you become a more accomplished writer who recognizes the connections between rhetoric, writing, communication, and citizenship.

Rhetoric, then, is an important tool to understand how we meet the challenges of communicating about important issues. In other words, when we see problems and events in our communities and the groups to which we belong, understanding rhetoric and how to use it effectively will help us solve problems, see how others might be using rhetorical strategies to accomplish their own goals, and make our way through the complexities of everyday life.

Writer Citizen

Now that you have a definition of rhetoric and an understanding of the specific characteristics of rhetorical communication, it is time to make an important connection to rhetoric's relevance to you as a student of writing and an active citizen in various communities.

Analyzing the Rhetorical Worlds Around You

You inhabit a very rhetorical world: rhetoric surrounds you. Through newspapers, advertisements, political speeches, television programs, movies, editorials, and many other forms, rhetoric informs and shapes our communities. The communities you create help shape your democracy. There are important connections to be made between rhetoric, citizenship, communities, and democracy. As concepts, these words are fairly easy to define and understand, but their interrelationships are more complex. It is especially important to understand how communities, practices of citizenship, and practices of democracy develop *out of* the practices of rhetorical communication. In other words, how does the rhetorical communication you see occurring around you, and in which you participate, contribute to the formation and sustenance (even the destruction) of community and democracy?

Let's start by considering these two questions:

What is a community?

How does a community come about as a result of the practice of rhetoric?

The roots of the word "community" come from the Latin *communitatem* (nom. *communitas*), meaning "community, fellowship," from *communis*, which means public and shared by many. This understanding of community is useful because it suggests that community is more than a group of people who live in geographic proximity. Instead, community also involves common interests, identities, and experiences. This expanded definition of community means that we can talk about communities that occur in cyberspace, in classrooms, or from common membership in oppressed groups, to name some interesting options. Further, these options allow you to delve more thoroughly into the everyday practices of rhetoric that serve to create, maintain, and often destroy such communities.

> **"What is a community?"**
> A community is a group of people who share interests, identity, and/or experiences and who are connected through communicative practices.

And now to the second question, "How does community come about as a result of the practice of rhetoric?" We have already determined that a community emerges when people share goals, interests, experiences, and/or group memberships in common. How do you discover that other people share such things with you? One useful concept to consider is that of identification.

The concept of **identification** is not as simple as it first appears because we are using it in its rhetorical sense. This idea was developed most thoroughly by Kenneth Burke (1897–1993), a rhetorical theorist. Burke, like Aristotle, recognized that understanding rhetorical practices in relationship to human communities creates opportunities for human connection and success in the public sphere. Burke also believed that such an understanding enables people to make the world a better place.

Kenneth Burke (1897–1993) was one of the first contemporary thinkers about rhetoric to consider forms of communication other than speech. Burke started his career as a music critic in New York City. Later in his life, though, he called himself a "word man," because he was fascinated by language and symbols. His books are significant to the study of rhetoric because:

- He developed a broad range of theories about rhetoric as **human action**.
- He thought about music, literature, poetry, and drama as **rhetorical events**.
- He built upon the work of Aristotle and other ancient theorists to recognize the importance of the audience and context to the meaning of discourses.

Burke's key idea about creating community is identification. He uses identification in a very particular sense, however—not just distinguishing, naming, or recognizing something. He uses a unique word to describe and define his notion of identification. Burke, in his book *Rhetoric of Motives*, says that "To identify A with B is to make A 'consubstantial' with B" (1950, p.21). Consubstantiality, in other words, means that two people are not identical to each other, but instead share important experiences, ideas, values—human substance. In fact, Burke defined consubstantiality as shared substance.

Think of consubstantiality as a tool in developing connections with other people. Imagine that you go to class on the first day and choose a random seat. The person next

CONSUBSTANTIAL *ADJ.*

Of the same substance, nature, or essence.

to you pulls out a notebook with your high school logo or mascot on the cover. You ask about the notebook, and it turns out that this person went to the same high school that you did, knows your brother, took math with the same teacher, and attended the same senior party.

- How do you find out all of this information? By communicating.
- How did the communication begin? Because of the symbol of your high school, which had shared meaning for both you and your new acquaintance.

It is the body of shared meanings, experiences, and knowing that identifies you with this person and establishes what Burke called consubstantiality and thus the beginnings of a community. A similar phenomenon happens on Facebook and other community websites. People find others with comparable quirks, interests, or experiences, and develop friendships, even forming groups. The groups and relationships that endure do so not only because of communication, but also because of sharing "substance, nature, or essence" among participants.

Consubstantiality in Action

Enraged at the senseless injury and deaths of their youthful daughters in crashes caused by drunk drivers, Cindi Lamb and Candace Lightner connected in 1980 to found Mothers Against Drunk Driving (MADD). Lamb lived in Maryland and Lightner lived in California, yet they had a terrible tragedy in common. Assisted by media reports, public figures, and fellow victims of similar crimes, these women built a movement and community of like-minded people that has become an institution in the United States.

You can probably understand how powerful a feeling it would be to recognize your loss in a public campaign to eliminate drunk driving. Because of MADD, people who lost children or loved ones in drunk driving crashes can recognize, understand, and share anger, devastation, loss, and anguish with others through the stories, advertisements, and presentations of the organization. The shared substance, or consubstantiality, of all of these like-minded people provided the momentum for the growth of MADD. The following statement from MADD Online demonstrates a very strong call to identify with others in the organization:

> We're dads and daughters, sons and uncles,
> friends and neighbors. And mothers.
> We're all ages and from all walks of life.
> We are many colors with one voice.

The MADD website statement unifies all people into a collective with one voice, implying that there is intense strength behind the effort against drunk driving. Someone motivated to join MADD is assured of meeting people who will share an important set of values and experiences molded by tragedy and concern. Here you can see the immense power of rhetorical communication and identification to create a community of national significance.

The fact that rhetoric can and does mobilize people to form groups and communities demonstrates that it is worth understanding how rhetoric works. Thus, it is important to acquire and practice the skills of effective rhetorical communication, whether we are writing or speaking. It is also important to develop critical skills of analysis or consumption of rhetorical communication as well, so that we don't buy every product advertised, join every group or cult, or believe everything that we hear or read. A healthy dose of skepticism goes a long way, as does understanding how powerful messages can be.

MADD Slogan, Used by permission of MADD National.

A Brief Review

The information in this chapter is important because the rest of the book builds from here. You should keep the following specific points in mind as you move through the next chapters:

- Rhetoric is the intentional use of language or symbols to accomplish a specific goal with a specific audience.
- Rhetoric:
  - Requires an audience
  - Has a purpose
  - Responds to a situation
- Human language and the use of rhetoric are the starting points of community.
- A community can be understood as a group of people who share interests, identity, and/or experiences and who are connected through communicative practices.
- Identification is:
  - A rhetorical strategy by which people share experiences, understanding, and meaning
  - The root of community building
- Democracy, in order to be effective, requires involvement and communication among citizens. This process occurs through:
  - The news—print, TV, the Internet
  - Blogging
  - Political campaigns and demonstrations
  - People caring about their communities
  - Many communicative media

Rhetoric in Action

- Select a website to analyze. It may be a site that you visit frequently to learn about news or current music or movies. Or you may choose a site new to you that deals with a current social problem. You will use the site to think about the formation of a community.

Developing Your Ideas: Thinking about Community

As noted in this chapter, a community is a group of people who share interests, identity, and/or experiences and who are connected through communicative practices. Communities often come about as a result of the practice of rhetoric. Take some time to read and analyze your selected website. Then, write a one- to two-page

Writer Citizen

response in which you: (1) describe the website; (2) identify the intended situation, audience, and purpose; and (3) explain how the website's rhetorical practices shape a community.

Looking Ahead

As you can see, the ability to understand, analyze, critique, and practice rhetoric will be useful to the person who wants to be an effective communicator, make a contribution to her or his community, or simply create the best possible life for his or her family. Rhetoric surrounds most facets of our lives, influencing our values, beliefs, and behaviors in important ways. As you move forward, you will need to hone your attention to detail through active, critical reading, which we discuss next. This type of activity and knowledge will enhance not only your reading, but also your writing and use of rhetoric.

Your Writer's Toolkit

Reading with a Critical Eye

Effective writing grows from effective critical reading. Reading critically means reading actively. In other words, you need to question the premises of the argument or ideas being presented, speculate on the ways in which evidence and support are being used, compare the statements of one writer with another, and consider what you think in response to what you're reading. In short, your goal is to engage with the text and not take the text at face value. There are key steps to reading actively:

Prereading. Active readers take time to consider key elements before diving into a text. These elements include considering the author, the title, the intended audience, and the assignment at hand. It's useful to keep in mind these questions when you first confront a text you have to read:

- What is the text's title? What does the title tell you about what you are about to read?
- Who is the author? What is his or her background? These questions might require some research, or your text might provide this information for you.
- Who is the intended audience? How do you know? Or is the audience something you have to determine after reading the text?
- What is your assignment? Are there specific questions you need to answer?

Prereading helps you prepare to read critically, to respond specifically to your assignment, and to attune your mind to the specific purposes and unique characteristics of the text you will read. This activity will also help you understand better what you read and, in the end, will help you become a stronger writer.

Annotating. Active readers take time to engage with the text on the page. Annotating means making notes in the margins, underlining key words, writing down questions, and marking sections of the text that stand out to you as you read.

Why annotate a text? Annotating helps you focus your reading and helps you develop an interpretation of the text, whether it's an essay, poem, play, novel, newspaper article, speech, or other type of document. Annotating builds upon your prereading activity. The most effective way to fully engage with a text and to figure it out, so to speak, is to question a text and work with it. In other words, you should "annotate" or mark up texts—write on them, make comments in the margins, draw symbols—whatever works for you so that you understand how the text works on a deeper level. Annotating means you are explicating your thinking process and figuring out how to approach and engage with a text. Also, annotating helps you remember what you've read. Keep these annotating actions in mind:

- Highlight key passages that you want to be familiar with.
- Circle words you don't understand so that you can go look them up.
- Underline or mark key terms that you need to know; write them at the top of the page or in the margins.
- At the end of a text, make notes about what you think the purpose of the text is.
- Put in marks where the text shifts so you can easily identify the turning points.

Ask questions. Active readers also question texts to discover how they work and what they say. You want to consider the issues and ideas you are reading, and how they are presented in the text. Here are some useful questions to ask when annotating a text:

- Who is the speaker?
- Who is the intended audience?
- What is the tone?
- What is the situation for the text?
- Who is the subject of the text?
- What is the text's purpose?
- How is the text organized?

Here are more questions that can help you further understand a text's content as you read:

- How does the author create his or her argument? Does he or she rely on examples, descriptions, statistics, analogies, interviews, or personal opinions?

Don't want to write in your book?

Buy a notebook and keep your annotations there.

Photocopy important pages you want to annotate by hand.

Remember, rhetoric:
- Requires an audience
- Has a purpose
- Responds to a situation

Writer Citizen

- What central problem, issue, or subject does the text explore? What are the causes and effects of the problem/issue/subject presented?
- How is the text structured? Does the author rely upon comparison/contrast techniques? Definition? Persuasive techniques? Deductive or inductive reasoning?
- How does the author's use of writing strategies affect how his or her ideas are expressed? Do the strategies help or confuse you?
- What type of tone does the author employ? Formal and traditionally academic? Sarcastic? Humorous? How does the tone affect you as a reader?
- Does the author succeed in conveying his or her ideas to you as a reader? Are you persuaded to believe the author? Why or why not?

Review and form your own ideas. Active readers read a text more than once and take time to formulate their own ideas in response to the text. Make sure to review your annotations and reread assignments before class. As you do so, consider whether you are ready to talk about what you have read. What ideas do you have about the reading? Develop your own thoughts and ideas on the reading and be ready to bring those thoughts and ideas up in conversation.

The following example shows an annotated text. As you explore this process, think about how annotating a text will make you a better writer.

topic *Audience is more than U.S.*

Recycling: A global work in progress

By Meg Bortin for the *International Herald Tribune*

Wednesday, February 21, 2007

Big Question

Why recycle? It is costly, time-consuming and takes more effort than simply chucking all the waste into a single bin.

Nonetheless, over the last two decades, recycling has become the norm in the Western world. Citizens pay higher taxes to cover the costs; municipalities enforce recycling regulations and refuse to pick up the garbage of households that do not comply.

Some people complain, but others get angry when they cannot apply what they see as eco-friendly solutions to problems like an overabundance of trash. In Britain, the 211,000 members of the Women's Institute, a respected civic group, staged a revolt last June, saving up food packaging for a week and taking it back to supermarkets around the country.

people "get" recycling as an issue/action

Even in France, where recycling got off to a slower start than in pioneering places like Germany and California, people have now come to accept it.

"A few years ago we had a hard time making people understand the need for recycling," said Reynald Gilleron, chief of sanitation for Paris's wealthy 16th district. "Now, given the importance that ecology and sustainable development have taken on in political life, it's become a no-brainer. There has been a collective wake-up call."

Still, there are issues.

What do we do with waste?

For one thing, various cities in Europe and the United States send their sorted waste to Asia for recycling, and one major buyer—China—may be having second thoughts. Last month the Chinese authorities ordered an investigation into reports that Britain, which ships paper and plastic to China, had sent harmful waste to Guangdong Province.

Who is responsible?

Some Westerners, too, are troubled by the notion of sending their garbage abroad and wonder whether Asia has sufficient safeguards to recycle used materials without creating risks to health or the environment. There is also the question of what will happen when Asian manufacturing powerhouses like India and China begin to produce even a fraction of the trash produced in the West.

Skeptics question recycling's cost-benefit relationship. If it costs less to bury trash in a landfill, they say, why sort and reprocess it? Wouldn't it be better to use the savings on other environment-friendly projects? *recycling? What are benefits o drawba_ _ = cos*

Proponents answer that recycling helps conserve natural resources and also reduces the greenhouse gas emissions held responsible for climate change because less energy is needed to transform goods than to obtain raw materials and manufacture new products. *+ = conservation, re_ global warn*

A deeper issue is how to create less waste. According to Gilleron, a new collective wake-up call is in order. "We need to reduce the amount of trash we make," he said. This, in turn, would cut back on the need for recycling. *How do we change?*

As for the actual process, the *International Herald Tribune* decided to board garbage trucks in seven cities to see firsthand what happens once people stash their trash in a recycling bin. *> Situation/issue of recycling is evolving*

What emerges is a global work in progress.

Reading actively enables you to participate fully in class discussions, as well as in other more public conversations with fellow citizens. Notice how the annotations ask important questions about the issues raised by the article. Following is another example of how annotation can help prepare concise responses to some key questions:

Reading Actively Means Asking Questions

What is the article's topic?
- Recycling

How does the article work?
- Introduces the question "Why recycle?"
- Explains that people understand the need for recycling
- Addresses pros and cons of recycling
- Suggests recycling is an evolving issue

What tone does the article employ?
- Objective and factual

Who is the article's audience?
- People concerned about waste
- People who don't know about recycling and the issues

What writing strategies?
- Author relies on interviews and current actions

What is the purpose of the article?
- To educate readers about recycling's current status and issues

Developing Your Skills: Close Reading

Now it's your turn to put your reading skills to work. Read Anna Quindlen's article "Write for Your Life." Annotate the article as you read, keeping in mind that your goal in reading is to understand more than the superficial meaning of the essay.

Write for Your Life

Anna Quindlen (1952–) was a columnist for the *New York Times* (1981–1994) and *Newsweek Magazine* (1999–2009). In 1992, she won the Pulitzer Prize for Commentary. She has gone on to write several successful novels, including *Object Lessons* and *One True Thing*. This column was published in *Newsweek*, January 22, 2007.

The new movie *Freedom Writers* isn't entirely about the themes the trailers suggest. It isn't only about gang warfare and racial tensions and tolerance. It isn't only about the difference one good teacher can make in the life of one messed-up kid. *Freedom Writers* is about the power of writing in the lives of ordinary people. That's a lesson everyone needs. The movie, and the book from which it was taken, track the education of a young teacher named Erin Gruwell, who shows up shiny-new to face a class of what are called, in pedagogical jargon, "at risk" students. It's a mixed bag of Latino, Asian and black teenagers with one feckless white kid thrown in. They ignore, belittle and dismiss her as she proffers lesson plans and reading materials seriously out of step with the homelessness, drug use and violence that are the stuff of their precarious existences.

And then one day, she gives them all marbled composition books and the assignment to write their lives, ungraded, unjudged, and the world breaks open.

"My probation officer thinks he's slick; he swears he's an expert on gangs."

"Sorry, diary, I was going to try not to do it tonight, but the little baggy of white powder is calling my name."

"If you pull up my shirtsleeves and look at my arms, you will see black and blue marks."

"The words 'Eviction Notice' stopped me dead in my tracks."

"When I was younger, they would lock me up in the closet because they wanted to get high and beat up on each other."

Ms. G, as the kids called her, embraced a concept that has been lost in modern life: writing can make pain tolerable, confusion clearer and the self stronger.

How is it, at a time when clarity and strength go begging, that we have moved so far from everyday prose? Social critics might trace this back to the demise of letter writing. The details of housekeeping and child rearing, the rigors of war and work, advice to friends and family: none was slated for publication. They were communications that gave shape to life by describing it for others.

But as the letter fell out of favor and education became professionalized, with its goal less the expansion of the mind than the acquisition of a job, writing began to be seen largely as the purview of writers. Writing at work also became so stylistically removed from the story of our lives that the two seemed to have nothing in common. Corporate prose conformed to an equation: information × polysyllabic words + tortured syntax = aren't you impressed?

And in the age of the telephone, most communication became evanescent, gone into thin air no matter how important or heartfelt. Think of all those people inside the World Trade Center saying goodbye by phone. If only, in the blizzard of paper that followed the collapse of the buildings, a letter had fallen from the sky for every family member and friend, something to hold on to, something to read and reread. Something real. Words on paper confer a kind of immortality. Wouldn't all of us love to have a journal, a memoir, a letter, from those we have loved and lost? Shouldn't all of us leave a bit of that behind?

The age of technology has both revived the use of writing and provided ever more reasons for its spiritual solace. E-mails are letters, after all, more lasting than phone calls, even if many of them r 2 cursory 4 u. And the physical isolation they and other arms-length cyber-advances create makes talking to yourself more important than ever.

That's also what writing is: not just a legacy, but therapy. As the novelist Don DeLillo once said, "Writing is a form of personal freedom. It frees us from the mass identity we see in the making all around us. In the end, writers will write not to be outlaw heroes of some underculture but mainly to save themselves, to survive as individuals."

That's exactly what Gruwell was after when she got the kids in her class writing, in a program that's since been duplicated at other schools. Salvation and survival for teenagers whose chances of either seemed negligible. "Growing up, I always assumed I would either drop out of school or get pregnant," one student wrote. "So when Ms. G started talking about college, it was like a foreign language to me." Maybe that's the moment when that Latina girl began to speak that foreign language, when she wrote those words down. Today she has a college degree.

One of the texts Erin Gruwell assigned was *The Diary of a Young Girl* by Anne Frank. A student who balked at reading a book about someone so different, so remote, went on to write: "At the end of the book, I was so mad that Anne died, because as she was dying, a part of me was dying with her." Of course Anne never dreamed her diary would be published, much less read by millions of people after her death at the hands of the Nazis. She wrote it for the same reason the kids who called themselves Freedom Writers wrote in those composition books: to make sense of themselves. That's not just for writers. That's for people. ➤

Now that you've finished reading the article, answer these questions:

- What is the article's topic?
- Who do you think the author's intended audience is? Why?
- How is the article structured?
- What is the purpose of the article?
- What tone does the article employ?
- What writing strategies do you notice?

Critical reading requires active engagement on your part. Each time you read a text, you should take time to annotate and ask questions of the text. Doing so will ensure that you remember what you read more thoroughly and understand the text's deeper meaning.

Summary

Much of the writing you will do in your college career and beyond will involve some combination of summary, paraphrasing, and synthesis. Mastering these processes gives you a powerful tool for effectively using information to support your own original ideas.

Before you summarize a piece of writing, you will need to read the material closely and carefully. After you have read carefully, annotating your text, you need to begin thinking about how to summarize what you have read. A good place to start is with the typical newspaper approach to information, ask *who, what, where, when, why,* and *how* of the material you've read. These questions provide a shorthand approach to summarizing what you've read, helping you develop your basic understanding of the material. If you can summarize what you have read in those terms, you've taken the first step toward processing the information for yourself.

To convey your understanding of information you find in articles, books, websites, blogs, and among other things you read, you'll need to take the next step toward communicating your understanding to others by deciding what shape your summary will take. Keep in mind that a summary should accurately and concisely include the key points of the original work.

There are two types of summaries:

Descriptive: A descriptive summary sounds like a report of each point of the text. In a descriptive summary, you'll want to systematically go through the original and reduce each paragraph to one concise sentence in your own words. Your goal is to take your audience through the source, point-by-point, in a narrative format.

Informative: An informative summary sounds like an introduction or conclusion of the text being discussed. Your goal is to present the main points of the source as concisely as possible. An informative summary is often more analytical than a descriptive summary, as you need to identify the source's main points clearly, while leaving out less essential information.

Keep in mind these objectives when writing summaries:

- Summaries contain the main ideas and most important points of the text you are discussing.
- Summaries in your own writing are used to lead up to or extend your argument as you draw upon an outside source for support.

Paraphrase

Although a summary is shorter than the original text and is intended to capture the key points of the work accurately, a paraphrase is a restatement of the original work *in your own words* that closely mirrors the original work. Summaries are short and concise; paraphrasing is often similar to the original work in terms of length and complexity.

The challenge in paraphrasing is to avoid plagiarism. **Plagiarism** is the use of someone else's words as your own. The act of paraphrasing requires that you rephrase the material and find a way to restate the key points, in full and in your own words. Your ability to paraphrase—to restate in your own words—what you've just read is crucial to being able to use sources effectively in your own writing. Paraphrasing what you have read is an integral part of the critical thinking process.

Writing effective summaries, as well as paraphrasing a writer's central statements, requires close critical reading. To practice these skills, take time to read the following essay by Joan Didion. Like Quindlen's article, Didion's essay discusses what draws her to the written word. Consider how you would write a descriptive summary of this essay and how you would write an informative summary. How would you paraphrase the key points of this essay?

Why I Write

Joan Didion (1934–) is an American writer known for her fiction and nonfiction. She has written several collections of essays commenting on contemporary life, beginning in 1968 with *Slouching Towards Bethlehem* and culminating with *We Tell Ourselves Stories in Order to Live*, published in 2005. She won the National Book Award in 2005 for her memoir, *The Year of Magical Thinking*.

Prereading: Why do *you* write? Freewrite in response to this question for 5 minutes.

Of course I stole the title for this talk, from George Orwell. One reason I stole it was that I like the sound of the words: *Why I Write*. There you have three short unambiguous words that share a sound, and the sound they share is this:

In many ways writing is the act of saying *I*, of imposing oneself upon other people, of saying *listen to me, see it my way, change your mind*. It's an aggressive, even hostile act. You can disguise its aggressiveness all you want with the veils of subordinate clauses and qualifiers and tentative subjunctives, with ellipses and evasions—with the whole manner of intimating rather than claiming, of alluding rather than stating—but there's no getting around the fact that setting words on paper is the tactic of a secret bully, an invasion, an imposition of the writer's sensibility on the reader's most private space.

I stole the title not only because the words sounded right but because they seemed to sum up, in a no-nonsense way, all I have to tell you. Like many writers I have only this one "subject," this one "area": the act of writing. I can bring you no reports from any other front. I may have other interests: I am "interested," for example, in marine biology, but I don't flatter myself that you would come out to hear me talk about it. I am not a scholar. I am not in the least an intellectual, which is not to say that when I hear the word "intellectual" I reach for my gun, but only to say that I do not think in abstracts. During the years when I was an undergraduate at Berkeley I tried, with a kind of hopeless late-adolescent energy, to buy some temporary visa into the world of ideas, to forge for myself a mind that could deal with the abstract.

In short I tried to think. I failed. My attention veered inexorably back to the specific, to the tangible, to what was generally considered, by everyone I knew then and for that matter have known since, the peripheral. I would try to contemplate the Hegelian dialectic and would find myself concentrating instead on a flowering pear tree outside my window and the particular way the petals fell on my floor. I would try to read linguistic theory and would find myself wondering instead if the lights were on in the bevatron up the hill. When I say that I was wondering if the lights were on in the bevatron you might immediately suspect, if you deal in ideas at all, that I was registering the bevatron as a political symbol, thinking in shorthand about the military-industrial complex and its role in the university community, but you would be wrong. I was only wondering if the lights were on in the bevatron, and how they looked. A physical fact.

I had trouble graduating from Berkeley, not because of this inability to deal with ideas—I was majoring in English, and I could locate the house-and-garden imagery in "The Portrait of a Lady" as well as the next person, "imagery" being by definition the kind of specific that got my attention—but simply because I had neglected to take a course in Milton. For reasons which now sound baroque I needed a degree by the end of that summer, and the English department finally agreed, if I would come down to Sacramento every Friday and talk about the cosmology of "Paradise Lost," to certify me proficient in Milton. I did this. Some Fridays I took the Greyhound bus, other Fridays I caught the Southern Pacific's City of San Francisco on the last leg of its transcontinental trip. I can no longer tell you whether Milton put the sun or the earth at the center of his universe in "Paradise Lost," the central question of at least one century and a topic about which I wrote 10,000 words that summer, but I can still recall the exact rancidity of the butter in City of San Francisco's dining car, and the way the tinted windows on the greyhound bus cast the oil refineries around Carquinez Straits into a grayed and obscurely sinister light. In short my attention was always on the periphery, on what I could see and taste and touch, on the butter, and the Greyhound bus. During those years I was traveling on what I knew to be a very shaky passport, forged papers: I knew that I was no legitimate resident in any world of ideas. I knew I couldn't think. All I knew then was what I couldn't do. All I knew then was what I wasn't, and it took me some years to discover what I was.

Which was a writer.

By which I mean not a "good" writer or a "bad" writer but simply a writer, a person whose most absorbed and passionate hours are spent arranging words on pieces of paper. Had my credentials been in order I would never have become a writer. Had I been blessed with even limited access to my own mind there would have been no reason to write. I write entirely to find out what I'm thinking, what I'm looking at, what I see and what it means. What I want to what I fear. Why did the oil refineries around Carquinez Straits seem sinister to me in the summer of 1956? Why have the night lights in the bevatron burned in my mind for twenty years? *What is going on in these pictures in my mind?*

When I talk about pictures in my mind I am talking, quite specifically, about images that shimmer around the edges. There used to be an illustration in every elementary psychology book showing a cat drawn by a patient in varying stages of schizophrenia. This cat had a shimmer around it. You could see the molecular structure breaking down at the very edges of the cat: the cat became the background and the background the cat, everything interacting, exchanging ions. People on hallucinogens describe the same perception of objects. I'm not a schizophrenic, nor do I take hallucinogens, but certain images do shimmer for me. Look hard enough, and you can't miss the shimmer. It's there. You can't think too much about these pictures that shimmer. You just lie low and let them develop. You stay quiet. You don't talk to many people and you keep your nervous system from shorting out and you try to locate the cat in the shimmer, the grammar in the picture.

Just as I meant "shimmer" literally I mean "grammar" literally. Grammar is a piano I play by ear, since I seem to have been out of school the year the rules were mentioned. All I know of grammar is its infinite power. To shift the structure of a sentence alters the meaning of that sentence, as definitely and inflexibly as the position of a camera alters the meaning of the object being photographed. Many people know about camera angles now, but not so many know about sentences. The arrangement of words matters, and the arrangement you want can be found in the picture in your mind. The picture dictates the arrangement. The picture dictates whether this will be a sentence with or without clauses, a sentence that ends hard or a dying-fall sentence, long or short, active or passive. The picture tells you how to arrange words and the arrangement of the words tells you, or tells me, what's going on in the picture *Nota bene:*

It tells you.

You don't tell it.

Let me show you what I mean by pictures in the mind. I began "Play It As It Lays" just as I have begun each of my novels, with no notion of "character" or "plot" or even "incident." I had only two pictures in my mind, more about which later, and a technical intention, which was to write a novel so elliptical and fast that it would be over before you noticed it, a novel so fast that it would scarcely exist on the page at all. About the pictures: the first was of white space. Empty space. This was clearly the picture dictated the narrative intention of the book- a book in which anything that happened would happen off the page, a "white" book to which the reader would have to bring his or her own bad dreams- and yet this picture told me no "story," suggested no situation. The second picture did. This second picture was of something actually witnessed. A young woman with long hair and a short white halter dress walks through a casino at the Riviera in Las Vegas at one in the morning. She crosses the casino alone and picks up a house telephone. I watch her because I have heard her paged, and recognize her name: she is a minor actress I see around Los Angeles from time to time, in places like Jax and once in a gynecologist's office in the Beverly Hills Clinic, but never have met. I know nothing about her. Who is paging her? Why is she here to be paged? How exactly did she come to this? It was precisely the moment in Las Vegas that made "Play It As It Lays" begin to tell itself to me, but the moment appears in the novel only obliquely, in a chapter which beings:

"Maria made a list of things she would never do. She would never: walk through the Sands or Caesar's alone after midnight. She would never: ball at a party, do S-M unless she wanted to, borrow furs from Abe Lipsey, deal. She would never: carry a Yorkshire in Beverly Hills."

That is the beginning of the chapter and that is the end of the chapter, which may suggest what I meant by "white space."

I recall having a number of pictures in my mind when I began the novel I just finished, "A Book of Common Prayer." As a matter of fact one of these pictures was of that bevatron I mentioned, although I would be hard to tell you a story in which nuclear energy figured. Another was a newspaper photograph of a hijacked 707 burning on the desert in the Middle East. Another was the night view from a room in which I once spent a week with paratyphoid, a hotel room on the Colombian coast. My husband and I seemed to be on the Colombian coast representing the United States of American at a film festival (I recall invoking the name "Jack Valenti a lot, as if its reiteration could make me well), and it was a bad place to have fever, not only because my indisposition offended our hosts but because every night in this hotel the generator failed. The lights went out. The elevator stopped. My husband would go to the event of the evening and make excuses for me and I would stay alone in this hotel room, in the dark. I remember standing at the window trying to call Bogotá (the telephone seemed to work on the same principle as the generator) and watching the night wind come up and wondering what I was doing eleven degrees off the equator with a fever of 103. The view from that window definitely figures in "A Book of Common Prayer," as does the burning 707, and yet none of these pictures told me the story I needed.

The picture that did, the picture that shimmered and made these other images coalesce, was the Panama airport at 6 A.M. I was in this airport only once, on a plane to Bogotá that stopped for an hour to refuel, but the way it looked that morning remained superimposed on everything I saw until the day I finished "A Book of Common Prayer." I lived in that airport for several years. I can still feel the hot air when I step off the plane, can see the heat already rising off the tarmac at 6 A.M. I can feel my skirt damp and wrinkled on my legs. I can feel the asphalt stick to my sandals. I remember the big tail of a Pan American plane floating motionless down at the end of the tarmac. I remember the sound of a slot machine in the waiting room. I could tell you that I remember a particular woman in the airport, an American woman, a *norteamericana, a thin norteamericana* about 40 who wore a big square emerald in lieu of a wedding ring, but there was no such woman there.

I put this woman in the airport later. I made this woman up, just as I later made up a country to put the airport in, and a family to run the country. This woman in the airport is neither catching a plane nor meeting one. She is ordering tea in the airport coffee shop. In fact she is not simply "ordering" tea but insisting that the water be boiled, in front of her, for twenty minutes. Why is this woman in this airport? Why is she going nowhere, where had she been? Where did she get that big emerald? What derangement, or disassociation, makes her believe that her will to see the water boiled can possibly prevail?

"She had been going to one airport or another for four months, one could see it, looking at the visas on her passport. All those airports where Charlotte Douglas's passport had been stamped would have looked alike. Sometimes the sign on the tower would say 'Bienvenidos' and sometimes the sign on the tower would say 'Bienvenue,' some places were wet and hot and other dry and hot, but at each of these airports the pastel concrete walls would rust and stain and the swamp off the runway would be littered with the fuselages of cannibalized Fairchild F-227's and the water would need boiling.

"I knew why Charlotte went to the airport even if Victor did not.

"I knew about airports."

These lines appear about halfway through *A Book of Common Prayer*, but I wrote them during the second week I worked on the book, long before I had any idea where Charlotte Douglas had been or why she went to airports. Until I wrote these lines I had no character called Victor in mind: the necessity for mentioning a name, and the name "Victor," occurred to me as I wrote the sentence. *I knew why Charlotte went to the airport* sounded incomplete. *I knew why Charlotte went to the airport even if Victor did not* carried a little more narrative drive. Most important of all, until I wrote these lines I did not know who "I" was, who was telling the story. I had intended until that moment that the "I" be no more than the voice of the author, a 19th-century omniscient narrator. But there it was:

"I knew why Charlotte went to the airport even if Victor did not.

"I knew about airports."

This "I" was the voice of no author in my house. This "I" was someone who not only knew why Charlotte went to the airport but also knew someone called "Victor." Who was Victor? Who was this narrator? Why was this narrator telling me this story? Let me tell you one thing about why writers write: had I known the answer to any of these questions I would never have needed to write a novel. ∿

Comprehending the Text

1. Why did Didion title her essay "Why I Write"?

2. According to Didion, what is the act of writing about? Summarize her ideas in one or two paragraphs.

3. What does Didion mean when she talks about "pictures in her mind"? How would you explain her concept in your own words?

Analyzing the Text

1. Who do you think Didion's target audience is? How do you know?

2. What type of tone does Didion employ and how does that tone affect you as a reader?

3. What do you think is the overall purpose of Didion's essay and how does she make you, the reader, understand that purpose?

Synthesis

Summary and paraphrase will lead you, ultimately, to synthesis. All sorts of writing situations require that you synthesize information; in other words, you need to combine various ideas from the texts you encounter into a new text that you create. Sounds simple, but it takes some practice to achieve an effective synthesis. Summary and paraphrase are often part of a synthesis. For example, you may be writing about the importance of the U.S. Census, which requires you to paraphrase a journal article *and* to summarize a newspaper feature as part of your own argument about the significance of the census process.

However, synthesis is more than just summarizing and paraphrasing other sources. Think of it like making brownies. You have the mix and you add the water and other ingredients. The elements for brownies are all there, but you have not yet achieved actual brownies. It's not until you mix the ingredients and bake them that they become brownies—that is, all of the ingredients have been synthesized into a new, more complex (and edible) set of ingredients.

Here's another way to think of synthesis. Imagine you are running for public office in your hometown. To help build your political platform, you poll your future constituents for their thoughts on current issues. At the same time, you read articles and public policy documents to build your understanding of those issues. Then, so people know what you believe and what you will work on while in office, you write a position statement that brings together the ideas of what you've learned from your poll and readings.

When you read and process information, whether it is from books, television, or the Internet, you are collecting ingredients for your synthesis. But rather than simply dropping that information into your essay by including a quote here and a summary there, you need to process that information through your own critical thinking process in order to synthesize it into some new, more complex, yet clear information. Synthesis is central to creating your own ideas and engaging with what you have read, viewed, or experienced.

The two kinds of synthesis you are likely to employ in your college career and beyond will take one of two forms: argument or explanation. For example, you might synthesize results from an experiment in your chemistry class with information from your chemistry textbook to explain a unique chemical phenomenon that you've observed. In an effort to argue for a policy on your campus to abolish plastic containers, you would support your original idea by synthesizing (melding together via your own critical thinking) evidence from a journal article on the harmful plastic BPA with your own interviews of campus officials commenting on the issues.

A successful synthesis will:

- Report information from sources accurately
- Make clear the source of information and how sources may overlap
- Help readers understand the information in new ways or greater depth

Developing Your Skills: Synthesizing Ideas

Many writers recognize the importance of language to our lives. Consider, for example, Joan Didion and the joy she finds in capturing the pictures in her mind, as well as her passion for writing. Anna Quindlen also discusses the power of writing in her essay "Write for Your Life." Now, create your own "Why I Write." In your own essay, discuss how writing works for you. As you do that, use summary and paraphrasing to help synthesize the ideas found in Didion's and Quindlen's work to help support your own ideas about the power of writing.

The Writing Process

Writing involves a process. Being a process, good writing does not just happen—it must be thoughtfully constructed from start to finish. Some writers might argue that the process potentially never ends, as any piece of writing can always be revised. At each round—from invention, to brainstorming, to first draft, to revised drafts—the piece of writing gets better and more refined as it comes closer to what you're really trying to say. What you learn here about the writing process can be applied to virtually any writing you'll ever be called upon to produce. Keep in mind what you've learned about rhetoric—your writing will be rhetorical. As such, think about your critical analyses of others' work, as well as the qualities of rhetorical communication.

Often people think that writing is an art form that requires little preparatory work. It's easy to see the processes associated with other art forms. For example, if you are a painter, there are many things you need to do to prepare to paint, such as mixing colors or stretching canvas. If you're a pianist, you're not going to just sit down and play a concerto without warming up, stretching your hands, and running a few scales before you perform. Yet, when it comes to writing, the assumption is that you simply sit down and write an essay, letter, report, blog, or even an email without prior preparation. Well, that's not how good writing happens. By preparing thoroughly and thoughtfully to write, you can discover what you think, and how you feel, and often you will find the right words and phrases to express those ideas, thoughts, and feelings.

Getting Going

Writing is messy. That perfect paper that you hand to your professor often starts with a scribbled list of words or random phrases you bang out on the computer, often containing the phrase "I hate this class." That's okay—in fact, that's exactly how it should be because every great piece of writing starts with a word on a page. You're beginning the process of invention.

Facing the blank page can be daunting, but there are ways to deal with that moment that will help take the fear and trepidation out of the process. First, get rid of the blank page—write something—anything—just get something on that page so you get past that moment immediately. It's a trick professional writers use all of the time as they type things like the title or song lyrics that come to mind or even phrases like "I have no idea what I'm going to write today." The psychological edge you gain in getting over that first hurdle can often propel you to the next step.

Free writing involves writing down whatever comes to mind, like song lyrics, or exclamations of frustration. If you were a concert pianist, free writing is like doing finger exercises. If you were a painter, you'd be mixing paints and imagining what you might like to paint today. As a writer, when you're free writing, writing down whatever comes to mind, you're greasing the wheels of your brain, loosening up muscles that power your creativity. It's a great strategy for busting through writer's block and coming up with ideas. What you write may not make sense to anyone, even you, but it works to get the wheels turning. Never throw out your free writing because you never know what hidden gems you might find there when you go back and read through what you've written.

Brainstorming helps you generate new ideas. It's a simple but very powerful tool for any writer, and you can use this strategy many times during the writing process. For example, you can brainstorm to generate topics for an essay, or to come up with a thesis, or to explore ideas about the opposition to your argument. As the word suggests, you're going to capture the storm of ideas flying around in your brain. "But I don't have any ideas," you might say. Well, this process can help you get some and can then help you in framing those ideas for a piece of writing. Here's how to brainstorm:

- Find a comfortable writing environment, whether it's with your laptop on your bed or a legal pad on a table in the library.

- Set a specific time frame for this brainstorming session, such as 15 minutes. Be true to that—for that time frame you are going to do nothing but brainstorm. Don't let anything distract you during that time, not an IM, not the phone, not your dog barking, or your stomach growling. Dedicate yourself to this task only for those 15 minutes.

- Take a moment to separate yourself from the rush of the world around you. Then focus intently on your topic. This is the beginning of the brainstorm.

- Pen in hand, or hands on the keyboard, start writing and *don't stop* for the full 15 minutes you've set aside for this task.
- Write everything that comes to mind, no matter how weird or wild or mundane, and keep writing. Do this without judgment, without editing, and don't bother to pay attention to correct spelling or usage. Try not to spend time reading what you're writing—just write and keep writing. Now you're capturing every drop of that brainstorm.
- Time is up. Now, have a look at what you've created. Sift through what's there. Delete or scratch out the nonsensical elements. Look for phrases or words that you feel connected to or that you feel like you have more to say about. Look for connections between phrases or words. Often what you'll find in a brainstorming session are the building blocks for the piece of writing you're getting ready to produce.

Another way to get rolling toward writing is by using a method called **clustering** or **mind mapping**. Mind mapping produces a visual representation of your thoughts and ideas about a topic. If you think in pictures rather than words, this process might help you in generating ideas for your writing. The following illustration shows how you might go about developing a mind map:

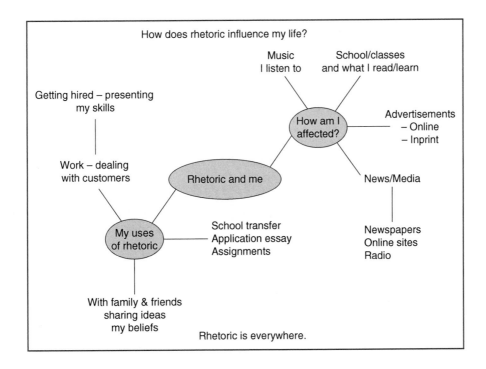

When developing a mind map, you begin by writing your topic in the middle of the page. Then, like brainstorming, begin writing words or phrases that come to your mind as you ponder that central element in the middle of your page. Follow your instincts as to where you place the words or phrases associated with your topic. Once again, generate the words and phrases without editing or censoring yourself and quickly jot your ideas wherever you want on the page.

If you are a visual thinker, you will start to see associations between the words and your topic. With circles, squares, arrows, and highlighters, you can graphically illustrate the associations between your ideas that you're discovering right there on the page. What you end up with might look like a tangled mess, but it could very likely be the road map to your next essay. If you'd like to see this mind mapping concept in action as it is applied to words and their synonyms, try an internet search for "mind mapping." There are several good websites that will give you helpful information. Here's an example from visualthesaurus.com:

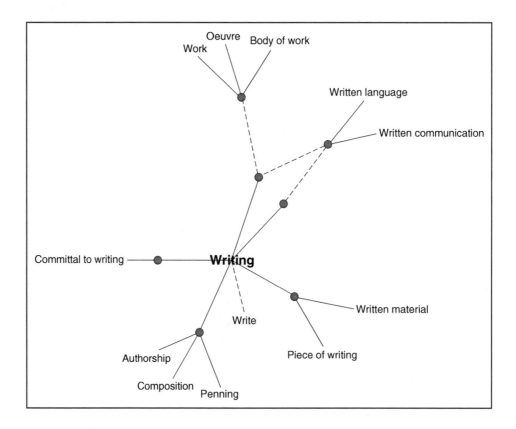

Getting a Plan

Now that you have generated some ideas about your topic, whether it's from your free writing and brainstorming list or from a color-coded mind map, you are ready to start thinking about shaping those ideas into a coherent essay. Your next step is to consider your audience and your purpose. Ask yourself these questions:

- Who are you trying to reach with your writing (your professor, a prospective employer, the newspaper editor, your senator)?

- What outcome do you want as a result (do you want to inform, or persuade, or entertain)?

> **An *effective thesis statement* needs to pass the "so what" test.**
>
> You need to construct a thesis that is debatable or controversial or at least has two sides to a question. Then you need to make the thesis statement matter by saying something new or in a new way about your subject or in a way that will speak to your defined audience.
>
> Your object is to avoid the "so what" response to your writing.

Questions often guide the most successful writers. For example, journalists shape much of the writing that you find in newspapers, magazines, and online by asking these questions: who, what, where, when, how, and why? If you look at your topic and your brainstorming or prewriting on your topic and ask yourself those questions, you may begin to discover the shape of your essay. Keep in mind that you will probably not use all of ideas, words, or phrases that come from your brainstorming or prewriting sessions. Asking questions and looking for answers there will help you eliminate those elements that fall outside the focus of a given writing assignment.

Another way to move from idea to essay is to begin fleshing out a thesis. A **thesis** is a clear statement identifying the point of your essay. A thesis serves to unify all of the ideas you choose to use in your essay. At this stage, you want to think in terms of a **working thesis**, which, as you organize your ideas and develop details in your essay, will likely be revised and refined along the way.

A thesis needs to reach beyond the basic book report form, which is, "I read the book and here's what the book said." Instead, an effective thesis does the following:

- Expresses a point of view about your topic and provides a road map for your essay

- Makes an assertion

- Focuses on a central and specific point

- Is specific and detailed

You want to be careful to distinguish between a topic and a thesis. A topic is your subject; a thesis is what you have to say about your subject—the point you want to make about it.

Examples:

Topic: The First Amendment

Thesis: College campus speech codes limiting a college student's free expression is a violation of the First Amendment.

Topic: Alternative energy

Thesis: Wind turbines designed to produce an inexpensive source of electricity do irreversible harm to wildlife and the environment.

Once you've narrowed your topic and come up with a working thesis, you need to think about what you intend—your purpose—in writing that thesis. The purpose of most writing falls into three broad categories: to inform, to persuade, or to entertain. The best writing often does all three at the same time.

If you're writing a test question essay with your professor as your main audience, you are most likely writing to **inform**—you are trying to show the professor that you know the information he or she wants you to know. You're conveying information to your audience.

If you're writing to your state representative complaining about the mandatory seat belt law, you're most likely writing to **persuade** him or her to see issue your way.

If you're writing fiction or satire or even a humorous nonfiction essay intending, primarily, to amuse your audience, you're writing to **entertain**.

Finding a Form

When you engage in writing, it's helpful if you can find a form—a way of shaping your use of language—that will provide a structure for your piece of writing, whether it's an essay for your composition class, a brief response on a written test in your sociology class, a letter to the editor, or a cover letter for a job application. Think of this process as you would build a house; you wouldn't start building without a foundation. Forms of discourse, just like forms laid for the foundation of a house, provide a foundation on which you can build any piece of writing you're called upon to produce.

If you've done your prewriting and brainstorming, you have a working thesis, and you've identified your audience and purpose, you have gathered all of the lumber you need to build an essay. Now you need a foundation. Unlike building a house, you don't necessarily need to go out and lay that foundation every time you sit down to write. In writing, the foundation is provided for you in a variety of narrative strategies, including:

- Narration
- Description
- Definition
- Comparison and contrast

- Process analysis
- Cause and effect
- Argument

Each of these forms has its own conventions, which provide a way to shape your writing for maximum effectiveness. Think of each of them as a tool for conveying your ideas in writing. You can use them individually or in combination with one another. If, in your decision-making process, you can learn to assess the writing situation and determine when to use which of these modes or strategies, you will be able to adapt your writing to suit any need or desire you have to communicate your ideas.

The goal of **expository writing** is to convey ideas that inform or explain. You encounter expository writing every day, as it is the primary form of nonfiction writing you find in newspapers, magazines, and instructional books like cookbooks and textbooks. In fact, if you've ever written an essay for class, you've engaged in expository writing.

Expository writing encompasses a broad range of writing, but it can be separated into categories based on the purpose of the communication event:

- If you're writing about yourself for yourself, you are using an **expressive** form of expository writing. Personal journals would fall into this category as would some blogs or personal profiles on Facebook.

- If you're writing to convey facts, you are engaging in **explanatory** writing. Much of the writing you will do in college will be explanatory writing. When you encounter a test question in your history class asking you to give the reasons why the United States became involved in World War II, you're going to write an explanation. Beyond your time in college, you will use explanatory writing if you have to write to the credit card company to tell them your identity has been stolen or if you have to write to a landlord to explain why you should get your security deposit back.

- If you intend to influence a specific audience with your writing, you are practicing **persuasive** writing. Your cover letter on your job application falls into this category, as did your college entry application. You can also think of advertising and public relations writing as examples of persuasive writing.

Expressive, explanatory, or persuasive, it's all expository writing. You will find expository writing in all kinds of writing—letters, reports, or presentations.

YOUR TURN: Creating Your Ideas

1. We now turn to the influence of rhetoric in your life. Create an essay that explains how you see and experience rhetoric. There are many questions you can ask yourself here, among them: What rhetorical practices influence you

the most and why? How do you see rhetoric as having an effect on your life? Do you find language to be powerful like Didion and Quindlen? How do you use language? The goal of this essay is to describe and explain how rhetoric and rhetorical practices affect you and your life.

2. Rhetoric is all around you. Find a newspaper or magazine editorial. In a brief essay, describe the publication in which you found this editorial. Then analyze the editorial according to the characteristics of rhetorical communication, providing evidence for your analysis. Who is the audience? What is its purpose? To what situation is the editorial responding? For each question, provide evidence to prove your assessment (in other words, how do you know?).

TECH TALK: Keeping Track of Your Work and Formatting Your Papers

More and more, we are becoming a digital world. This means that most assignments you write will be created on a computer. You will have to figure out a way to organize your various files so that you can keep track of your work. Here are a few tips for maintaining your computer files:

1. Set up folders on your computer for each class you are taking. These folders can be in your *My Documents* area or on your desktop. You can store your files in the folders for easy access and locating.

2. Follow a set format for naming your documents and other files so that you can easily identify a file when looking for it. Here are some suggestions:

   Your last name_abbreviate assignment name
   For example: Torrens_response_1

   Class number, title of assignment, date
   For example: ENL101_Paper1_09-01-2010

Note: Never include spaces or symbols in your file names. Why? If your instructor asks you to upload your file into a learning management system (LMS), sometimes the LMS cannot read file names with spaces or symbols.

Whatever format you decide upon for your file-naming system, be consistent. It will save you time in the future.

And, don't forget: *back up your files!* Technology often fails us. Computers can and will crash, and you don't want to lose your work. You should back up your computer at least once a month. You can purchase a 1 GB flash drive and back up your course files there.

For composition classes, papers typically follow a format required by the Modern Language Association (MLA), which we'll discuss in more depth in Chapter 7 when we talk about using sources and citing those sources.

Here's an example of how your paper should be formatted:

Smith—1

Joe Smith
English 101
Professor Jones
September 5, 2010

Title of Paper

Indent each new paragraph five spaces (you can use the Tab key to do this), and

then make sure that your paper is double-spaced.

Chapter 2

Understanding the Rhetorical Tradition

One key point you have learned so far is that public rhetoric is an integral part of democratic communities and societies. As you know, rhetorical discourse, whether being used ethically or unethically, is communication

- With a purpose and an audience
- Planned around a response to some situation
- That enables the conversations and displays on which democracy depends

Consequently, you are learning a skill that will help you make choices in terms of oral and written communication and that will reflect your decisions when you make statements in public and observe public rhetoric. As an educated citizen—particularly one with an understanding of rhetorical strategies—you possess the skills to contribute to your community in many ways. Your participation in your classes in school, in online communities like *Facebook*, in your local community, and in organizations throughout your life is an important feature of living in a democratic—and rhetorical—world.

Democracy has a long history and a strong place in the United States and other countries, as evidenced by countless documents, symbols, speeches, and protests expressing the views of citizens like you. You are on your way to greater involvement in your community, through identifying with people around you and engaging in active citizenship. This chapter

What is the "rhetorical tradition"?

The rhetorical tradition is simply how we describe the history of thinking and theorizing about rhetoric, public communication, and rhetorical ideas in general. Usually, the rhetorical tradition takes a predominately Western view and begins its survey of rhetorical thinking, as we do, with the ancient Greeks.

takes you through the rhetorical tradition to explore how rhetoric, from ancient Greece to our contemporary era, affects the creation and sustenance of democratic principles, institutions, and communities.

The Rhetorical Tradition and Democracy

In contemporary culture, we tend to understand democracy—rule by the people—as having the following essential qualities:

- A democracy is a system of government where everyday citizens of a country participate in the governing processes of that country.
- A democracy stands in opposition to a monarchy or dictatorship, where one individual governs a country.

Many definitions of democracy contrast its form and function with other types of governance, with the principal distinguishing characteristic being the amount of power or control each type offers to its people. Most contemporary democracies hold to fundamental principles like:

- Free elections
- The right to vote in elections
- Freedom of speech
- The right to affiliate with groups of their choice

> Free and fair elections allow people living in a representative democracy to determine the political makeup and future policy direction of their nation's government.

Despite transformation from ancient times to today, democracy still relies on the active participation of citizens through verbal and written communication practices like letter writing, speeches, meetings, demonstrations, and—recently, via the World Wide Web—in blogs and websites.

Rhetoric and Democracy

Talking about the foundations of democracy, even from a rhetorical perspective, could consume this entire book. Therefore, this discussion will focus on a few central issues that we can consider pillars of democracy—key, important features. For example, you will consider

- The role of education in the development of citizens and governments
- The social and/or political environments that thrive upon citizen engagement and participation
- The personal accountability or investment expected from individuals in developing, maintaining, and protecting the state

By the end of this discussion, you will understand how various contexts, political or otherwise, make citizenship possible, impossible, attractive, or not at all appealing. Neither democracy nor citizenship are easily attained or maintained. Historical contexts teach us that old ideas—ancient ideas—have relevance as people today try to make decisions about policies and actions about important issues.

Ancient Greece: The Roots of Democracy

The kind of governmental and citizenship system we now know as democracy took root in ancient Athens, Greece. Understanding the ideals upon which democracies are founded makes people better able to make critical choices about their participation in that kind of system, whether that means voting, writing letters to their lawmakers, contributing financially to various causes, or any of the other myriad avenues provided by democracy.

As a contemporary thinker, writer, and citizen, you need to explore the rhetorical foundations of democracy. The Sophists of ancient Greece offer a starting place for understanding the rhetorical foundations of democracy and citizenship.

The Sophists: Practical Skills for Democracy

The Sophists of ancient Greece were itinerant teachers of public skills, with a clear focus on persuasive speaking. They did not have permanent schools, for the most part, but instead traveled from place to place (hence "itinerant"), stopping where they found students interested in their services. Sophism gained many followers due to a growing demand for education in 5 BCE Greece, particularly for skills that would enable men to be successful in public venues, including the courts, business, and politics—especially politics.

Although the Sophists taught any subject that students demanded, such as mathematics, physics, grammar, or history, most of them focused on rhetoric and persuasion. Their students, because of the

> Athenian democracy was different from the much later American form, not only because it was the expression of a single city-state but because it was a direct, rather than a representative, democracy.... The continual buzz of conversation, the orotund sounds of the orators, the shrill shouts from the symposia—this steady drumbeat of opinion, controversy, and conflict could everywhere be heard. The *agora* (marketplace) was not just a daily display of fish and farm goods; it was an everyday market of ideas, the place citizens used as if it were their daily newspaper, complete with salacious headlines, breaking news, columns, and editorials.
>
> —**Thomas Cahill, *Sailing the Wine-dark Sea: Why the Greeks Matter***

B.C.E.

"Before common era." This abbreviation replaced "B.C" ("before Christ"). The abbreviation is now used to indicate the period of history prior to the birth of Christ.

civic culture of the time, understood the connection between rhetorical skills and political success. At any point, a citizen might be elected by lottery to sit on a jury, function as a political policy maker, or be a military leader. To prepare for these potential opportunities, citizens needed to learn effective communication and argument, both central skills associated with rhetoric.

Such skills were considered crucial to the man (for only men could be citizens and communicate publicly during this time period) who wished to participate in the political realm and have an impact on his community. Ancient Athenian culture encouraged public engagement. Every male citizen had the right to speak in the public assemblies, where voting and other legalities occurred. Consequently, the skills of rhetoric and public communication formed the foundation of the Sophists' teachings. They practiced a pragmatic approach to everyday life, focusing on reasoning, personal virtue, and practical wisdom.

The sophic approach to personal success started with the notion that a person had to appear knowledgeable and good in order to get people to listen to him, believe his words, and ultimately be persuaded by his message. So, whether a man was defending himself in court, negotiating a business transaction, or running for a public office, his ultimate success began in the demonstration of his personal qualities. His rhetorical communication was intended to exemplify his excellence and credibility. These ideas have real relevance to our public world today.

The philosophy and perspective taught by many sophists centered around four primary attributes:

- Personal virtue (*arête*)
- Knowing the right word or phrase for the right time (*kairos*)
- Two-fold or two-sided arguments (*dialectic*)
- A sense of justice as centered in social agreement or convention (*nomos*), rather than arbitrary dictate

You might be asking yourself right now if these elements are relevant to our thinking and writing today. The answer is "yes." The qualities of personal virtue, knowing the right thing to say, two-sided arguments, and everyday wisdom influence one's style of communication and effect on an audience. Why does a business person need to know how to demonstrate personal virtue or goodness? Simple. Do you really want to buy your car, home,

Student Voices

What do the sophists teach us today? That there might not be a right answer. There will always be two sides to everything. If you have an argument with a friend, you should think about what you are arguing against. You might not be 100% right.

—Greg

or insurance from someone who comes across as self-interested? By the same token, should our school principals or civic leaders be good people at heart or bad? Of course, there is no guarantee that our perceptions of other people's virtue are accurate, but you can see the value of being skilled in demonstrating your ethics and motives.

Knowing how and when to say something (*kairos*) is a very valuable skill as well, whether one is in business or politics. If you are a restaurant manager, for instance, and your best waitperson gets upset because the kitchen is slow, your skills of mediation and calm negotiation will come in very handy in defusing a potentially unpleasant situation. If your job is selling copy machines to offices, your ability to identify the exact moment when your customer is ready to buy will guarantee a better paycheck for you. At the same time, it's important to know when to remain silent. For example, if you're a real estate agent showing a great home to potential buyers, it's often wiser to let the clients absorb their surroundings rather than talking their ears off. Can you think of instances in your own life when you would have been better off saying nothing?

The sophists understood the need to evaluate the situation and carefully analyzed their audience, purpose, and the limitations placed upon them by time or other factors. This process ensured that they understood the various perspectives that influence decision making.

In turn, they taught their students to analyze all possible sides to an argument or subject. You could say that they answered most questions by saying, "It depends." When you really think about it, how many times is there absolutely only one way to consider a subject?

The example from *WitnessLA* helps us to understand the value of a relative definition of justice, or one founded in *nomos* as argued by the Sophists. *Nomos*, or convention, gives rise to laws imbued with a certain amount of flexibility. In the situation of Chelsea Fraser, writing one word on her school desk, an arbitrary definition of right and wrong with accompanying arbitrary punishments would validate the call to the police, for there could be no argument with the claim that Chelsea did something *wrong*. However, as pointed out by the author of the blog entry, the punishment—being handcuffed and taken to the police station—did not fit the minimal severity of the infraction. Rather, she suggests that one must consider the entire circumstance or situation of the infraction

---

"Of Girls and Crime and Desks," by Celeste Fremon, April 6, 2007. Reprinted by permission of Celeste Fremon, editor of WitnessLA.com and the author of *G-Dog and the Homeboys*.

before determining the punishment. The Sophistic ideal, the legal system governing the United States, allows for various definitions of issues and considerations of circumstances when determining actions and outcomes.

The Skills of Public Life

The attributes of *arête, kairos, dialectic,* and *nomos* teach several things about the skills people learned from the Sophists. First of all, the focus on virtue indicates confidence in individual ethics in public communication. Isocrates, an early Sophist, believed that educating people in the ways of citizenship would ensure that they would not use public oratory or writing for evil uses, instead concentrating on the good of the state or community. Although this idea may sound naïve to modern sensibilities, it establishes an ideal of ethical uses of rhetoric. Furthermore, being able to both determine the appropriate word for the moment and understand that there are two sides (or more) to every story or argument increases the ability of any communicator to make his or her point clearly and accurately.

Conversely, of course, we can see the possibilities for someone to manipulate his or her point in such a way to cover up the truth, which is why the Sophists were often mistrusted in their day. Additionally, locating justice in social agreement rather than some ideal that is etched in stone meant that justice became contingent on circumstance or context (much like it is today, if you think about it), which also made many Athenians nervous. Today, the notion of sophistry often carries negative connotations, much like rhetoric does. In both cases, the negative associations are rooted in ancient misuses and misunderstandings.

It is important to recognize that these communication skills opened the doors for more people to join public conversation and deliberation in the politically charged environment of Athens. Rather than assuming that only people in power were naturally endowed with the capabilities to govern and communicate, other people could learn to communicate well and participate in the governance of their communities. A participative government, though not perfect, allowed for much more diversity of opinion and for the contributions of more people.

The new political and economic system in place in Athens at the time privileged the art of oratory, or public speaking. Political decisions were made by an assembly with the majority vote holding forth, even in decisions of warfare. As contemporary rhetorical scholar Takis Poulakos explains in *Speaking for the Polis,* these votes were "open to any Athenian citizen willing to attend and, when important decisions were to be made, regularly drew an attendance of over five thousand people" (1997, p. 65). Clearly, the political scene was one of participation, and knowledge of rhetorical practices helped men to find success in public life, whether as speakers or writers of speeches. Additionally, recall that possessing such rhetorical skills heightens one's critical awareness of the discourse he or she witnesses, as you have found in learning to read critically. So citizens would not only be able to construct effective arguments in speech and writing, but would also be able to analyze and critique the speeches and writings of other citizens.

According to scholar George Kennedy, in *Classical Rhetoric and Its Christian and Secular Tradition*, "Those planning public careers would benefit from instruction in composing a speech, but it might have been even more important that they have an understanding of rhetoric as it was being used by others and be able to make sound judgments about speeches they heard" (1999, p. 78). Critical readers and listeners, then, are empowered citizens, for they are less likely to blindly accept arguments that do not ring true or sound credible. They will interrogate what they read and hear, ask for supporting evidence, and insist on sound reasoning. Rhetorical prowess or skill, then, enables a lively public sphere.

Although you may not plan to run for public office, teach, or become a social activist, it's hard to know when, where or why such skills might be required of you. As a student, you will be asked to display your knowledge and possibly argue for changes in your campus. As a citizen of different and various communities, you may need to advocate for someone less powerful than you, like your children or siblings, to stand up for yourself in court, or buy a home. In all of these situations, the ability to skillfully use rhetoric to your advantage will assist you in achieving your goals.

Aristotle's ideas emerged from the need for a lively public sphere. His theories of rhetoric and his ideas about public ethics and engagement still influence thinking and teaching about rhetoric and public communication. The son of a court physician to the rulers of Macedon, Aristotle lived from 384 to 322 BCE and left behind numerous writings and notes covering the natural sciences, philosophic ideas and dilemmas, and metaphysics. Perhaps because of his father's influence as a scientist and methodical investigator, Aristotle took a systematic approach to understanding the world he lived in, from natural phenomena to ethics, communication, and politics. His analysis of rhetoric and public discourse categorizes types of communication, methods of persuasion and argumentation, and audiences. His attention to detail continues to help students today determine how best to accomplish the goals of effective communication.

As you know from Chapter 1, Aristotle defined rhetoric as "an ability, in each particular case, to see the available means of persuasion." His definition requires a communicator to think situationally and strategically because each situation calls for a unique response to its issues. Aristotle determined that the successful accomplishment of rhetorical goals could be evaluated according to three things: the truth and logic of the topic (*logos*); the speaker's ability to convince the audience of his or her trustworthiness (*ethos*); and the emotions a speaker arouses in an audience so they are likely to accept the views presented to them (*pathos*). These rhetorical elements—logos, ethos, and pathos—are the foundation of good communication. As you will discover in Chapter 3, improving your writing and rhetorical skills will require you to lean heavily on these three forms of rhetorical proof.

For Aristotle, success in the public arena was closely tied to the ethical practice of rhetoric in writing and in speaking. Although the political culture of Aristotle's day was not perfect or ideal, it was definitely grounded in communication among citizens. As we have already discussed, the better one is at forming an argument and evaluating the arguments of others, the better a citizen one will be. Aristotle's public sphere, like yours today, dealt with new ideas and technologies as democracy took hold. There is much to gain from understanding Aristotle's approach to reasoning, argument, and rhetoric.

The Educated Citizen

Citizen participation in public deliberation has been and is important in democratic governments. The ancient Greeks developed the concept of government based on community involvement. Today, many countries around the world operate under a similar notion of a government that is representative of and accountable to its citizens. Not surprisingly, during historical periods of tyranny or oppressive regimes, the skills of public communication, whether writing or speaking, tended to be constrained to messages and formats acceptable to those in charge.

For example, under the Roman Republic (approximately 500–44 BCE), which operated as a limited democracy, people were educated in rhetoric with an eye to the public participation of educated citizens. However, when the Republic fell to the Roman Empire and tyranny was established, people had to be very careful about what they said about their government, the emperors, and social issues. Even though some emperors were less brutal than others, the Roman Empire has been characterized as moving from civilization to a time of tyranny and greed enacted by those in power. This era was not a time for citizens to speak out against their government or to try to change things.

Between the fall of Rome in about 411 CE and the early Renaissance, the study and practice of rhetoric as effective public communication was at a low. In part, this lack of emphasis was due to the primacy of the newly powerful Christian church, general turbulence of the age including the pestilence of the plague and the lack of democratically oriented systems of government. What emerges from the challenges of such times is a renewed focus on the educated citizen.

During the Renaissance (roughly 1300–1600 CE), important social principles began to emerge, such as:

- Personal ethos (or credibility)
- Communicative competence
- The significance of audience
- A publicly deliberated vision of justice and society

Many scholars claim that the Renaissance (the word means "rebirth") is where the roots of subsequent historical developments rest, in part because of the many social, scientific, and mechanical developments of the time period, as well as a revived interest in the arts and communication.

During this time period of rebirth, there was a general reawakening of interest in human endeavors, education, and empowerment. The church relinquished some of its absolute control over public decision making and deliberation. This was also a time of great discoveries and inventions, such as the printing press and the microscope. More people began to participate politically, as well as socially. Once again, the need arose for political wisdom, ethical statesmen, and citizens educated in rhetorical skills. The age also saw renewed interest in the Roman era works by Cicero and Quintilian, both of whom advocated for the development of orator–statesmen and ideal citizens. Quintilian's ideas were particularly popular among scholars of rhetoric during this time period due to his emphasis on ethical citizenship and education. The successful person was the man educated in many areas—a well-rounded individual. This person would be versed in rhetoric, science, and humanities, in order to be able to converse intelligently with other public figures.

The ideals, developments, and discoveries of the Renaissance era laid the groundwork for the intellectual movement, exploration, and challenge of the Enlightenment (1600–1800 CE). The Enlightenment period, also known as the Age of Reason, highlighted the importance of logic, reasoning, and rationality to thinkers during this era. In Britain, rhetoric played a particularly important role in education. In part, this was due to an emerging sense of "the public" as composed of participants—that is, real people—instead of being a faceless concept. In other words, because citizens had more access to each other and to modes of communicating like writing pamphlets, participating in debate societies, and gathering in public spaces like coffeehouses, demand grew for instruction in effective

A basic list of Enlightenment values would include the following:
- a deep commitment to reason,
- a trust in the emerging modern sciences to solve problems and provide control over nature,
- a commitment to the idea of progress in material wealth and in human civility,
- a belief in the essential goodness of human nature,
- an emphasis upon the individual as master of his fate and fortune, and
- an engagement with the public sphere of discussion and action.

In short, the Enlightenment thinkers believed in the powers of humankind and saw themselves as part of a revolutionary development in history that would replace superstition and tired rituals and corrupt traditions with reason and productive energy.

communication. Public speaking was once again considered to be an important art, and the ability to express oneself effectively marked a person as of high quality.

The Roots of Western Democracy

The privileging of human reason during the Enlightenment significantly influenced the development of American democratic principles. In this view, the individual person is endowed with great importance and is considered to be capable of participating fully in public deliberation. Accordingly, enlightened society was expected to cultivate that participation and rationality through education, freedom of expression, and representative government with the goal of the overall advancement of humanity.

In general, as the world's population has increased and as human abilities to invent, manipulate, and extend technologies have multiplied, conflicts and tensions have also grown. International disputes and wars, national debates and issues, and local struggles over resources and power have drawn the attention of rhetorical scholars. Efforts to understand the role of public communication—writing, speaking, and protesting in all of its varying forms—have resulted in many theories about and approaches to the role of rhetoric in communities and democracies.

To this point, you have explored a bit of the development of democracy throughout history. During every age where democratic principles were fostered, education and personal investment in citizenship were significant. Further, democratic principles did not thrive in contexts where the rule of law was through tyranny, oppression, or the elite. In addition, the free practice of rhetorical communication was dangerous during such eras. The Greek ideals of ethical principles may have seemed far-fetched to you when this discussion began, but by now it should be clear that a democracy will succeed only if most of its citizens agree to common rules of engagement and behavior that protect the people and the state.

A Brief Review

- **The rhetorical foundations of democracy:**
  - The roots of democracy extend back to the ancient Greek educators known as **sophists**. These teachers focused on developing their students' rhetorical skills in an effort to help them be engaged citizens in the political realm. The philosophy taught by many sophists centered around four primary attributes:
    - Personal virtue (*arête*)
    - Knowing the right word or phrase for the right time (*kairos*)
    - Two-fold or two-sided arguments (*dialectic*)
    - A sense of justice as centered in social agreement (*nomos*) and situation, rather than arbitrary dictate

- The ideas of the Greek philosopher Aristotle about ethical communication, as well as *ethos*, *pathos*, and *logos*—the three artistic proofs available to help writers and communicators make logical, credible arguments—will be useful tools as you develop your skills as a writer–citizen.
- Throughout history, education has been the key to preparing citizens for participation in government.
- The Renaissance and Enlightenment eras developed the focus on education, as a successful person was considered one who was educated in many subjects including rhetoric.
  - In particular, the Enlightenment privileged human reason, a viewpoint that fostered the development of democratic principles, as people were encouraged to participate in public deliberations thoughtfully and with rationality.

Rhetoric in Action

"Why I Write," Ellis Cose

Ellis Cose (1951–) has been a contributing editor and columnist for *Newsweek* magazine. A well-known journalist, he is also the author of several books, including *The Envy of the World* and *Color-Blind*. He has appeared on several television and radio shows, and has received Clarion awards and National Association of Black Journalist awards, among others. Here, Cose shares with readers what drew him to writing.

Pre-reading: Spend five minutes completing a freewrite answering the question, "Why do you write?"

I DID NOT SEEK OUT THE '60S; THEY FOUND ME: IN MY LIVING ROOM where, as a kid during a hot summer night, I bore witness to the madness of the times. That madness took the form of a massive police assault unfolding outside two buildings just across the way. As my parents, my brothers and sisters and I sat huddled away from the windows, listening in horror to the gunshots and screams, I knew that something huge was happening outside and that the world I thought I knew was about to change.

The assault was a response to a sniper attack. Upwards of 100 policemen flooded the area and eventually evacuated the two huge buildings about a block away and cater-cornered to my own. This happened during the riot that broke out on Chicago's West Side in July 1966, after police turned off a fire hydrant sprinkling water on residents trying to escape the heat. That riot was only a prelude to the explosion to come. Two years later, in April 1968, my neighborhood was among those that erupted after the assassination of Martin Luther King Jr.

I lived in a housing project a couple of blocks away from the Madison Street commercial strip that was the epicenter of the '68 explosion. Some 1,500 National Guardsmen were rushed to the area as Madison Street went up in flames. Some days after the worst was over, I took a walk and was amazed that I could still feel the heat from fires extinguished hours earlier.

The high school I attended, Lane Technical, was for boys who tested well. Its mission had nothing to do with integration, but with giving bright young men who could not afford private school the kind of education public-school kids didn't typically get. Attending Lane meant that, every day, I left my almost all-back community to go into one that was virtually all white. After the riot, I pondered why it was that my city, my world, was so divided by color. And why was it that the distance between those two worlds seemed so difficult to bridge?

My obsession with such matters led me to write a paper on race and riots in America that grew into a manuscript of more than 100 pages. My English teacher, Helen Klinger, suggested I send the opus to Gwendolyn Brooks, then poet laureate of Illinois. Brooks invited me into her writers' group and told me to focus on becoming a writer.

Both the Chicago Sun-Times and the Chicago Tribune, the city's two mainstream dailies, did an impressive job covering the chaotic events of 1968. But they covered my community, for the most part, as if it were a dark, forbidden universe. "The white man trespasses on West Madison Street. He has crossed into a foreign country, he bears no passport, and the natives mistrust him," the Tribune observed in one article I recently reread. At another point, the same article refers to the "West Madison Street Jungle," and notes there were "only 2,500 policemen . . . to control about 300,000 blacks." Reading such stuff years later, it's easy for me to remember why I concluded I might be able to produce better journalism than the writers I was reading. I, at least, knew I didn't live in a "jungle" and that my 300,000 (generally law-abiding) neighbors did not need to be controlled by the cops.

After the riots of April, my interest in journalism grew. The more I read, the more convinced I became that I had something to contribute. In many news accounts, the 1968 Democratic National Convention, held in Chicago, was chronicled as a war between the forces of order and deranged hippies—with innocent newsmen caught in the middle. I suspected the real story was much more complicated and regretted not being able to report on and tell the story myself. I also suspected that, with the streets in seemingly constant turmoil, there would be plenty of things worth writing for some time. So I endeavored to follow Brooks's advice. I wrote editorials and edited stories for a college publication. And at some point after my 18th birthday, I decided I was ready for the big time. I applied to the Sun-Times for a columnist job that had not been advertised and did not really exist. Instead of laughing me out of their offices, editor James Hoge and managing editor Ralph Otwell took me under their collective wing. They gave me a column in a small Sun-Times publication; and when I was 19, still in college but presumably somewhat better prepared, they gave me an op-ed column in the newspaper itself. Their decision confirmed, at least for me, the sagacity of Brooks's counsel and set me on a new life course.

The building where I spent my childhood has since been torn down; a condominium development is going up in its place. The new residences will feature fireplaces, granite kitchen counters, balconies, private backyards, garages and other luxurious amenities, according to prominently placed signs. The old neighborhood, in others words, is no more, finally having reached the end of a cycle of destruction and renewal that began with the fires of '68: the same fires that shook my world, upended my life and turned me into a writer. ➶

Comprehending the Text

1. Summarize Cose's article in one paragraph.

2. Explain how Cose came to writing. What motivated him to become a writer? Paraphrase Cose's ideas in your response.

3. How does Cose end his essay? Why does he end it this way?

Analyzing the Text

1. Cose is engaging in public life. What is the purpose behind his essay? What does he want readers to learn?

2. How does Cose's essay contribute to the ongoing development of community and democracy?

3. Describe an experience in which you witnessed an event that motivated you to take action. What happened? What did you do?

Developing Your Skills: Building Your Ideas

Now, consider the Bill of Rights of the United States. The Bill of Rights grew out of community action during the period of the American Revolution. Following the writing of the Declaration of Independence, concerned citizen legislators argued for a "bill of rights" that would protect individual civil liberties and shape how their new country would operate on behalf of its citizens. On September 25, 1789, the first Congress of the United States put forth 12 amendments. Of the 12 amendments, 10 were ratified to become the Bill of Rights.

Take time to read the Bill of Rights, then turn to the writing assignment after the postreading questions.

Prereading: Can you identify the 10 amendments that make up the Bill of Rights of the United States? Make a list here of as many rights as you can.

The Bill of Rights

Amendments 1–10 of the Constitution

The Conventions of a number of the States having, at the time of adopting the Constitution, expressed a desire, in order to prevent misconstruction or abuse of its powers, that further declaratory and restrictive clauses should be added: And as extending the ground of public confidence in the Government will best insure the beneficent ends of its institution.

RESOLVED, by the Senate and House of Representatives of the United States of America, in Congress assembled, two-thirds of both Houses concurring, that the following Articles be proposed to the Legislatures of the several States, as amendments to the Constitution of the United States, all or any of which articles, when ratified by three-fourths of the said Legislatures, to be valid to all intents and purposes as part of the said Constitution; viz.

ARTICLES in addition to, and Amendment of the Constitution of the United States of America, proposed by Congress, and ratified by the Legislatures of the several States, pursuant to the fifth Article of the original Constitution.

Amendment I

Congress shall make no law respecting an establishment of religion, or prohibiting the free exercise thereof; or abridging the freedom of speech, or of the press; or the right of the people peaceably to assemble, and to petition the government for a redress of grievances.

Amendment II

A well regulated militia, being necessary to the security of a free state, the right of the people to keep and bear arms, shall not be infringed.

Amendment III

No Soldier shall, in time of peace be quartered in any house, without the consent of the Owner, nor in time of war, but in a manner to be prescribed by law.

National Archives

Amendment IV

The right of the people to be secure in their persons, houses, papers, and effects, against unreasonable searches and seizures, shall not be violated, and no Warrants shall issue, but upon probable cause, supported by Oath or affirmation, and particularly describing the place to be searched, and the persons or things to be seized.

Amendment V

No person shall be held to answer for a capital, or otherwise infamous crime, unless on a presentment or indictment of a Grand Jury, except in cases arising in the land or naval forces, or in the Militia, when in actual service in time of War or public danger; nor shall any person be subject for the same offense to be twice put in jeopardy of life or limb; nor shall be compelled in any criminal case to be a witness against himself, nor be deprived of life, liberty, or property, without due process of law; nor shall private property be taken for public use, without just compensation.

Amendment VI

In all criminal prosecutions, the accused shall enjoy the right to a speedy and public trial, by an impartial jury of the State and district wherein the crime shall have been committed, which district shall have been previously ascertained by law, and to be informed of the nature and cause of the accusation; to be confronted with the witnesses against him; to have compulsory process for obtaining witnesses in his favor, and to have the Assistance of Counsel for his defense.

Amendment VII

In Suits at common law, where the value in controversy shall exceed twenty dollars, the right of trial by jury shall be preserved, and no fact tried by a jury, shall be otherwise reexamined in any Court of the United States, than according to the rules of the common law.

Amendment VIII

Excessive bail shall not be required, nor excessive fines imposed, nor cruel and unusual punishments inflicted.

Amendment IX

The enumeration in the Constitution, of certain rights, shall not be construed to deny or disparage others retained by the people.

Amendment X

The powers not delegated to the United States by the Constitution, nor prohibited by it to the states, are reserved to the States respectively, or to the people.

Comprehending the Text

1. What purpose does the Bill of Rights play in the United States?

2. Which amendment do you think is most important and why?

3. What does it mean to "plead the Fifth" or "be tried by your peers"?

Analyzing the Text

1. How does the Bill of Rights speak to the needs of the citizens of the United States?

2. Choose an amendment and demonstrate how the amendment is open to interpretation and debate by the public.

3. Why is it important that the Bill of Rights is open to interpretation?

Choose an amendment you agree or disagree with and write a one- to two-page response that explains your point of view. Your goal is to thoughtfully express your ideas as an American citizen or non–American citizen about the Bill of Rights.

Looking Ahead

Writing and public speaking tie into how you, as a citizen, engage with your communities and your government. As you learned in this chapter, the emphasis on rhetoric has evolved over time, but a clear focus has stayed on the importance of engaging with and responding to the world around you. Developing your ability to do so requires the building of your writer's toolbox and practice using various writing strategies to help you express your ideas. Often, writers rely on the strategies of definition, description and even narration to express themselves, which is where you turn next.

Your Writer's Toolkit

Writing Strategies: Narration

Narration organizes and conveys action and information, and is one of the oldest forms of human communication. Simply put, narration is the act of telling a story. In creative writing, the narrative you create is an imaginary series of events used to entertain your audience. In nonfiction and expository writing, the narrative you create has a point, and in telling a story, you provide insight into your subject. In the real world, police officers use narrative to construct the story of an accident, a lawyer uses narration to walk a jury through a course of events in a trial, and historians narrate the course of civilization. A nonfiction narrative has a point, answering the big "so what?" question. A successful narrative contains some key elements.

A good narrative establishes a **context** for the action it conveys. Your introduction needs to capture the reader's attention and give the reader a sense of the world you're writing about.

A good narrative offers a **reliable sequence for the action**. You can construct a sequence based on time—the moment, the day, the day, the season, the year, or the decade—and tell your story based on the progression of time through your narrative. For example, if you're a nurse keeping a record of a patient's progress, you would rely on a time sequence, what is called a time-based method, to convey that information. But time-based narratives can be clinical and monotonous, especially if your purpose is to entertain or persuade.

Establishing a context

It was 1968, the summer of love, and the anti-war movement was beginning to gain momentum in communities throughout the United States.

Notice how the statement sets the time and describes the atmosphere of this moment in time in the United States.

The **temporal approach** is another way of writing about a successive series of events that is not as rigid as the time-based method. With this method, you can use a variety of transitional terms to show the passage of time or to place events in context with other events in your narrative. The word "meanwhile" is often used as the temporal transition that moves the reader on to the next action in your narrative.

A good narrative adopts a **stable point of view** and uses **active verbs** to convey action. Most narratives are either in first or third person. First person, the "I" point of view, offers immediacy and intimacy, and the third person, which uses he/she/it pronouns, offers a more broad and distant point of view. One of the decisions you will make in constructing your narrative is to decide whether you're going to write it in first or third person, but the important thing to remember is that you must stay with one or the other.

Establishing a stable point of view and using active verbs

When I **challenged** the property tax assessment, I **discovered** the town mistakenly **identified** many houses in my town.

Notice how the verbs create a sense of action in the sentence.

Because you are writing about a series of actions or events, it's also good to think in terms of active verbs to tell that story. A verb carries the action of a sentence, and active verbs express meaning more vividly than passive verbs. The most passive form of verbs is the "to be" verb in all of its forms (am, is, was, are were, and so on), as they simply capture a state of being rather than action.

A good narrative incorporates **dialogue at key points in the story**. Even the nurse recording a patient's progress in a clinical, time-sequenced narrative can use dialogue to capture the patient's state of mind when recording the answer to the question, "How are you feeling?" It's important to incorporate dialogue when you are writing nonfiction (essays, response papers, letters, reports, interviews) and when you're writing fiction (short stories, novels, and anything else you "make up").

Using dialogue to enliven your narrative

My father, being an avid baseball fan, always said, as I left the house, "*Keep your eye on the ball.*" As a kid, that never made sense to me, but as I grew older I began to understand the wisdom in that simple statement.

Notice how the dialogue adds to the narrator's description.

In nonfiction, you need to be true to the facts represented in dialogue. You may not walk around with a notebook recording what people say to you, but you can fairly and accurately represent the facts when you're recreating dialogue. For example, if your grandfather told you stories about his life when he came to this country as a new immigrant, you may not have written down exactly what he said, but you can use dialogue to enliven your account of the experience. You can qualify your dialogue by introducing it in ways such as, *I remember my grandfather saying, "It was the hardest thing I'd ever done."* That way, you qualify that this is your memory of the event and you've captured the essence of what he said. Using dialogue in realistic ways helps you capture how people speak. For example, that nurse whose patient responds, "I feel like an elephant is sitting on my chest," needs to write the statement exactly as the patient has said it, because although the patient doesn't use the words *heart attack*, his statement does describe very accurately the feeling the patient is having at that moment.

Writing Strategies: Description

Narration and **description** often go hand in hand; you can hardly have one without the other, yet the elements of each form are separate and distinct. Writing relies on the reader's imagination to make meaning of the words on the page. So it's up to the writer to be as detailed, specific, and concrete as possible, in order to represent the world he or she is writing about fully and accurately for the reader. You accomplish that with description.

You know the world through your senses—you see, hear, taste, touch, and smell your way through the world. You continually make judgments based on the information you get through your five senses. Imagine the power you could inject into your writing if you had the power to appeal to a reader's five senses. You have that power through the effective use of descriptive detail.

Consider this passage from Thomas Mann's *Confessions of Felix Krull, Confidence Man:*

> It was a narrow room, with a rather high ceiling, and crowded from floor to ceiling with goodies. There were rows and rows of hams and sausages of all shapes and colors—white, yellow, red and black; fat and lean and round and long—rows of canned preserves, cocoa and tea, bright translucent glass bottles of honey, marmalade and jam.
>
> I stood enchanted, straining my ears and breathing in the delightful atmosphere and the mixed fragrance of chocolate and smoked fish and earthy truffles. I spoke into the silence, say: "Good day" in a quite loud voice; I can still remember how my strained, unnatural tones died away in the stillness. No one answered. And my mouth literally began to water like a spring. One quick, noiseless step and I was beside one of the laden tables. I made one rapturous grab into the nearest glass urn, filled as it chanced with chocolate creams, slipped a fistful into my coat pocket, then reached the door, and the next second was safely round the corner.

Here, Mann writes with words that are specific and concrete in their appeal to the senses. We see: narrow room, high ceiling, hams, sausages, preserves, and more. We smell: fragrance of chocolate, smoked fish, earthy truffles. We hear: "Good day," unnatural tones, stillness. We taste: mouth, water like a spring. We touch: grab, slipped, fistful into my coat pocket. Now, he could have simply said something like, "I was poor and I'd never seen such an array of food." Dull, dull, dull. It's the vivid detail that Mann uses that invites you into the experience of that moment.

Descriptions often come alive through the use of **figurative language**, which is the artful use of elements like metaphors and similes. **Metaphors** offer a way of understanding one thing by comparing it to another. This type of comparison creates a new way of seeing and understanding the thing you're describing. For example, "my memory is a little foggy" gives the intangible "memory" a physical point of reference "foggy," so that we can picture fog clouding someone's ability to remember something accurately. **Similes** offer a more direct comparison using the word "like" or "as." For example, "biting into a hot pizza is like molten lava spreading across the roof of your mouth." Here, you've taken an ordinary event—eating pizza—and brought it to life in a way that allows the reader to instantly relate to that experience.

In getting the reader to see what you see, you need to use specific detail that describes the scene and make comparisons that are both somewhat provocative and make logical sense. You are trying to create a picture in the reader's mind, so the more specific

---

Thomas Mann, *Confessions of Felix Krull*, New York: Vintage Books, 1955.

Writer Citizen

detail you can provide, the more likely you will be to succeed at conveying exactly what you mean. Good descriptions create a unifying, dominate impression, as Maxine Hong Kingston, an Asian American writer, does here, explaining her experience when first speaking English publicly in *The Woman Warrior*:

> I became silent. A dumbness—a shame—still cracks my voice in two, even when I want to say "hello" casually, or ask an easy question in front of the check-out counter, or ask directions of a bus driver. I stand frozen.

In this descriptive passage, Kingston, the daughter of Chinese immigrants, captures the shame that sets the tone for this passage in her book. If you were to read on in that section, you see and feel that sense of shame reverberating through each paragraph. It is that kind of unification of ideas that you strive for in writing descriptive essays or simply in using description as a technique in all forms of writing.

For many writers, this kind of clarity often comes only in the revision process. During that process, you are able to see all of the elements you've included in your essay and can ask the hard questions about what fits and what doesn't; what contributes to that unifying feeling and what detracts from it. In the editing process, you have the chance to sharpen that vision.

Exemplifying Narration and Description

Cherry

Mary Karr

Mary Karr (1955–) is a poet and a memoirist known for her searing accounts of growing up in America in the 1950s and 1960s. Her latest book, *Lit*, has been nominated for a National Book Award.

Prereading: As you read, note how Karr is telling the story (narration). How does she draw you in? How does she keep your interest and compel you to read on? What narrative strategies does she use (the context, the sequencing of events, the use of active verbs and dialogue)? Note, too, how she chooses to describe the events she is telling you about. How does she make these scenes vivid? What metaphors does she use to paint the picture in your mind? What figurative language does she employ? How does she appeal to your senses in her descriptions?

Only one girl showed outlaw tendencies nearly as wild as mine: Clarice Fontenot, who at fourteen had three years on me, which discrepancy didn't seem to matter at first.

The only obstacle to our spending every conceivable second together that summer was her Cajun daddy's tight rein on her, which consisted of seemingly innumerable chores and capricious rules he ginned out.

The Fontenots lived in a celery-green house on the corner that seemed to bulge at its seams with her wild-assed brothers. They all slicked back their hair on the sides and walked with a sexy, loose-hipped slouch. If they looked at you at all, the glance came from the sides of their faces. Like their tight-lipped father, they barely spoke, just radiated a sly disapproval.

Clarice's role in that Catholic household seemed to be serving their needs. While they ran the roads, she scrubbed and hung laundry and baby-sat a variety of black-eyed cousins whose faces (like hers) were spattered with freckles as if flicked from a paintbrush. Her blights and burdens put me in mind of Cinderella's, though Clarice rarely whined. Still, her circumstances defined her somehow, for her jittery, electric manner seemed to have formed itself solely to oppose both her station in life and her brothers' quiet surliness.

Clarice would have hung out at my house every day for the abundant food and the air conditioning if not my somewhat peculiar company. But her daddy's strictness was the stuff of neighborhood legend. A compact, steel-gray man, he was about the only guy on our block who didn't do refinery work (I think he worked for the gas company). That he wore a tie to work made him not exotic but peculiar. No one's daddy knew his schedule or ever heard him say more than a passing hey. Usually, Clarice could only play at my house an hour or so before she'd be called home for chores. I didn't take these partings lightly.

Once she was back home, I'd patrol the strip of road before her house, skate-boarding past palmettos and the dog run and back again, trying all the while to predict her return by the advance of her work. Window by window, the glass she was washing would lose its grease smears and begin to give back blue sky and flickers of sun when I rolled by. Or I'd watch through those windows while Clarice unhooked each venetian blind. I'd try to measure how long it would take for her to lower those blinds into the Clorox-fuming bathtub, to wash each slat, then towel it off and reappear to hang the blind, giving me an exasperated wave before moving to the next.

Sometimes her daddy just summoned her home for no reason. Which infuriated me. She'd joke that his fun-meter had gone off, some invisible gauge he had that measured the extent of her good time and sought to lop it off. He'd insist she stay in her own yard, and forbid me to cross over the property line. I'd pace their yard's edge for an hour at a pop, or just sit cross-legged along their hurricane fence line reading while their deranged German shepherd loped and bayed and threatened to eat my face off. From my lap I'd flip him the permanent bird using a Venus pencil to keep my fingers cocked in place. A few times, Clarice joined me in this border-holding action. She'd loiter in the heat on her side of the fence, glancing over her shoulder till her dad's gray face slid into a window or his gravelly voice shouted her in.

Doubtless her daddy meant this all as some kind of protection. Plenty of girls her age "got in trouble," and there were countless lowlife characters circling like sharks to pluck any unwatched female into libidinal activity in some hot rod or pickup truck. But my own parents were so lax about corralling me at all ("You can do anything you're big enough to do," Daddy liked to say) that I found Mr. Fontenot's strictures mind-boggling. In my head I engaged in long courtroom soliloquies about him, at the ends of which he and his feckless sons were led away shackled while a gavel banged and Clarice and I hugged each other in glee.

Clarice bridled against her daddy's limits but never actually broke the rules. She lacked both the self-pity and the fury I had in such abundance. She laughed in a foghorn-like blast that drew stares in public. She could belch on command loud enough to cause old ladies in restaurants to ask for far tables. I never mastered this. But thanks to her, I can whistle with my fingers, execute a diving board flip, turn a cartwheel, tie a slip knot, and make my eyeballs shiver like a mesmerist. While other people worried what would come of Clarice if she didn't calm down, for me she had the absolute power of someone who fundamentally didn't give a damn, which she didn't (other than toeing her father's line, which she seemed to do breezily enough).

My first memory of her actually comes long before that summer. It was from the bleached-out time before we'd passed through the school doors, so we had no grade levels by which to rank ourselves.

A cold sun was sliding down a gray fall sky. Some older boys had been playing tackle football in the field we took charge of every weekend. In a few years, they'd be called to Southeast Asia, some of them. Their locations would be tracked with pushpins in red, white, and blue on maps on nearly every kitchen wall. But that afternoon, they were quick as young deer. They leapt and dodged, dove from each other and collided in mid-air. Bulletlike passes flew to connect them. Or the ball spiraled in high arc across the frosty sky one to another. In short, they were mindlessly agile in a way that captured as audience every little kid within running distance of the yellow goalposts.

We could not help watching. Even after I stepped accidentally in a fire-ant nest and got a constellation of crimson bites on my ankles. Even after streetlights clicked on and our breaths began to spirit before us and to warm my hands I had to pull my arms from my sweatshirt sleeves, then tuck my fingers into my armpits so the sleeves flapped empty as an amputee's. In fact, even once the game had ended, when the big boys had run off to make phone calls or do chores, we stayed waiting to be called for supper. I can almost hear the melamine plates being slid from the various cupboards and stacked on tile counters. But having witnessed their game, we were loath to unloose ourselves from the sight of it.

It was before the time of stark hierarchies. Our family dramas were rumored, but the stories that would shape us had not yet been retold so often as to calcify our characters inside them. Our rivalries had not yet been laid down. No one was big enough to throw a punch that required stitches or to shout an invective that would loop through your head at night till tears made your pillowcase damp. Our sexual wonderings seldom called us to touch each other, just stare from time to time at the mystery of each other's pale underpants or jockey shorts, which we sometimes traded looks at under a porch or in the blue dark of a crawl space. For years our names ran together like beads on a string, John and Bobbie Clarice and Cindy and Little Mary (as opposed to Big Mary, who was Mary Ferrell). With little need to protect our identities from each other, we could still fall into great idleness together—this handful of unwatched kids with nowhere to be.

At some moment, Clarice figured out as none of us had before how to shinny up the goalpost.

That sight of her squiggling up the yellow pole magically yanks the memory from something far-off into a kind of 3-D present. I am alive in it. There's early frost on the grass, and my ant bites itch. Clarice's limbs have turned to rubber as she wraps round the pole. She's kicked off her Keds, so her bare feet on cold metal give purchase. About a foot at a time she scoots up, hauls herself by her hands, then slides her feet high. And again. She's weightless as an imp and fast.

At the top of the pole, she rises balletic, back arched like a trapeze artist. She flings one hand up: *Ta-da,* she says, as if she were sheathed in a crimson-spangled bathing suit with fishnet hose and velvet ballet slippers, then again *ta-da.* We cheer and clap, move back to the ten-yard line to take her in better. This is a wonder, for her to climb so far above us. And there we align ourselves with the forces of awe that permit new tricks to be dreamed up on chilly fall nights when nothing but suppers of fried meat and cream gravy await us, or tepid baths.

For a few minutes, Bobbie Stuart tries to weasel up the other pole, but he's too stiff. His legs jackknife out from under him, and his arms can't hold his long thin body.

Then Clarice does something wholly unexpected for which she will be forever marked.

She sticks her thumbs in the gathered waistband of her corduroy pants with the cowgirl lassos stitched around the pockets. With those thumbs, she yanks both her pants and her underpanties down around her bare feet. She then bends over and waggles her butt at us as I later learned strippers sometimes do. Screams of laughter from us. John falls over and rolls on the ground like a dog, pointing up and laughing at her bare white ass, which still holds a faint tan line from summer.

We've just about got used to the idea of her butt when she executes another move. She wheels around to face us and show us her yin-yang, a dark notch in her hairless pudendum. Her belly is round as a puppy's jutted forward. Then our howls truly take on hyena-like timbre. And there across the ditch, which marks the realm of adult civilization, appears the fast moving figure of Mrs. Carter through leaf smoke of a ditch fire. She's holding the spatula in her hand with which she intends to blister our asses, Clarice's most specifically.

But she's a grown-up, Mrs. Carter. Her steps on the middy slope are tentative. Not wanting to funk up her shoes with mud, she hesitates before she leaps across. And in that interval, Clarice slithers down the yellow pole and tears off in a streak. And the rest of us flee like wild dogs.

Decades later, I asked Clarice point blank why she did it. We were in our forties then, living two thousand miles apart, and talking—oddly enough—on our car phones. Her voice was sandpaper rough with a cold, but it still carried the shimmer of unbidden amusement. I'd only seen her every two or three years—the occasional holiday, at my daddy's funeral, and after Mother's bypass surgery when she kept vigil with me. Still, there's no one who'd be less likely to tell me a flat-footed lie. Across the hissing static, I asked why she took her pants down that day, whether somebody had dared her to and I just didn't remember.

The answer that she gave remains the truest to who she was and who I then so much needed her to be: "Because I could, I guess," she said. "Wasn't anybody around to stop me." ✒

Comprehending the Text

1. Why did Karr select this particular scene for her book?

2. What does this scene reveal about character—both Karr's and Clarice's—and their circumstances?

3. What "outlaw tendencies" does Clarice display in this passage?

Analyzing the Text

1. Identify five sensory details that Karr uses and explain how those details work in this piece.

2. Identify one piece of dialogue that reveals Clarice's character.

3. Identify five action verbs that keep this narrative moving forward.

Developing Your Skills: Narration

You probably use narration every day as a strategy for communicating. Every time you tell a friend what you did over the weekend, you tell the story of your weekend—you're using narration. Think about a time when you heard some shocking news. Perhaps it was a news report—the attack on the World Trade Center, the earthquake in Haiti, or even an event closer to you, such as the death of a grandparent or someone close to you. Or maybe it was some kind of news that came from popular culture—Brad and Angelina fighting, your favorite contestant getting cut from *American Idol,* or the crazy antics of the Kardashians. Think about where you were, and whom you were with when you heard the news. What was your reaction? What did you say? How did you feel? What did you do in reacting to the news? Now write a narrative that tells the story of that moment. Remember to use active verbs and employ a logical progression of ideas so that your reader can comprehend this event and its impact on you.

Developing Your Skills: Description

You may or may not recognize this photograph. Regardless of whether you know the real story here, take a minute and imagine what is going on in this photograph. Your job here is to explore your imagination as you look at this scene and then describe, in detail, what you see and what you imagine to be the story behind this scene. Tell the story of this scene.

Jeff Widener/AP Images

Imagine the identity of the man standing in front of the tank. Why is he there? What is he feeling? Is his heart pounding? Is he angry? What's in that bag he's carrying? How old is he? Where does he work? What country is this? What does the air smell like? Imagine what the crew in the tanks feel when this man walks out in front of them. Who are they? What is their mission here rolling their tanks down a city street? What is going on just outside the frame of this photograph? Who is taking the picture? What is his or her intent? Remember to use concrete and specific details and incorporate as many sensory details as you can in your description.

Writing Strategies: Definition

When considering the role of rhetoric in creating the world around you, you will realize the importance of the precise use of language and how we arrive at our common understanding of the world. That's where the rhetorical strategy of *definition* comes into play. What does it mean to be "an educated citizen" in the twenty-first century? How would you define that term for a contemporary audience?

Defining your terms, and making sure your audience is clear about what your definitions are, is essential to effective communication. What is citizenship? What is patriotism? What is terrorism? What constitutes a threat? Ask any five people those questions and you are likely to get a hundred different answers. What's the right answer? It all depends on how you define your terms. Definitions of the same word may change, depending on the context and situation. For each of those five people, you may find five definitions of each of those words.

We use **definition** as a way of making sense of our world routinely and often unconsciously. Your first instinct may be to go to the dictionary to find the definition of a word. That literal application of definition is useful when you have unfamiliar terms, technical language, or jargon. For example, maybe you don't know the word "jargon" that we used in the previous sentence. So here is how you might construct a **literal definition**: Jargon often refers to technical or specialized language used by a group to communicate to others in the group. For example, "Lawyers often lobby against tort reform" might be the kind of sentence you'd find lawyers and lawmakers using when talking about legislation that might limit their ability to sue people for damages.

Definition is also useful when you're dealing with **controversial terms** that elicit strong emotional reaction. If you have any chance of communicating with your reader, you'll need to be very specific about supercharged terms such as "terrorism" or "weapons of mass destruction" or even "politically correct." You should put your terms in context and define them specifically for the purpose you intend in your writing.

To be persuasive, writers often need to define **abstract concepts** in concrete ways so that the reader can more easily understand the concept. This brief example from Barbara Ehrenreich's book *Nickel and Dimed* shows a way of defining the abstract term "extreme poverty":

> You would come across news of a study showing that the percentage of Wisconsin food-stamp families in "extreme poverty"—defined as less than 50 percent of the federal poverty line—has tripled in the last decade to more than 30 percent.

The origin of a word often provides insight into the terms you're using in your writing. The **etymology** of a word shows the origin and the historical evolution of a word. For example, you might say, "She is luminous" in describing someone you see on the subway. If you look that up in the dictionary, you'll find that "luminous" comes from the Latin word *lumen*, meaning "light." It's not likely that you'll use the etymology of a word in routine definitions of terms or in a definition essay. However, etymology can add to your understanding of a word and give you a fuller sense of how the language works.

Barbara Ehrenreich, *Nickled and Dimed: On (Not) Getting By in America*, New York: Henry Holt and Company, 2008.

Another way to clarify your definition of a term involves identifying what it is like, that is, by using a **synonym**: a word or phrase closely related in meaning that you use in place of another word or phrase. For example, in trying to further clarify the definition of "frozen," you might say, "The lake was iced over"; in doing that, you're not only expanding on your term "frozen," but you're also writing about it in a more vivid and expressive way. Of course, you can also define your terms by clarifying what they are not, that is, by **negation**. Here is a typical example: "Freedom isn't free."

In your college career, you will likely be called upon to write all kinds of definitions. To do that, you'll employ one or several of the techniques we've talked about so far. For example, you may be called upon to write a definition of "nihilism" on a philosophy exam; to do so, you might use a synonym like "nonexistence" to clarify that term. You may also remember the etymology of that word and note that it comes from the Latin word *nihil*, meaning "nothingness." If you do that, you'll be well on your way to defining that term. In cases in which you need to do more than just give a logical, literal definition of word or a phrase, consider writing an **extended definition**. You will find extended definitions in technical, science, and business writing, as one might define the parameters of a particular use of memory, or you might find an extended definition of "recession" as it applies to a small business.

Consider this example from John Dewey and his work *Education and Democracy*, as he defines the concept of *education*:

> We have seen that a community or social group sustains itself through continuous self-renewal, and that this renewal takes place by means of the educational growth of the immature members of the group. By various agencies, unintentional and designed, a society transforms uninitiated and seemingly alien beings into robust trustees of its own resources and ideals. Education is thus a fostering, a nurturing, a cultivating, process . . . . Etymologically, the word education means just a process of leading or bringing up. When we have the outcome of the process in mind, we speak of education as shaping, forming, molding activity—that is, a shaping into the standard form of social activity.

In this passage, Dewey takes the abstract concept "community" and defines it as sustaining itself "through continuous renewal." Dewey builds his definition by describing what "education" and by tracing the etymology of the word.

An extended definition focuses on a word or phrase and discusses it in detail, often using elements of other modes of discourse. To return to Dewey, consider his extended definition of the word "democracy":

> A democracy is more than a form of government; it is primarily a mode of associated living, of conjoint communicated experience. The extension in space of the number of individuals who participate in an interest so that each has to refer his own action to that of others, and to consider the action of others to

give point and direction to his own, is equivalent to the breaking down of those barriers of class, race, and national territory which kept men from perceiving the full import of their activity.

Dewey defines democracy by comparing the concept to "associated living." He adds to his definition through the use of metaphor explaining that democracy is "the breaking down of barriers."

Using Definition

You have taken on the environment as a topic and you have come up with the focus of your essay. Your tentative title is: Environmentalist or Conservationist: Which One Are You? In thinking about the modes of discourse, you could *narrate* the history of those two words; you could *describe* the characteristics of each; you could offer *examples* of environmentalists and conservationists; you could *compare and contrast* the two terms; and you could *argue* your perspective on which one you believe you are and why.

When **structuring a definition essay**, you might use the logical definition constructed as a thesis statement and then expand on the category and what differentiates your terms in that category. Using the environmentalist or conservationist example (see the box "Using Definition"), you might construct your extended definition essay like this:

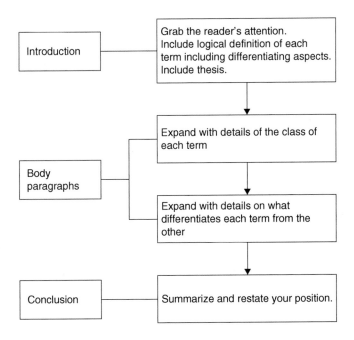

Developing Your Skills: Definition

Definition can be highly dependent on who is defining what. Following are two terms, liberal and conservative, with synonyms attached to them that offer a particular point of view:

LIBERAL

- **Tolerant, generous, open-minded, enlightened, broadminded, charitable**

CONSERVATIVE

- **Biased, prejudiced, stingy, narrow-minded, regressive, closed**

What's your reaction when you read this? How would you define "liberal" and "conservative"?

YOUR TURN: Creating Your Ideas

1. Read through the following definitions:
    - Rhetoric—Requires an audience, has a purpose, and is a response to a situation
    - Community—A group of people who share interests, identity, and/or experiences and who are connected through communicative practices
    - Narration—A method of organizing and conveying action and information; the act of telling a story that will have a point and in telling the story you will provide insight into your subject

    Write an essay where you create a *narrative* in which you tell a story about something that has happened in your community. You must be an active participant in the story—you cannot just stand by and tell us something happened. Use detail and *description* to show the readers the richness of your community and the importance of the "incident." Try to work toward showing the reader the importance of this community in your life, as well as your importance to the community. Remember that your story must have a point and provide insight into your subject.

2. Write an essay in which you define the democratic environment you live in. For example, do you have a say in your family life? What kind of democracy do you live in there? What kind of democracy do you live in your campus life? Do you vote? Have you ever voted for someone on *American Idol* or in some online poll? Select a slice of your life where you feel as though you're living in a democratic culture. Now, define what *you* mean by democratic culture. Describe how rhetorical practices (participating in a family discussion, casting a vote, etc.) play an important role in determining how that democratic culture works. Describe how are communities are formed from your rhetorical practices.

Writer Citizen

(For example, if you participate in an online poll, do you also add comments and form relationships with other people who comment there? What kind of community are you forming?)

3. Identify a current example of rhetoric in action from your own life that you feel exemplifies citizenship (a song, an advertising campaign, a website, a blog). Then, in a two page response, (1) define the term "citizen" according to you; and (2) draw upon your example to describe how the rhetoric in action exemplifies citizenship.

TECH TALK: Forms of Contemporary Rhetoric

Technology and the development of the Internet have changed how we experience communication in our lives. The Internet has created a place where communication happens 24 hours a day, and we can turn to the Internet to find out all types of information, ranging from directions for our next road trip to recent news reports and political debates. In particular, the development of online communication devices like email, blogs, and podcasts are increasingly carrying messages to us each day.

Blogging: In the early 1990s, we came upon a new form of communication called **blogging**, which is articles written on web logs, or the more informal name "blogs." Blogs originally began as online journals created by everyday people. Since then, they have grown to include the news, politics, pop culture, and more. Blogs are similar to talk radio. Within minutes of an event taking place, a blog writer can have information up on the Web for the public to read. Many blogs also invite feedback and responses, thus enabling people from all over the world to comment on and discuss an issue of common interest. Increasingly, we see media outlets such as CNN and MSNBC turning to blogs to report on politics and world events. In addition, blogs are where we see communities forming over common interests, ranging from book clubs to hobbies to political activist groups.

Podcasting: Podcasting, which has emerged on the Internet scene most fully in the early twenty-first century, is an online media delivery system. Podcasters create audio files, which are then accessible via the Internet to the public—often for free. For example, National Public Radio offers its daily news hour via a podcast. Individuals can download the file onto their personal audio player and head off to the gym or to take a walk while catching up on the news. Like blogs, podcasts have changed how we receive information on a daily basis. Moreover, podcasts have become rhetorical tools for politicians looking to reach a wider audience, activist groups looking to persuade you to join them, and media sources looking to disseminate current news information.

Chapter 3

The Rhetorical Moment

*E*ach and every time you are called upon to use your rhetorical skills, you face a particular rhetorical moment or situation. Rhetoric responds to some stimulus or problem and, as such, must be crafted to fit the requirements of the situation. In this chapter, you will explore the many decisions that you must make as an effective writer and communicator in any rhetorical situation.

Understanding the Rhetorical Moment

Consider this scenario: Nicole's first job after graduating from college is as a research assistant for a nonprofit organization in Washington, D.C. The organization works on women's issues around the world, including health, economics, and legal protections. As part of her job, Nicole analyzes information gathered from surveys of women in the United States. Her boss asked Nicole to prepare a report of her analysis of that information that the organization would use for fundraising purposes. In particular, Nicole's boss requested that the report be presented in a multimedia format.

Nicole faces a huge challenge. Not only does she have to make her report into a polished document, she must also translate a lot of information into an interesting media format. But Nicole first has much research to do before she can start shaping her information into a presentation. In order to produce a document that would fulfill her assignment, Nicole needs to discover and understand the following elements of the situation:

1. Her audience
2. The kinds of settings in which her report will be read
3. The goal her organization seeks to achieve by publishing her report

4. The resources available to her as the producer of the report

5. How long her report should be

6. What kinds of media are and are not appropriate

7. What deadlines she has to meet

8. How to talk about her information in ways that will be interesting and strategically appropriate for a fundraising document

As this list demonstrates, constructing a strategic document—whether a report of the magnitude of Nicole's, a letter to a newspaper editor, a blog entry, or a writing assignment for this class—involves many choices and decisions. Effective and strategic communication—whether written or spoken—goes beyond good grammar and presentation.

Nicole's best starting place will be with a consideration of the three most basic elements of her assignment: the writer/speaker, the audience, and the subject, or, as noted earlier, *ethos*, *pathos*, and *logos*. Her success depends on the interaction of all of these elements in her final product. As the writer, Nicole must demonstrate her knowledge of the subject, her ability to communicate that subject clearly to her audience, and her ability to adjust to the various demands of her boss regarding the report. This interconnected relationship between writer and audience is known as the **rhetorical triangle**:

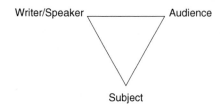

Keeping in mind these essential components of effective communication will assist you in preparing efficiently and successfully for each rhetorical moment you encounter.

Defining the Rhetorical Moment

A theoretical concept developed by Lloyd Bitzer, a contemporary rhetorical scholar, offers some guidelines and structure for such challenges. Bitzer articulated the idea of a "rhetorical situation" in which rhetorical communication comes about as a response to an issue, problem, or concern. The ability to break down the rhetorical situation or moment into conceptual and real elements will go a long way toward increasing your skills as an effective communicator. All rhetorical moments consist of exigencies (defined in the following section), the audience, and the limitations and opportunities of the moment. These elements are important to consider when planning a written or other type of communication project.

According to Lloyd Bitzer's theory, a rhetorical situation contains three elements:

1. The exigence = a problem that needs fixing or an issue that needs to be addressed.
2. The rhetorical audience = the audience that can fix the problem or address the issue.
3. Constraints = the people or events or situations that can affect the decisions or actions necessary to affect the exigence.

Overall, the exigence is that which brings a rhetorical response into being.

Understanding Exigencies

An **exigence** is a problem that needs fixing or an issue that needs attention. The exigence is that to which you, the communicator, respond. When discussing the idea of exigence, though, it is important to recognize that there may be many exigencies in a particular situation. In other words, you will rarely face only one simple issue that requires a rhetorical response.

Consider Nicole's situation once more. What are the various exigencies that Nicole faces when writing a report for her boss?

- It's an assignment from her boss and she wants to keep her job.
- If she does well on this report, Nicole may earn a raise.
- The organization needs funds, so the report is a fundraising tool.
- There are serious problems in the United States (and beyond) that Nicole's organization can help to solve. The report is one way to share information and initiate change.

Exigence in Action

The exigence determines the focus of a person's written or verbal communication. For example, consider President Ronald Reagan's well-known speech on the space shuttle *Challenger* disaster in January 1986. President Reagan opened his speech with the following lines:

> Ladies and gentlemen, I'd planned to speak to you tonight to report on the state of the Union, but the events of earlier today have led me to change those plans. Today is a day for mourning and remembering. Nancy and I are pained to the core by the tragedy of the shuttle *Challenger*. We know we share this pain with all of the people of our country. This is truly a national loss.

> Nineteen years ago, almost to the day, we lost three astronauts in a terrible accident on the ground. But we've never lost an astronaut in flight. We've never had a tragedy like this.

Due to the *Challenger* loss, President Reagan's exigence—the issue that needed attention for his national address—changed from the state of the union to the national tragedy. (The full text of Reagan's speech is included in the "Rhetoric in Action" section at the end of this chapter.)

This list demonstrates that there are several reasons why Nicole is preparing her report. It would be too simple to state that she has to make her report solely because her boss told her to do so. That's only a small part of the thinking process that Nicole must go through to accomplish the bigger task—producing a document that will serve a strategic, argumentative, and persuasive purpose for her organization.

Exigencies and Your Writing

Most of the writing you do in college will likely be in response to an assignment. These assignments should encourage you to learn how to respond to the world around you, to deal with problems and issues with which you are concerned. Can you complete writing assignments that serve both purposes? Of course. Does that complicate the assignment? You bet.

Similar to Nicole's report assignment, an assignment to write in response to "real-world" issues or exigencies means that you must consider your instructor and his or her expectations as well as relevant "real-world" decision makers. Whether you major in writing, engineering, nursing, or education, you carry with you the ability to discern the multiple layers of issues and problems that require your rhetorical response.

Imagine, for example, that your college campus has no recycling program. As a result, the campus is littered with printer cartridges, newspaper, printer paper, plastic bottles, and other waste simply added to the local landfill. In your Introduction to Sociology class, you have been assigned the task of creating a brochure that addresses the issue of recycling on your campus in an effort to increase awareness among the faculty and students.

> **Did you know:**
>
> According to the Environmental Protection Agency,
>
> - The amount of waste you create every day has gone from 2.7 pounds to 4.5 pounds from 1960 to 2008.
> - Yard trimmings such as grass and leaves contribute up to 26 percent of waste in the United States.

The assignment will be graded not only on content and layout, but also on how well you mold the information for the audience. Can you forget the teacher? Of course not. But your audience—college students and faculty—is of critical importance to the assignment. In other words, your goal is not to teach your instructor about recycling, but to educate your peers and others in the campus community and to lead them to take action.

In order to address your audience, you first need to consider the various problems (the exigencies) relevant to this assignment:

- **Your grade.** If you don't do the assignment, you will likely receive a zero, lowering your overall grade in the course.

- **Waste as a social and environmental problem.** Key information about recycling will come in handy when creating your assignment. For example, consider the

Writer Citizen

facts in the text boxes. This information detailing the amount of waste in communities and on campuses brings relevance to a problem that students and faculty may have tried to ignore.

- **Multiple issues related to the environment.** Issues associated with the environment range from greenhouse gases, vehicle emissions, melting glaciers, endangered animals like penguins and polar bears, overflowing landfills, government regulations on corporations, and irresponsible waste on college campuses. The list is pretty overwhelming. Even on your campus, there are probably several areas you could target, from campus buses and safety vehicles, to student and faculty carpooling, to a focus on recycling computer parts, aluminum, paper, or glass—you must be selective and specific when deciding which issue to tackle for your project. As you have been asked to focus on recycling, you might focus on one of the last few issues.

In order to determine what kinds of information you should provide, you must work through the layers of associated problems or exigencies in order to arrive at your **controlling exigence**: the key problem you seek to address through your informational brochure.

Determining Your Controlling Exigence

First, you need to decide which problem is the most important or which is the one you will have the most impact upon. Let's say that you discover that a large percentage of campus waste is in the form of paper, glass, and aluminum that ends up in the garbage cans. That waste could become the controlling exigence for your brochure.

With the controlling exigence, you have a basis on which to shape your response to the topic. Understanding the problem helps you determine how to shape your rhetorical communication—what kinds of evidence to use, how to understand and achieve your goals, and how to determine your audience. In other words, your definition of the exigencies or problems you're responding to raise lots of additional questions that you must answer, and require decisions about how you will communicate most effectively. Some of the most critical decisions of this process will involve your audience.

The Rhetorical Audience

Every time you engage in a rhetorical practice, multiple decisions must be made. You have to decide on a topic, which means engaging in prewriting or some sort of brainstorming activity. You also need to determine what rhetorical situation you are addressing. Are you writing a paper for your composition class? Or are you adding to your personal blog that you created to draw attention to campus issues facing students today? This decision making process is complicated further by the need to decide who your audience is—whom do you want to affect with your rhetorical actions and why? Therefore, it is important to consider your purposes for engaging in rhetorical actions, as well as to learn to analyze your audience so that your words have the desired impact.

> ## Who is your audience?
> The audience consists of only those people with an interest in and ability to do something about the problem you seek to address.

In the same manner that you had various levels of issues or exigencies, you have various audiences that are connected closely to those issues. For example, one audience for the informational brochure in your Introduction to Sociology class was the instructor. This audience, your instructor, will establish requirements for the brochure that you need to satisfy in order to achieve a high score or grade. What were some of the other reasons for making this brochure?

- To appeal to college students and faculty
- To persuade your peers and faculty about the benefits of recycling on campus

Your additional goals in accomplishing your assignment indicate that your instructor is not the sole audience for your message. Rather, if you intend to initiate change on your campus, your audience includes the students and faculty as well. Thus, it is important that you identify the audience you wish to target with your message.

Identifying Your Audience

Every rhetorical message has an audience. Returning briefly to the characteristics of rhetoric established early in this book: the audience is an integral and defining part of any rhetorical situation. If you have a specific goal in mind, whether you want to persuade or inform someone of your point of view, there is a particular someone you have in mind when you craft your message.

For example, imagine that your campus is experiencing growth in student numbers but has not created enough parking spaces for everyone. Now, let's imagine that you and some of your classmates decide that you want to voice your opinion on this problem. What do you do? If you really want to make an impact and move toward solving the problem, you need to decide who the decision makers are on your campus regarding parking. You are not going to have much luck changing the situation if your only action is to complain loudly in class, engage in parking lot rage, or park illegally.

Who might be the important people you need to talk to about the problem? If your campus has a Parking Services Department or something similar, that might be the place to begin. You have just identified your **target audience**. Next, you must decide what mode of rhetorical discourse you want to employ in your message. Will you speak to the parking folks? Write them a let-

> **Target audience:**
> The particular someone you have in mind when you develop your message

ter? Send an email? Design a website and send them a link to the page? These questions should start you thinking about the tools you have at your disposal to appeal to your audience, as well as other audiences you might want to target. You could rally support behind your cause with a campus-wide blog or a podcast sent out on a RSS feed to the campus community, for example. The choices you have in any rhetorical situation are potentially overwhelming. Therefore, it is essential that you clarify to yourself what your goals are and how you want to achieve them.

Let's return to your assignment for sociology class. Your informational brochure will require that you further plan and refine your goals so that you arrive at an understanding of the audience. From your controlling issue, you can examine where the root of the problem lies, and from there identify the audience of people who will be able to work on the problem. These questions will help you narrow your scope:

- Why is so much potentially recyclable material ending up in the trash?
- Why is there no campus recycling program? Is it because of a lack of resources like recycling bins, or is it because people on the campus are uninformed?
- Is there a group on campus (i.e., students, staff, or faculty) more responsible for the problem than another?

The answers to these questions—and any other questions you ask—will help you determine what information your audience needs. For example, students may need (and respond to)

Thinking About Audience

A recent letter to the editor of a local college paper was written by a professor who had given a presentation on campus. Her talk had been covered by a student reporter, who apparently misquoted the professor and misrepresented the message. The professor's letter was clearly intended to correct the public's impression and understanding of her speech. She addressed the editor and the readership of the paper, but did not refer directly to the reporter who had written the story. One could imagine that her message to the reporter would not be for public consumption!

Why didn't the professor address the reporter directly?

The professor had a specific goal: to rectify how her speech might be perceived by those reading the paper. Thus, the reporter was not a key member of her target audience. Notice how the goal of the rhetorical act influenced who the writer addressed.

information presented in a different format than faculty (i.e., using social networking tools or examples referring to the future facing the younger generation). In other words, you must analyze your audience and their motivations to read your brochure and take action based on your brochure's points.

You have to remember that not everyone is going to be interested in what you have to say. Your brochure may be compelling, important, and extraordinarily well-written, but if a person doesn't care about the issue you're focusing on, chances are your comments and information will have no effect on that person. On the other hand, careful reflection on the people interested in recycling and likely to recycle will lead you to produce a brochure that will appeal to their interests and values. Analyzing your audience will enhance your understanding of your audience's values and motivations and will help you determine the most appropriate strategies to achieve your goal.

Analyzing Your Audience

Once you have identified your audience through careful reflection upon your goals, you must learn as much as you can about them. **Audience analysis**, an important process, will help you fulfill your rhetorical purpose. You will be able to communicate more efficiently and effectively with more knowledge about those whom you wish to receive, understand, and respond to your message.

Audience analysis seeks to discover general characteristics of your audience, their likely attitudes and values, their willingness to listen to you, and how able they are to be influenced by your message. Although this list may seem long, overly inquisitive, and potentially impossible to discover, remember that your interest lies in getting as much information as possible, recognizing that you will not be able to interview every person alive who might read, like, and be affected by your brochure on recycling. A general sense of your audience will, however, be possible and very helpful.

Some questions you should ask about your audience include:

- What does my audience expect?
- What is my objective in my rhetorical message?
- What kind of information should I use to develop my paper?
- How should I organize and present the information?
- How can I gain and hold the audience's attention?
- What kinds of examples will be most effective for this audience?

For example, if you know that you are most interested in college students and faculty, you can identify characteristics of those populations that **most** of them will hold in common. You're not interested in the specifics of a population, but in the general tendencies, general attitudes, and so on. Because of their association with your campus, they automatically have at least one attribute in common.

One type of audience analysis that can be useful to you is called **demographic analysis**, which is demonstrated by Jeff's story (see following text box). **Demographics** are general characteristics of a population such as age, gender, religion, economic status, and ethnicity. Knowing something about the demographic makeup of your audience can help you understand where they might stand in relation to your message and your purposes. For example, though college students may range widely in age, there are still some issues they will be concerned about, simply because they are students. How many can you think of?

Audience Analysis:

Jeff spent his first college semester living in the dorm, enjoying his first time away from home. He enjoyed the sense of freedom he felt! In fact, Jeff enjoyed making new friends, staying out late, and learning about his new campus home so much that he frequently "forgot" about classes or homework, often convinced by his friends that he could easily catch up. Jeff barely had a GPA after his first semester; he was excused from the next semester. However, the dean of the college informed Jeff that he could be readmitted for the following school year if he wrote a letter of appeal that would explain his previous behavior and how Jeff planned to become a successful student at the college.

When Jeff sat down to write his letter of appeal, he had to figure out exactly what he wanted to accomplish in his letter to the dean. If he genuinely wanted to be readmitted to the school, Jeff had to be clear about that goal, as well as have some ideas about how to accomplish that goal. Further, he needed to think carefully about how to approach the dean in the letter. The dean, Jeff's audience, held Jeff's immediate future in his hands.

Jeff decided that his goal was readmission and that he was willing to work very hard to be a good student, earn good grades, and participate productively in campus life. He realized that his audience, the dean, was a highly educated person to whom education and learning were important, as well as the college itself. A little research revealed to Jeff that the dean had no patience with students who came to school and played around. However, the dean had established scholarship funds and other support for students who excelled at their studies, represented the campus in the community and with various groups, and were good citizens of the school. In short, Jeff had to prove to the dean that he held similar concerns, had a strong work ethic, had ambition, and, importantly, would not replicate his first semester. To craft the letter, Jeff adopted a strong tone and was very careful to use proper grammar and intelligent language. His letter sounded professional, respectful, and educated. Jeff was readmitted to the college, where he is looking forward to graduation!

(Continued)

Jeff obviously made some assumptions about the dean based on his position in the college and level of education. Therefore, we can conclude that Jeff, regardless of whether he knew it, did some demographic analysis for his letter. In addition to demographic analysis, though, Jeff also considered the dean's attitudes toward education and hard work, as evidenced by some of the dean's official acts while holding his position in the college. When we think about the types of questions Jeff might have asked himself about the audience for his letter, he probably asked "What does my audience expect?" This question gives Jeff guidelines for what to include in the letter (information about the job he has held while waiting to be reinstated, how he performed as a high school student, the volunteer opportunity he recently discovered and is anxious to begin, and so on) *and* what to leave out (what Jeff was doing during his first semester of college, Jeff's favorite music, and how angry Jeff's parents were when he told them the news of his expulsion, to name a few things). The expectations of your audience need to be one of your most important considerations when beginning to craft your rhetorical message.

Demographic analysis offers insights into general tendencies your audience may hold. From these general tendencies, then, you can figure out how to tailor your messages for targeted members of your audience.

Targeting Your Audience

From your analysis of the audience, you will have more ideas about targeting your audience. Jeff's story might be a clue to the most difficult part of the process of dealing with your audience. Many decisions must be made in order to correctly fulfill the audience's expectations, connect with them, and achieve your goal. Once you have gathered some information about the audience who will be the target of your message, you must peruse your rhetorical toolbox for the most appropriate tools.

In order to communicate effectively and rhetorically, you have to make a wide range of decisions, including how best to address, or target, your audience. Your job is not to tell the audience what they want to hear, but to craft your message so that they will hear, understand, and respond to what you have to say. In other words, if your audience analysis has shown that you are likely to have a tough time convincing your audience of your point of view (i.e., Jeff's argument to the dean of his college), your goal doesn't change, but the way you go about accomplishing that goal must adjust to the audience.

For example, the dean of Jeff's college was probably not inclined to let Jeff come back to school. Given that knowledge, Jeff could have decided to forget all about it, go to trade school, and become an auto mechanic or hair dresser. However, he decided he really wanted to pursue college and become a public relations specialist. As a result, he had to

> **Audience analysis helps writers determine:**
> - What kind of language to use
> - What modes of writing or speaking to engage in
> - What examples will resonate with an audience
> - How many examples might be necessary to have an impact
> - How much an audience might know about the writer's topic
> - Whether an audience is likely to agree or disagree with the writer's point of view, or the audience is willing to learn from the writer

find a way to tailor a message that would overcome the dean's objections and ultimately change the dean's mind about readmitting Jeff to school.

The key points to targeting your audience center on making your message acceptable to those who are interested in your message, affected by your concerns, able to be influenced by your message, and able to help you achieve your goals. The choices you need to make concern all the strategies you have in your rhetorical toolbox:

- Language
- Form
- Examples
- Evidence
- Strategies of style

How you use those tools is a direct function of your audience analysis.

Addressing Your Audience

Now that you have identified, analyzed, and targeted the audience for your rhetorical message, it is time to actually address that audience. Aristotle's ideas about *ethos*, *pathos*, and *logos* offer you some strategies that have stood the test of history.

If you recall, Aristotle worked to figure out and describe how people actually communicated in practice, rather than in theory. Granted, his world was enormously different than yours, but his agenda is worth remembering today. Remember Aristotle's definition of rhetoric? In Chapter 1, we agreed that his definition was important because of his attention to the situation in which communication was occurring. That situation included the audience. His attention to the situation—and the audience—involved strategies that Aristotle called the "artistic proofs" because they are within the art, or control, of the message creator.

Here again, you will be faced with a set of choices as you determine precisely how you will present your message. Each message will, in a way, be a specially tailored recipe or combination of Aristotle's artistic proofs: *ethos*, *pathos*, and *logos*. We can relate this recipe to the triangle of essential components introduced at the beginning of the chapter: the writer/speaker, the audience, and the subject. Although the audience ultimately decides whether you have met the requirements of demonstrating *ethos*, *pathos*, and *logos* in your communication, we can visualize their relationship like this:

> **Artistic proofs:** materials that the message creator finds, like research or testimony. The artistic proofs then determine how that material is used.

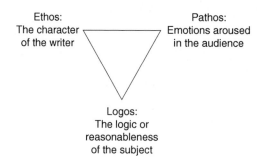

Ethos:
The character
of the writer

Pathos:
Emotions aroused
in the audience

Logos:
The logic or
reasonableness
of the subject

Ethos: The Appeal Exerted by the Character of the Writer

Ethos is the writer's character or credibility. Aristotle believed that a person making an argument needed to exhibit good sense, good will, and good character in order to earn the audience's trust. Establishing your ethos means that you must demonstrate a command of your subject (good sense), show that you are responsible and ethical (good will), and prove that you are a good person (good character). How do you do this? Well, you'd sound pretty silly if you

> **Demonstrate your Ethos in Your Writing or Speech Act**
> - Give accurate information
> - Cite credible sources
> - Document your findings correctly

started your letter to the editor with, "I have a lot of ethos." So, it isn't quite as easy as simply telling your audience to trust you. Rather, you have to demonstrate ethos. Ethos is the appeal to the audience that tells them that you have their best interests at heart, that you are not an evil person out to manipulate them, and that your information—and you!—are trustworthy.

Demonstrating ethos requires that you give accurate information and cite the credible sources of that information in your messages. If you have accumulated research, you want your audience to see the hard work you've done and to understand that the facts, statistics, and quotations you are presenting are true and support the point you want to make. In other words, you're neither making up the information nor plagiarizing it from another source. Citing your sources also tells your audience that you have consulted experts who are also of high ethos or credibility, making your argument that much more worthy of their time and trust. Doing high-quality, creative research and using good information shows your audience that you have considered the sources available to you and made wise choices about which to consult. All of these features point to you as someone of good sense, good will, and good character.

Demonstrating ethos mean being consistently ethical. In other words, if you regularly write letters to the editor or participate on a political weblog, your appearances in those mediums should always demonstrate the qualities of an ethical communicator if you wish to gain your audience's sense of trust. Our current media-saturated life makes such consistency a bit of a challenge. Perhaps you know of students and friends who have been embarrassed by pictures posted on the Web, either in MySpace, Facebook, or other networking sites. Some people post such images of themselves, but others have no knowledge that their face has been plastered on the Web by friends as a good joke. Needless to say, trying to establish your credibility with someone (say, an employer) who may have seen any embarrassing images of you is going to be really difficult. This is not to say that you shouldn't have a good time with your friends! But rather, it is to demonstrate that you live in a world where your rhetorical message enters a vast theater of past behaviors, writing, speaking, and imagery that may not always be complimentary to your ethos or your goals. It is important to think about because—at least according to Aristotle—character, or ethos, is possibly the most significant factor in obtaining an audience's agreement. Therefore, if you want to be as effective as possible in your writing and other forms of communicating, your audience should perceive you as believable, trustworthy, and intelligent about your topic, regardless of whether you seek to inform, persuade, or entertain them.

Logos: The Appeal to Reason

Logos is the rationality or reasonableness of the argument. It's about arranging your facts and information in such a way that your audience will make sense of your point. Logos is obviously important because if your message doesn't make sense to your audience, you will look a little foolish. Further, they won't believe you, agree with you, or be persuaded by you. Remember Jeff's challenge to get back into college? Imagine how

Using Logos Effectively

You must determine the best way in which to appeal to your audience's sense of reason. Once again, ask yourself some questions:

- How does your audience reach decisions?
- How much evidence do they require before they will believe a fact?

the dean would have reacted to Jeff's letter if it were one sentence long—just a regular sentence. Then think about how the dean might have reacted if Jeff had written a two-page letter—all one sentence. Not only would that be very poor grammar, but it also just wouldn't make any sense. As a result, it is very likely that the dean would have refused to consider Jeff's application for reinstatement with the school.

As the creator of a rhetorical message, you need to think through how you plan to structure your message. Sometimes, as in Jeff's case, it will be important to lay out all of your important points along with their supporting materials. Jeff thought carefully about how the dean would read and interpret his argument to be reinstated as a student. Arranging his points in an appropriate logical order strengthened his case.

In other situations, particularly if you are communicating with an audience you know very well and with whom you share common knowledge and understanding (like a member of your family, for instance), you may be able to count on them understanding your logic, so you don't need to carefully lead them through your points or include every detail. For example, if you want to tell your friends about the new club you are forming on campus, they are likely to know and understand your interests (whether in chess, global warming, or diversity) and won't need to hear every single detail about why you want to start the group. Logos, like others of Aristotle's concepts, involves very practical approaches to your audience.

Pathos: The Appeal to Emotions

Jeff may have been successful in his letter of appeal to the dean because he was able to arouse some kind of emotional response in the dean to his case. Consider the range of emotional responses that Jeff may have been able to evoke. Jeff's letter could have made the dean angry, sad, happy, irritated, proud, embarrassed, hostile, afraid—the list of normal emotional responses that people experience goes on and on. This is where your audience analysis comes in handy, as well as a keen sense of your ability to touch people's emotions.

The MADD website illustrates effective use of pathos as well as the need to balance pathos with ethos and logos. Thinking about emotional responses also requires that you keep a close eye on the overall goal that you hold for your message, and measure just how much emotional response is appropriate. Persuasive messages regarding the environment frequently feature stories and images of endangered arctic animals, wide-eyed children, and messages of imminent environmental chaos and disaster.

If you have seen or read such messages and felt touched emotionally—whether moved to sadness or fear—you have experienced the pull of pathos. Remember that Aristotle recognized—and that you also need to recognize—the need to balance the proofs of ethos, pathos, and logos. Each rhetorical situation calls for a unique equation of the three that depends on the audience, the goals of the message, and the situation.

Pathos in Action: MADD

Take a moment to consult MADD's main website and consider their options for arousing emotion in their audiences. The story of MADD's origins is an emotional narrative of young children losing their lives to drunk-driving incidents. Yet, the story is not highlighted on the website, nor is there an "in-your-face" sense of the deep tragedies that have driven the expansion of the organization. However, you see faces of what seem to be real people, young and old, black and white. No matter what page you navigate to within the site, you are accompanied by the motto:

> We're dads and daughters, sons and uncles,
> friends and neighbors. And mothers.
> We're all ages and from all walks of life.
> We are many colors with one voice.

The motto emphasizes a common thread by using the word "we." The wording of the motto is friendly, nonthreatening, and calm. There is material on the site to make people feel calm (like the motto), material to make people angry (the statistics and research on drunk driving and underage drinking), material that will make people sad (knowing that the 21-month-old son of the 2007 MADD president was killed in a 1988 drunk-driving crash), and information that will make people feel safe and confident (the many avenues others have taken to address and prevent drunk driving in their communities).

In other words, the MADD website is full of pathos or appeals to audience emotions. What is important here, though, is that the emotion evoked does not always have to be intense sadness or pity. We have a wide range of emotions that we feel naturally, and it is those that the skillful message creator will address. Think about it: if what you accomplish is making someone cry hopelessly, chances are pretty good that they're not going to heed your message.

Now that you have learned about exigencies and the importance of your audience to each rhetorical situation, it is time to think about other elements of the rhetorical moment that ultimately help you shape your message. In every situation, there are expectations—whether held by the audience or simply put in place because of circumstances—that must be considered if you want to achieve your rhetorical goal.

Limitations and Opportunities: Shaping your message

Any rhetorical moment presents limitations on what you can and cannot (or should and should not) say, as well as opportunities to further your goals and expand your points, beyond the immediate objective of your rhetorical effort. Your Introduction to Sociology assignment for the brochure about campus recycling is useful to consider for

---

MADD Slogan, Used by permission of MADD National.

the limitations and opportunities of that rhetorical moment. The limitations on the message are pretty easy to distinguish, in part because they have been established by the parameters of the assignment:

- You are limited to the topic of recycling.
- Your format is a brochure.
- Your general purpose is informational.
- The focus of your concern is your campus.

Beyond those basic restrictions, though, what other limitations can you identify? Return to the elements of the rhetorical moment you identified earlier.

What is your controlling exigence?

The most important issue or exigence was that too much recyclable material was not being recycled. How does that fact limit your informational brochure? You can't explore the entire issue of pollution or global warming, or even recycling. You must be selective about your facts, so that you demonstrate the problem that needs the attention and action of your audience. This limitation follows not only from your exigencies, but also from the limitations imposed by the brochure format. A brochure, to be informative, interesting, and accessible, should not be dense with facts, numbers, examples; in other words, avoid too much information.

Who is your audience?

The information you do include, how you arrange it, and the overall message is also limited by your audience. Your audience has been identified as people on your campus interested in and willing to do more about recycling. Thus, your audience analysis should seek information about what these people think and know about recycling so that

An Opportunity for Change

The work you do in your classes might have benefits outside the classroom. For example, pulling together important information on recycling that will help your campus can actually bring about useful change at your school. Your college might take your information and ideas into consideration and work toward different tactics of recycling. Individuals may seek further information about how to recycle more effectively in order to be involved in effective environmental practices. Most importantly, once you begin thinking of the assignment as something other than an assignment and place it within its appropriate rhetorical context, you should begin to see the potential significance your rhetorical communication can contain. When you are asked to address issues of substance and community import, your school projects can become vehicles for actual change.

you know how much background information to include in your brochure. The knowledge level and emotional involvement of your audience will determine the kinds of information you include, whether cold, impersonal facts, personal stories or narratives, or threatening facts about possible mounds of garbage and their influence on your campus, or a combination of all types. Recycling campaigns at other schools might make good examples, as well as local information on how recycling occurs and works.

However, the audience also provides important opportunities for rhetorical communication. Consider the brochure, the response to an assignment by your teacher. This assignment provides the opportunity to showcase your knowledge, effective communication strategies, strong writing skills, and efficient grasp of research tools. Naturally, all of these abilities help you get a good grade, but they also help you take advantage of other opportunities within your rhetorical moment.

The concept of **kairos**, or knowing the right word or phrase for the right time, is another way to explain how a rhetor, the speaker or writer, should respond to her or his rhetorical situation. As you remember from Chapter 2, *kairos* was the rhetorical skill taught by the Sophists in ancient Greece. In preparing a response to a rhetorical situation, whether a report for your boss, an informational brochure for a class assignment, a letter to the editor of your community newspaper, a blog entry, or any other message, you must decide what is the right thing to say or do, how, and when, in order to be successful. Your decisions, if approached properly, will reflect all of the issues and constraints of the rhetorical situation as you determine what strategies, words, examples, and methods are appropriate to the rhetorical moment.

Adding *kairos* to this discussion allows you to think about the importance of credibility in accomplishing your rhetorical goals. Because *kairos* functions as one of the indicators of good sense, according to Aristotle, the able analysis of a rhetorical situation and resultant good decisions will aid in impressing your audience, achieving your goals, and furthering your career, whether in school, the workplace, or elsewhere.

A Brief Review

Let's take a moment to review the key concepts from our discussion.

- When confronting a rhetorical situation, there are three key elements to consider and analyze:
  - **The exigence:** A problem that needs fixing or an issue that needs to be addressed. When responding to an issue or situation, a writer must determine the **controlling exigence**; in other words, the writer must determine what he or she wants to get the audience to think and do about the issue being addressed. Every rhetorical situation contains multiple potential exigencies.
  - **The rhetorical audience:** The audience that can fix the problem or address the issue. Every rhetorical message has an audience, or a particular someone

for whom the message is intended. The writer must identify, analyze, and target her audience for maximum success.

- **Limitations and opportunities:** The people or events or situations that can affect the decisions or actions necessary to have an impact on the issue you are addressing.

- Effective communication requires careful analysis of the rhetorical situation.
- Each rhetorical situation also requires a unique equation of:
  - **Ethos:** Appeals based on the writer's character
  - **Logos:** Appeals based in reasoning and arrangement
  - **Pathos:** Appeals to the emotions of the audience

Rhetoric In Action

"The Clan of the One-Breasted Woman"

Terry Tempest Williams (1955–), American writer, naturalist, conservationist, activist. A fifth-generation Mormon, Williams writes out of her experiences as a Southwesterner. Her works include *Red: Passion and Patience in the Desert*, *Unspoken Hunger*, and *Leap*. This essay is the closing chapter to her well-known memoir, *Refuge: An Unnatural History of Family and Place*.

Prereading: When you have confronted an injustice or an issue you care deeply about, what have you done to take action?

Epilogue

I belong to a Clan of One-Breasted Women. My mother, my grandmothers, and six aunts have all had mastectomies. Seven are dead. The two who survive have just completed rounds of chemotherapy and radiation.

I've had my own problems: two biopsies for breast cancer and a small tumor removed between my ribs diagnosed as "a borderline malignancy."

This is my family history.

Most statistics tell us breast cancer is genetic, hereditary, with rising percentages attached to fatty diets, childlessness, or becoming pregnant after 30. What they don't say is living in Utah may be the greatest hazard of all.

We are a Mormon family with roots in Utah since 1847. The "Word of Wisdom" a religious doctrine of health, kept the women in my family aligned with good foods: no coffee, tea, tobacco, or alcohol. For the most part, these women were finished having babies by the time they were 30. And only one faced breast cancer prior to 1960. Traditionally, as a group of people, Mormons have a low rate of cancer.

Is our family a cultural anomaly? The truth is, we didn't think about it. Those who did, usually the men, simply said, "bad genes." The women's attitude was stoic. Cancer was a part of life. On February 16, 1971, the eve before my mother's surgery, I accidentally picked up the telephone and overheard her ask my grandmother what she could expect.

"Diane, it is one of the most spiritual experiences you will ever encounter."

I quietly put down the receiver.

Two days later, my father took my three brothers and me to the hospital to visit her. She met us in the lobby in a wheelchair. No bandages were visible. I'll never forget her radiance, the way she held herself in a purple velour robe and how she gathered us around her.

"Children, I am fine. I want you to know I felt the arms of God around me."

We believed her. My father cried. Our mother, his wife, was 38 years old.

Two years ago, after my mother's death from cancer, my father and I were having dinner together. He had just returned from St. George, where his construction company was putting in natural gas lines for towns in southern Utah. He spoke of his love for the country: the sandstone landscape, bare-boned and beautiful. He had just finished hiking the Kolob trail in Zion National Park. We got caught up in reminiscing, recalling with fondness our walk up Angels Landing on his fiftieth birthday and the years our family had vacationed there. This was a remembered landscape where we had been raised.

Over dessert, I shared a recurring dream of mine. I told my father that for years, as long as I could remember, I saw this flash of light in the night in the desert. That this image had so permeated my being, I could not venture south without seeing it again, on the horizon, illuminating buttes and mesas.

"You did see it," he said.

"Saw what?" I asked, a bit tentative.

"The bomb. The cloud. We were driving home from Riverside, California. You were sitting on your mother's lap. She was pregnant. In fact, I remember the date, September 7, 1957. We had just gotten out of the Service. We were driving north, past Las Vegas. It was an hour or so before dawn, when this explosion went off. We not only heard it, but felt it. I thought the oil tanker in front of us had blown up. We pulled over and suddenly, rising from the desert floor, we saw it clearly, this golden-stemmed cloud, the mushroom. The sky seemed to vibrate with an eerie pink glow. Within a few minutes, a light ash was raining on the car."

I stared at my father. This was new information to me.

"I thought you knew that," my father said. "It was a common occurrence in the fifties."

It was at that moment I realized the deceit I had been living under. Children growing up in the American Southwest, drinking contaminated milk from contaminated cows, even from the contaminated breasts of their mothers, my mother—members, years later, of the Clan of One-Breasted Women.

It is a well-known story in the Desert West, "The Day We Bombed Utah," or perhaps, "The Years We Bombed Utah." Aboveground atomic testing in Nevada took place from January 27, 1951, through July 11, 1962. The winds were blowing north, covering "low use segments of the population" in Utah with fallout and leaving sheep dead in their tracks, and the climate was right. The United States of the 1950s was red, white, and blue. The Korean War was raging. McCarthyism was rampant. Ike was it and the Cold War was hot. If you were against nuclear testing, you were for a Communist regime.

Much has been written about this "American nuclear tragedy." Public health was secondary to national security. The Atomic Energy Commissioner, Thomas Murray, was quoted as saying, "Gentlemen, we must not let anything interfere with this series of tests, nothing."

Again and again, the public was told by its government, in spite of burns, blisters, and nausea, "It has been found that the tests may be conducted with adequate assurance of safety under conditions prevailing at the bombing reservation." Assuaging public fears was simply a matter of public relations. A news release typical of the times stated, "We find no basis for concluding that harm to any individual has resulted from radioactive fallout."

On August 30, 1979, during Jimmy Carter's presidency, a suit was filed entitled "Irene Allen v. The United States of America." Allen was the first to be alphabetically listed with 24 test cases, representative of nearly 1,200 plaintiffs seeking compensation from the United States government for cancers caused from nuclear testing in Nevada.

Irene Allen lived in Hurricane, Utah. She was the mother of five children and had been widowed twice. Her first husband, with their two oldest boys, had watched the tests from the roof of the local high school. He died of leukemia in 1956. Her second husband died of pancreatic cancer in 1978.

In a town meeting conducted by Utah Senator Orrin Hatch, shortly before the suit was filed, Allen said, "I am not exactly blaming the government, I want you to know, Senator Hatch. But I thought if my testimony could help in any way so this wouldn't happen again to any of the generations coming up after us . . . I am really happy to be here this day to bear testimony to this."

God-fearing people. This is just one story in an anthology of thousands.

On May 10, 1984, Judge Bruce S. Jenkins handed down his opinion. Ten of the plaintiffs were awarded damages. It was the first time a federal court had determined that nuclear tests had been the cause of cancers. For the remaining 14 test cases, the proof of causation was not sufficient. In spite of the split decision, it was considered a landmark ruling. It was not to remain so.

In April 1987, the 10th Circuit Court of Appeals overturned Judge Jenkins' ruling on the basis that the United States was protected from suit by the legal doctrine of sovereign immunity, the centuries-old idea from England in the days of absolute monarchs.

In January 1988, the Supreme Court refused to review the appeals court decision. To our court system, it does not matter whether the United States government was irresponsible, whether it lied to its citizens, or even that citizens died from the fallout of nuclear testing. What matters is that our government is immune: "The King can do no wrong."

In Mormon culture, authority is respected, obedience is revered, and independent thinking is not. I was taught as a young girl not to "make waves" or "rock the boat."

"Just let it go—" my mother would say. "You know how you feel, that's what counts."

For many years, I did just that—listened, observed, and quietly formed my own opinions within a culture that rarely asked questions because it had all the answers. But one by one, I watched the women in my family die common, heroic deaths. We sat in waiting rooms hoping for good news, always receiving the bad. I cared for them, bathed their scarred bodies, and kept their secrets. I watched beautiful women become bald as cisplatin, Cytoxan, and Adriamycin were injected into their veins. I held their foreheads as they vomited green-black bile and I shot them with morphine when the pain became inhuman. In the end, I witnessed their last peaceful breaths, becoming a midwife to the rebirth of their souls. But the price of obedience became too high.

The fear and inability to question authority that ultimately killed rural communities in Utah during atmospheric testing of atomic weapons was the same fear I saw being held in my mother's body. Sheep. Dead sheep. The evidence is buried.

I cannot prove that my mother, Diane Dixon Tempest, or my grandmothers, Lettie Romney Dixon and Kathryn Blackett Tempest, along with my aunts, contracted cancer from nuclear fallout in Utah. But I can't prove they didn't.

My father's memory was correct: the September blast we drove through in 1957 was part of Operation Blumbbob, one of the most intensive series of bombs to be initiated. The flash of light in the night in the desert I had always thought was a dream developed into a family nightmare. It took 14 years, from 1957 to 1971, for cancer to show up in my mother—the same amount of time, Howard L. Andrews, an authority on radioactive fallout at the National Institutes of Health, says radiation cancer requires to become evident. The more I learn about what it means to be a "downwinder," the more questions I drown in.

What I do know, however, is that as a Mormon woman of the fifth generation of "Latter-Day Saints," I must question everything, even if it means losing my faith, becoming a member of a border tribe among my own people. Tolerating blind obedience in the name of patriotism or religion ultimately takes our lives.

When the Atomic Energy Commission described the country north of the Nevada Test Site as virtually uninhabited desert terrain, my family members were some of the "virtual uninhabitants."

One night, I dreamed women from all over the world were circling a blazing fire in the desert. They spoke of change, of how they hold the moon in their bellies and wax and wane with its phases. They mocked at the presumption of even-tempered beings and made promises that they would never fear the witch inside themselves. The women danced wildly as sparks broke away from the flames and entered the night sky as stars.

And they sang a song given to them by Shoshoni grandmothers:

Ah ne nah, nah	Consider the rabbits
nin nah nah—	How gently they walk on the earth—
Ah ne nah, nah	Consider the rabbits
nin nah nah—	How gently they walk on the earth—
Nyaga mutzi	We remember them
oh ne nay—	We can walk gently also—
Nyaga mutzi	We remember them
oh ne nay—	We can walk gently also—

The women danced and drummed and sang for weeks, preparing themselves for what was to come. They would reclaim the desert for the sake of their children, for the sake of the land.

A few miles downwind from the fire circle, bombs were being tested. Rabbits felt the tremors. Their soft leather pads on paws and feet recognized the shaking sands while the roots of mesquite and sage were smoldering. Rocks were hot from the inside out and dust devils hummed unnaturally. And each time there was another nuclear test, ravens watched the desert heave. Stretch marks appeared. The land was losing its muscle.

The women couldn't bear it any longer. They were mothers. They had suffered labor pains but always under the promise of birth. The red-hot pains beneath the desert promised death only, as each bomb became stillborn. A contract was being drawn by the women who understood the fate of the earth as their own.

Under the cover of darkness, ten women slipped under the barbed-wire fence and entered the contaminated country. They were trespassing. They walked toward the town of Mercury in moonlight, taking their cues from coyote, kit fox, antelope ground squirrel, and quail. They moved quietly and deliberately through the maze of Joshua trees. When a hint of daylight appeared they rested, drinking tea and sharing their rations of food. The women closed their eyes. The time had come to protest with the heart, that to deny one's genealogy with the earth was to commit treason against one's soul.

At dawn, the women draped themselves in Mylar, wrapping long streamers of silver plastic around their arms to blow in the breeze. They wore clear masks that became the faces of humanity. And when they arrived on the edge of Mercury, they carried all the butterflies of a summer day in their wombs. They paused to allow their courage to settle.

The town, which forbids pregnant women and children to enter because of radiation risks to their health, was asleep. The women moved through the streets as winged messengers, twirling around each other in slow motion, peeking inside homes and watching the easy sleep of men and women. They were astonished by such stillness and periodically would utter a shrill note or low cry just to verify life.

The residents finally awoke to what appeared as strange apparitions. Some simply stared. Others called authorities, and in time, the women were apprehended by wary soldiers dressed in desert fatigues. They were taken to a white building on the other edge of Mercury. When asked who they were and why they were there, the women replied, "We are mothers and we have come to reclaim the desert for our children."

The soldiers arrested them. As the ten women were blindfolded and handcuffed, they began singing:

You can't forbid us everything
You can't forbid us to think—
You can't forbid our tears to flow
And you can't stop the songs that we sing.

The women continued to sing louder and louder, until they heard the voices of their sisters moving across the mesa.

Ah nenah, nah
nin nah nah—
Ah ne nah, nah
nin nah nah—
Nyaga mutzi
oh ne nay—
Nyaga mutzi
oh ne nay—

"Call for reinforcements," one soldier said.

"We have," interrupted one woman. "We have—and you have no idea of our numbers."

On March 18, 1988, I crossed the line at the Nevada Test Site and was arrested with nine other Utahns for trespassing on military lands. They are still conducting nuclear tests in the desert. Ours was an act of civil disobedience. But as I walked toward the town of Mercury, it was more than a gesture of peace. It was a gesture on behalf of the Clan of One-Breasted Women.

As one officer cinched the handcuffs around my wrists, another frisked my body. She found a pen and a pad of paper tucked inside my left boot.

"And these?" she asked sternly.

"Weapons," I replied.

Our eyes met. I smiled. She pulled the leg of my trousers back over my boot.

"Step forward, please," she said as she took my arm.

We were booked under an afternoon sun and bused to Tonopah, Nevada. It was a two-hour ride. This was familiar country to me. The Joshua trees standing their ground had been named by my ancestors who believed they looked like prophets pointing west to the promised land. These were the same trees that bloomed each spring, flowers appearing like white flames in the Mojave. And I recalled a full moon in May when my mother and I had walked among them, flushing out mourning doves and owls.

The bus stopped short of town. We were released. The officials thought it was a cruel joke to leave us stranded in the desert with no way to get home. What they didn't realize is that we were home, soul-centered and strong, women who recognized the sweet smell of sage as fuel for our spirits.

Comprehending the Text

1. Summarize the events in this chapter. What process does the author undergo?

2. How does Williams challenge her religion?

3. What has happened to Williams and her family that makes her write this essay?

Analyzing the Text

1. What argument does Williams make about protecting our environment?

2. How does Williams convince you, the reader, to see her point of view? What writing strategies does she employ? Are they effective?

3. How is this essay a political document?

Developing Your Skills: Identifying Exigence and Rhetorical Strategies

Terry Tempest Williams' essay "The Clan of the One-Breasted Women" is drawn from the final chapter to her memoir *Refuge: An Unnatural History of Family and Place*. In the essay, Williams considers her family's battle with cancer and the connection she sees to governmental testing of nuclear weapons in Nevada. After reading Williams' essay, write a short response that considers the following questions. Be sure to explain and support your claims.

- What is Williams' purpose in this essay?
- Is Williams responding to an exigence? What is it?
- Does Williams strive to create identification with the reader? If so, how?
- What language does Williams use to evoke emotion?
- In what ways does Williams employ the strategies of *ethos*? *Logos*?
- Does Williams understand the concept of *kairos*? How do you know? Cite evidence from the essay.

Looking Ahead

This chapter has provided you with several ways to analyze communicative acts, whether written or spoken, for their effectiveness. Understanding the exigence that motivates a rhetorical act, as well as identifying how and why that act affects an audience in the way that it does, means you are able to engage thoughtfully and critically with the world around you. Rather than simply accept what you read or hear, you are building the tools to question and analyze what you read and hear to determine in your own mind the effectiveness and validity of the discussions. A central strategy to understanding broad discussions and important issues in our communities is that of comparison and contrast, which is where we turn next.

Your Writer's Toolkit

Writing Strategies: Comparison/Contrast

During your lifetime, great change has occurred in the United States. The presidential election of 2008 was similar to past elections, yet it was also like no other. By comparing and contrasting the presidential elections of the past, we can see the evolution of a country. Similarly, as we have seen in this chapter, comparing and contrasting types and methods of public communication tell us a great deal about the development of public ideals and communities.

Comparison is the process of examining two or more people, places, objects, events, or ideas in order to establish their similarities.

Contrast is the process of establishing the differences between two or more of those same things.

Photography by Russell Lee (1939)

Negro mother teaching children numbers and alphabet of sharecropper. Transylvania, Louisiana

As you consider how rhetoric works for you and how it is used in your communities, you will find that comparison and contrast is a part of virtually every kind of writing. Technical writers use comparison and contrast to demonstrate differences and similarities among a variety of elements; lawyers use the strategies of comparison/contrast when studying case law to build their arguments; stockbrokers use it to evaluate and recommend investment opportunities; and politicians use it to illustrate how and why they differ from their opponents (and should be elected).

You have probably used comparison and contrast, perhaps without knowing what the strategy was called. You may have employed this strategy to evaluate issues and build an argument for change based on similarities and differences. For example, you might want to suggest eliminating the grading system at your school and argue for changing to a pass/fail system. A comparison/contrast analysis of other schools' experiences in using pass/fail could help make your point.

To develop a comparison/contrast essay, you need to analyze two or more subjects by studying the parts of each and discussing the subjects in relation to each other. However, it is not enough to simply discuss the similarities and differences. You need to *do* something with the information you're discussing. Three ways to do something are to **classify**, **evaluate**, or **interpret**.

Your first step is to determine what elements the subject matter have in common in order to create a **basis for comparison**. In other words, you must identify the similarities and differences. For example, consider dogs and cats. You might begin your comparison and contrast analysis this way:

Photography by Dorothea Lange (1936)

Immigrant Worker

- **Classify the subject:** Dogs and cats are both animals (**classifying** your subject).
- **Interpret the situation and state commonalities:** Dogs and cats learn appropriate behaviors from their owners (**interpreting** the situation and stating commonalities).
- **Evaluate the situation and identify a contrast:** Dogs are smarter than cats because they can learn tricks and they tend to obey their owners more often than cats.

Observe these two photographs and take note of the similarities and differences between the two. Make a list. In a brief freewrite, note down your observations.

Note that your evaluation and identification of the differences between cats and dogs also leads you to your thesis—the idea or point of view you're going to prove with your comparison and contrast. Even though dogs and cats may learn different behaviors, the writer can still analyze the differences because of the common element that exists: *both are animals and both are trainable*. From those common elements, you can analyze the contrasts in order to prove your thesis that dogs are smarter. Remember that without any common element present, the writer has no basis for analysis and, essentially, no basis for an essay.

In your free write about the previous photographs, your classification might have included the basic information that they are both images of women. Your interpretation probably considered the poverty of their surroundings, which is conveyed by the physical location and by the bleakness of the black-and-white images. Your thesis might focus on the differences in photographic composition (a close-up vs. a more distant shot) or make assumptions about the circumstances of the women and children in the photographs. In any case, your basic process in preparing for a comparison and contrast essay requires the same essential steps.

The discussion of similarities and differences should take the reader beyond the obvious similarities and differences. That's where your thesis comes in—the point you're trying to make in this comparison/contrast. Note that when two subjects are very similar, the contrast may be what is worth writing about. For example, your discussion of cats and dogs might focus on proving the differences in intelligence between the two. When two subjects are very different, the comparison may be what is worth writing about. For ease of writing, though, your thesis should provide the focus of the essay.

Organizing Your Comparison and Contrast Writing

Once you're clear on how to focus your comparison and contrast writing, you'll need to decide on the proper organizational structure for you to make the most compelling case. There are two common organizational forms for the comparison/contrast essay: by subject or point by point.

In an **arrangement by subject**, the writer sets up a thesis that indicates a comparison is coming, and then discusses each subject separately within the paragraph using separate paragraphs if the subject matter is dense or needs more explanation. Here's how each organizational structure looks:

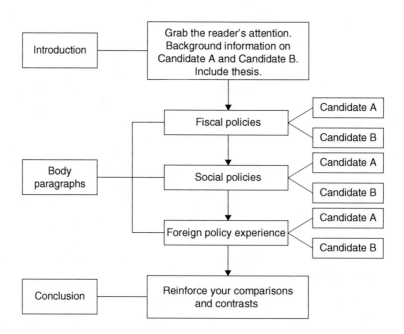

A subject arrangement breaks down in the following manner:

Thesis

Introduce Subject A

    Discuss Subject A in terms of the first point to be discussed

    Discuss Subject A in terms of the second point to be discussed

Introduce Subject B

    Discuss Subject B in terms of the first point to be discussed

    Discuss Subject B in terms of the second point to be discussed

    Conclude with a summary of the similarities and differences, as well as what the writer's point is

Or, you could do the following:

Paragraph One

Topic Sentence

    Discuss Subject A in terms of the first point to be discussed

    Discuss Subject A in terms of the second point to be discussed

Paragraph Two

Transition sentence to new subject

    Discuss Subject B in terms of the first point to be discussed

    Discuss Subject B in terms of the second point to be discussed

Paragraph Three

Transition sentence to explain why the writer is making the comparison/contrast

Sum up and discuss the similarities/differences and make analysis—conclude with thesis

Note: The second organizational technique takes up more time and space. As discussed in earlier chapters, a writer's approach all depends on the subject matter(s) that the writer is choosing to discuss, what the writer's purpose is, and who the writer's audience is.

In the **point-by-point arrangement**, the structure allows the writer to mingle observations about the subject as he or she wishes. A point-by-point arrangement breaks down in the following manner:

Topic sentence

Introduce the first point to be compared and contrasted

    Discuss Subject A in terms of this point

    Discuss Subject B in terms of this point

Introduce the second point to be compared and contrasted

Discuss Subject A in terms of this point

Discuss Subject B in terms of this point

Note: These points may also be discussed in separate paragraphs, depending upon the density of the subject matter and the writer's wishes. What follows are some actual examples.

Comparison/Contrast by Subject

Observe the subject arrangement of this example from John Morreal's book, *Taking Laughter Seriously*:

> When the person with a sense of humor laughs in the face of his own failure, he is showing that his perspective transcends the particular situation he's in, and that he does not have an egocentric, overly precious view of his own endeavors. This is not to say that he lacks self-esteem—quite the contrary. It is because he feels good about himself at a fundamental level that this or that setback is not threatening him. The person without real self-esteem, on the other hand, who is unsure of his own worth, tends to invest his whole sense of himself in each of his projects. Whether he fails or succeeds, he is not likely to see things in an objective way; because his ego rides on each of the goals he sets for himself, any failure will constitute personal defeat and any success personal triumph. He simply cannot afford to laugh at himself, whatever happens. So having a sense of humor about oneself is psychologically healthy. As A. Penjon so nicely said, it "frees us from vanity, on the one hand, and from pessimism on the other by keeping us larger than what we do, and greater than what can happen to us."

At the start of the passage, the author compares and contrasts how a sense of humor works in people who have good self-esteem versus those who have weak self-esteem. Then, Morreal discusses the differences between the two types of people, with the passage ending with a comment about the similarities among individuals who possess a good sense of humor. The passage effectively outlines for readers the differences between people, as well as adding in a main point—which we can consider the thesis of the paragraph—about why having a sense of humor is beneficial for one's life.

Comparison/Contrast Point by Point

This excerpt from Carl Sagan's book, *The Dragons of Eden* shows how a point-by-point structure works:

> How densely packed is the information stored in the brain? A typical information density during the operation of a modern computer is about a million bits per cubic

---

John Morreal, Taking Laughter Seriously, Albany: State University of New York, 1983.
Carl Sagan, The Dragons of Eden: Speculations on the Evolution of Human Intelligence, New York: Random House, 1986.

Writer Citizen

centimeter. This is the total information content of the computer, divided by its volume. The human brain contains, as we have said, about 10^{13} bits in a little more than 10^3 cubic centimeters, for an information content of $10^{13}/10^3 = 10^{10}$, about ten billion bits per cubic centimeter; the brain is therefore ten thousand times more densely packed with information than is a computer, although the computer is much larger. Put another way, a modern computer able to process the information in the human brain would have to be about ten thousand times larger in volume than the human brain. On the other hand, modern electronic computers are capable of processing information at a rate of 10^{16} to 10^{17} bits per second, compared to a peak rate ten billion times slower in the brain. The brain must be extraordinarily cleverly packaged and "wired," with such a small total information content and so low a processing rate, to be able to do so many significant tasks so much better than the best computer.

Sagan's passage demonstrates for you the effectiveness of moving point by point through information. As the passage opens, Sagan poses the question that guides the discussion. Then, he moves to make his first point about how the human brain compares to a computer. After summarizing his comparison, Sagan contrasts the brain with computers, showing how computers process information much more quickly than a human brain. The passage ends with Sagan's conclusion about the human brain and the computer, as he points out that the brain must be "cleverly packaged" to do "so many significant tasks so much better than the best computer." This closing comment also put forth Sagan's main point.

Of course, you can use both structures in the same essay, as in the following example. David Bosco, writing for *The New Republic Online*, authored an essay called "Gulag v. Gitmo" that included a point-by-point comparison of the two detention facilities. Here's an excerpt to demonstrate how Bosco uses comparison/contrast:

Typical Treatment:

Gulag: For the most part, Gulag prisoners provided labor for the Soviet system. Treatment varied widely, but most prisoners lived in overcrowded barracks, and prisoners occasionally killed one another in an effort to find space to sleep. Deadly dysentery and typhus outbreaks were common. Prisoners often had inadequate clothing to protect themselves from the elements, and most camps lacked running water and heat.

Guantánamo: A recent *Time* magazine report found that "the best-behaved detainees are held in Camp 4, a medium-security, communal-living environment with as many as 10 beds in a room; prisoners can play soccer or volleyball outside up to nine hours a day, eat meals together and read Agatha Christie mysteries in Arabic. Less cooperative

"Gulag vs. Guantanamo: Equivalency Test" by David Bosco from *The New Republic*, June 3, 2005. Used by permission from TNR, www.tnr.com.

detainees typically live and eat in small, individual cells and get to exercise and shower only twice a week." Human Rights Watch and other watchdog groups have collected firsthand testimony from prisoners alleging abuses, including the use of dogs, extended solitary confinement, sexual humiliation, and "stress positions." An official investigation uncovered only minor abuses, and most detainee accusations have not been verified.

Bosco begins by making the point that in the Gulag, prisoners were required to work for the Soviets. He builds his discussion as he makes a point about the dismal living conditions in the Gulag. Turning to Guantánamo, Bosco makes the point by comparing and contrasting the facts that the prisoners there are *not* required to work, but instead get to read and play soccer. Simply in describing the accommodations at Guantánamo, Bosco illustrates the contrast in living conditions with the Gulag and a previous historical event.

Developing Your Skills: Comparing and Contrasting

The president of the United States often delivers speeches covering a range of issues from government policies to the economy to national issues such as health care. Presidents are also called upon to speak to the nation in times of tragedy, as President Ronald Reagan did when the space shuttle *Challenger* exploded shortly after lift off in 1986. We even encounter speeches from presidents about their personal transgressions, as we did with President Bill Clinton in 1998. Take time to read these two speeches. As you do so, consider the respective rhetorical moments to which each president finds himself responding. Also, read critically to identify the various rhetorical strategies they employ. Once you have read the speeches, you will turn to comparing and contrasting them to determine how they work rhetorically and which speech, based on your analysis, is the most effective.

Bill Clinton's August 17 Speech to the American Public re: Monica Lewinsky

William Jefferson Clinton (1946–), 42nd president of the United States from 1990–1998. Here, President Clinton addresses the nation regarding his infidelity.

Prereading: What do you know about President Clinton? Jot down a short list of things you know or remember or have heard about President Clinton.

"Good evening.

This afternoon in this room, from this chair, I testified before the Office of Independent Counsel and the grand jury.

I answered their questions truthfully, including questions about my private life, questions no American citizen would ever want to answer.

Still, I must take complete responsibility for all my actions, both public and private. And that is why I am speaking to you tonight.

As you know, in a deposition in January, I was asked questions about my relationship with Monica Lewinsky. While my answers were legally accurate, I did not volunteer information.

Indeed, I did have a relationship with Miss Lewinsky that was not appropriate. In fact, it was wrong. It constituted a critical lapse in judgment and a personal failure on my part for which I am solely and completely responsible.

But I told the grand jury today and I say to you now that at no time did I ask anyone to lie, to hide or destroy evidence or to take any other unlawful action.

I know that my public comments and my silence about this matter gave a false impression. I misled people, including even my wife. I deeply regret that.

I can only tell you I was motivated by many factors. First, by a desire to protect myself from the embarrassment of my own conduct.

I was also very concerned about protecting my family. The fact that these questions were being asked in a politically inspired lawsuit, which has since been dismissed, was a consideration, too.

In addition, I had real and serious concerns about an independent counsel investigation that began with private business dealings 20 years ago, dealings I might add about which an independent federal agency found no evidence of any wrongdoing by me or my wife over two years ago.

The independent counsel investigation moved on to my staff and friends, then into my private life. And now the investigation itself is under investigation.

This has gone on too long, cost too much and hurt too many innocent people.

Now, this matter is between me, the two people I love most—my wife and our daughter—and our God. I must put it right, and I am prepared to do whatever it takes to do so.

Nothing is more important to me personally. But it is private, and I intend to reclaim my family life for my family. It's nobody's business but ours.

Even presidents have private lives. It is time to stop the pursuit of personal destruction and the prying into private lives and get on with our national life.

Our country has been distracted by this matter for too long, and I take my responsibility for my part in all of this. That is all I can do.

Now it is time—in fact, it is past time to move on.

We have important work to do—real opportunities to seize, real problems to solve, real security matters to face.

And so tonight, I ask you to turn away from the spectacle of the past seven months, to repair the fabric of our national discourse, and to return our attention to all the challenges and all the promise of the next American century.

Thank you for watching. And good night."

Comprehending the text:

1. What does President Clinton admit to?
2. What are President Clinton's reasons for putting off admitting to his indiscretion?
3. What does President Clinton say about "private lives"?

Analyzing the text:

1. How do you see the rhetorical triangle (writer/speaker, situation, audience) at work in this speech?
2. Where does President Clinton appeal to *ethos* in this speech? Is his use of *ethos* effective? Why or why not?
3. Does the speech make use of *logos* and/or *pathos*? Where? How effective are these strategies?

The Space Shuttle Challenger Tragedy Address

Ronald Reagan (1911–2004). Ronald Wilson Reagan was the 40th president of the United States from 1981–1989. Here, President Reagan addresses the people of the United States on the eve of the space shuttle *Challenger* tragedy in 1986.

Prereading: What do you think is the role and responsibility of the president of the United States in times of tragedy?

"Ladies and gentlemen, I'd planned to speak to you tonight to report on the state of the union, but the events of earlier today have led me to change those plans. Today is a day for mourning and remembering. Nancy and I are pained to the core by the tragedy of the shuttle *Challenger*. We know we share this pain with all of the people of our country. This is truly a national loss.

Nineteen years ago, almost to the day, we lost three astronauts in a terrible accident on the ground. But we've never lost an astronaut in flight. We've never had a tragedy like this. And perhaps we've forgotten the courage it took for the crew of the shuttle. But they, the *Challenger* Seven, were aware of the dangers, but overcame them and did

NASA

their jobs brilliantly. We mourn seven heroes: Michael Smith, Dick Scobee, Judith Resnik, Ronald McNair, Ellison Onizuka, Gregory Jarvis, and Christa McAuliffe. We mourn their loss as a nation together.

For the families of the seven, we cannot bear, as you do, the full impact of this tragedy. But we feel the loss, and we're thinking about you so very much. Your loved ones were daring and brave, and they had that special grace, that special spirit that says, 'Give me a challenge, and I'll meet it with joy.' They had a hunger to explore the universe and discover its truths. They wished to serve, and they did. They served all of us.

We've grown used to wonders in this century. It's hard to dazzle us. But for twenty-five years the United States space program has been doing just that. We've grown used to the idea of space, and, perhaps we forget that we've only just begun. We're still pioneers. They, the members of the *Challenger* crew, were pioneers.

And I want to say something to the schoolchildren of America who were watching the live coverage of the shuttle's take-off. I know it's hard to understand, but sometimes painful things like this happen. It's all part of the process of exploration and discovery. It's all part of taking a chance and expanding man's horizons. The future doesn't belong to the fainthearted; it belongs to the brave. The *Challenger* crew was pulling us into the future, and we'll continue to follow them.

I've always had great faith in and respect for our space program. And what happened today does nothing to diminish it. We don't hide our space program. We don't keep secrets and cover things up. We do it all up front and in public. That's the way freedom is, and we wouldn't change it for a minute.

We'll continue our quest in space. There will be more shuttle flights and more shuttle crews and, yes, more volunteers, more civilians, more teachers in space. Nothing ends here; our hopes and our journeys continue.

I want to add that I wish I could talk to every man and woman who works for NASA, or who worked on this mission and tell them: "Your dedication and professionalism have moved and impressed us for decades. And we know of your anguish. We share it."

There's a coincidence today. On this day three hundred and ninety years ago, the great explorer Sir Francis Drake died aboard ship off the coast of Panama. In his lifetime the great frontiers were the oceans, and a historian later said, "He lived by the sea, died on it, and was buried in it." Well, today, we can say of the *Challenger* crew: Their dedication was, like Drake's, complete.

The crew of the space shuttle *Challenger* honored us by the manner in which they lived their lives. We will never forget them, nor the last time we saw them, this morning, as they prepared for their journey and waved goodbye and 'slipped the surly bonds of earth' to 'touch the face of God.'

Thank you. 🖋️

Comprehending the text:

1. What do you think President Reagan's purpose was in giving this speech?

2. Though President Reagan clearly honors the crew of the *Challenger*, he also suggests that space exploration must continue. How does he do this without losing focus on the loss of the crew's lives?

3. What does he say about "the way freedom is ..."?

Analyzing the text:

1. Research the origin of "slipped the surly bonds of earth" and "touch the face of God" to find out who the original author of those lines is. Why do you think President Reagan quoted from this particular author? Or was it simply the words he was drawn to?

2. Identify at least one repeating theme of this speech. How many times does he refer to this that theme?

3. Where in the speech does President Reagan employ *ethos*, *logos*, and/or *pathos*? Does he use these strategies effectively? Why or why not?

After reading President Clinton's speech regarding the Monica Lewinsky affair and President Reagan's speech about the tragedy of the space shuttle *Challenger*, take some time to research each event. What is the rhetorical situation in which each president finds himself? How many exigencies can you identify? Which is the controlling, or most important, exigence for each speech? Think about the following questions and respond to as many of them as you can, clearly detailing your reasoning and support.

- Who is the audience (or what are the various audiences) for each speech?
- What is each president's main purpose in his speech?
- How do Presidents Clinton and Reagan structure their speeches?
- What are their main points?
- Does President Clinton and/or President Reagan attempt to create identification with his audience/s? If so, how?
- What kind of language do President Clinton and President Reagan use? Does the language help each President accomplish his goals? If so, how? If not, why?
- Which, if any, of the artistic proofs (*ethos*, *pathos*, and *logos*) can you identify in each speech? How does the use of these rhetorical elements affect the content and/or effectiveness of each speech?
- In your opinion, does each president achieve his goal? Why or why not?
- If you determine that one or both presidents do not achieve their goals, what do you think should have been done differently from a rhetorical point of view?

After analyzing both speeches carefully, write a short essay comparing and contrasting Clinton's and Reagan's responses to their rhetorical situations. In your opinion, who is more successful? Why?

YOUR TURN: Creating Your Ideas

1. Consider an issue in your daily life that you have strong opinions about. This issue could be something on your campus (for example, do you pay a parking fee? If so, do you think you should be charged on top of your tuition to park on campus?), or it could be a local community issue or a national issue. Then, write a letter that is directed toward the *audience* you want to share your opinion with in an effort to *persuade that audience* to see your point of view. Your goal here is to (a) consider the significant elements of the rhetorical situation you face; (b) focus on targeting a particular audience; (c) employ *ethos, pathos, and logos* in your work; and (d) work to affect that audience using the strategies discussed in this chapter.

2. Visual arguments can employ the same strategies to affect audiences. Review the two following images. The one of the left is the famous "Rosie the Riveter"

poster from World War II. The one on the right is from a 2007 *Time Magazine* cover for a focus on national service in the United States.

Write an essay in which you discuss these two images and compare and contrast their relationship to one another and to their respective historical moments. Some questions you might consider and answer include:

- Why do you think *Time* chose to mimic the Rosie the Riveter image?
- What is the message of the *Time* cover?
- Do the two images carry similar messages?
- What is being said by the imagery in each case?
- The original image of Rosie was an immensely powerful rhetorical act in its time period. Does the image of the contemporary "Rosie" have as much power in your historical moment? Why or why not?
- Who do you think the audience is for each of these images?

TECH TALK: Email

Electronic mail, or email, has become a part of daily life. You most likely have a school email account, and you most likely use email to communicate with your friends and receive information from your school about events, news, and classes. You also may use email to communicate with professors or administrators in your school, or you might even be using email to apply for an internship or a summer job. One way in which email has emerged as a important contemporary communication tool is in its use by political groups. How many of you have received a request from an organization asking you to send an email to your senator or local state representative about a current issue? Political groups have discovered the power of email to generate large responses to national events, for fundraising, and more. Email, in many ways, has replaced the traditional letter campaign and made public responses and addresses to government leaders more immediate.

Considering your audience is an important element of crafting an effective email. Email, just like other forms of communication that you use to persuade someone to listen to your point of view, needs an appropriate tone and also proper punctuation and grammar. Don't fall into the instant messaging practice of abbreviations, lack of capitalization, and lack of punctuation. You want your audience, whom you cannot see when they read your email, to consider your message carefully. Careless errors and an improper tone can turn your audience off and cause them to hit the delete button!

Chapter 4

Rhetoric, Publics, Community, and You

hetoric is found in the building of communities and nations, in the development of movements for social change, and in your everyday life as a student. Although this chapter may seem like a history lesson, the goal is to explain how rhetoric has been used in various formats and public arenas to shape the world you know. Learning about the public sphere and the concept of publics will allow you to understand various ways that rhetoric works to establish connections between individuals and groups, to foster the common bonds of identification, and to develop communities of people. Several documents and events from United States history exemplify these rhetorical processes. Throughout the chapter, keep making comparisons between the historical examples and how you see and use rhetoric today. The principles of rhetoric remain the same. As you develop your understanding of rhetoric in action, you should also begin to connect with the rhetorical events of your own historical moment.

The Rhetorical Tradition and the Public Sphere

You have probably noticed that most of the rhetorical actions discussed so far occurred in the realm of the public through:

- Public decision making
- Politics
- Community building

Rhetorical communication has the following essential components:

- An audience
- A purpose

- Response to a situation
- Engagement with issues of social concern

Whose "Public" Are You Talking About?

Consider the following example: Victor is a college student in the United States. He comes from Zimbabwe. He is not a U.S. citizen. He watches the President's State of the Union address, where the President asks for support from "the people" and Congress for increased funding for public schools.

Because Victor is not a citizen and cannot vote, either for Congressional representation or local school issues, his ability to make any strategic choices or to take any action on the President's request for support is extremely limited. Victor may care about public schooling, but he is not likely part of the audience the President and her or his speechwriters had in mind when crafting the State of the Union Address.

So, just because someone makes a public statement, that statement does not infiltrate every aspect of "the public," nor does it relate to every potential member of "the public." As a result, it makes sense to talk about different types of publics.

The very nature of rhetoric and its usefulness for bringing people together through identification and the creation of mutually understood visions and goals places it firmly in the realm of public communication. As a result, it is worth considering what "the public" actually means, whether it is the audience you are addressing with your letters to the editor or public speeches, the people for whom you design your Facebook profile, or classmates and teachers in a composition course.

Publics: A New Concept

When people use the words "the public," they sometimes mean "the population" or the great faceless group of individuals who are "out there" somewhere—individuals whom politicians address, individuals who read newspapers, groups of individuals that care about issues. Yet, if you think about "the public," can you really say whom it might include? Is such a vague term really useful? There is another way to think about the issue of "the public," and it involves dividing the concept up into more concrete and specific groups of people.

It may surprise you at first to think about different levels and configurations of publics. This conversation is important to you as a student of writing and communication because you will have the opportunity—even in this class—to address various publics in your assignments while in college. As a global citizen, you will also benefit from these ideas as you make choices about the issues you care about and choose to address.

For the most part, when people talk about "the public" or "the people," it seems that they have a vague, yet specific, idea of whom they are addressing, whether they are giving a political speech, reviewing a film, or planning an advertising campaign. In other words, "the public" seems to be a monolithic, easily identified but faceless audience envisioned by public communicators. But if you think about this concept carefully and strategically, can any single magazine article, TV ad, weblog, or speech actually speak to *everyone*? Remember, as you saw in Chapter 1, rhetoric is constructed with a specific audience in mind—a particular audience that needs to receive the message in order to accomplish the goal of the writer or speaker. Logically speaking, that audience cannot be everyone. Just because you *hear* a message, *read* the article, or *see* the ad does not mean that you are part of the audience for that particular message.

Gerard Hauser, in his book *Introduction to Rhetorical Theory*, describes "the public" as "a large, diverse, and mobile aggregate of citizens who rely on representatives to protect their interests" (2002, p. 16). That is a pretty vague definition. Yet Hauser's definition fits the vague understanding that pervades most talk about the public. It's big and full of a lot of people, but does not have much shape or definition.

Considering a more specific image is much more helpful in understanding this notion of the public. If citizens, for example, want to participate actively in public issues that affect and concern them, they form a group separate from those who "rely on representative to protect their interests," as defined by Hauser. When groups of people care about issues, whether because those issues (such as global warming, taxes, health care policies, education policies) affect them or people they care about or because of some other reason, those people should have access to particular information that will help them become informed and to participate effectively to the fullest possible extent.

Although average people may not be invited to meet with government leaders to discuss their favorite issues, there are plenty of avenues available for other forms of participation. And people who elect to participate—whether by writing letters, blogging, writing articles or editorials, or choosing other strategies—are definitely distinct from the vague idea of a public that most of us have carried in our heads. So we need to define a public more carefully. Hauser offers this more detailed definition of a public:

> that portion of the populace engaged in evolving shared opinion on a particular issue, with the intent of influencing its resolution. Publics are not fixed, they are not idealized constructs; they are *emergences* that arise from rhetorical experience (p. 85).

In other words, a public comes into existence in response to rhetorical communication, which might take the form of a speech, a new law or policy, or a film or museum exhibition. These types of actions raise issues or questions people wish to resolve. A public may consist of a small number of people at its inception and may grow over time, particularly as more rhetoric is shared throughout the public.

For example, in early 2007, an intergovernmental board of scientists declared global warming to be a serious, continuing problem that was undeniably the result of human activity. Prior to this announcement, many people had been debating the seriousness (and even the existence) of global warming and climate change, as well as whether human activity had anything to do with the issue. Further, prior to the front-page, lead story announcement of the scientists' conclusions, the public concerned about global warming was much smaller than after the announcement. Suddenly the news was inescapable and many more people were concerned about taking action to save endangered species, Arctic glaciers, the ozone layer, and the planet.

> Participating in the rhetorical actions of a particular public is an act of citizenship.

The public, though, contains people concerned about the issue, regardless of their position or opinion on the topic. So the people who continue to argue that global warming is a hoax are part of the public in the same way that those people driving hybrid cars and advocating for a conservation of our resources are part of the public. Additionally if global warming were, theoretically, stopped or contained, the public that cohered around the issue would diminish—perhaps even disappear.

The Public Sphere

A public is further categorized by its operation within a **public sphere**. In other words, individual members of a public and smaller groups operate in a wider public sphere. The public sphere is the location where public deliberation about public issues occurs. The word "public" is important here because of the need to distinguish between private or personal decisions and debates (you and your friends discussing the value of hybrid cars and recycling, for example) and public decisions and debates (you and your friends decide to lobby your school for special parking spots for carpoolers and those driving hybrid cars, for instance). The distinction is important here because of our focus on citizenship and democracy.

Participating in the rhetorical actions of a particular public is an act of citizenship, as it takes a person out of her or his personal sphere of deliberation and activity into the public sphere, where their acts can affect or influence the entire community. For example, your personal decision to drive a hybrid car affects the world because you are polluting the atmosphere less, but your group's decision to ask your school to delegate special parking privileges to people who pollute less has policy implications on a broad scale. Further, if the school's policy on parking for carpoolers and hybrid vehicles influences students, faculty, or staff to purchase hybrids and/or carpool, you have just had an influence not only on your local community, but also on the planet.

Your decisions and actions throughout your life will span several publics and inhabit several public spheres of varying influence. Democracy relies on the rhetorical actions of its citizens. The public spheres in which people participate must be spaces of inclusion so that all voices and opinions can be heard and so democratic principles and privileges remain intact.

Shaping Communities: Rhetorical Actions in History

Rhetoric is an important tool of the democratic process. Rhetoric draws people together into publics and communities, enabling varying levels of participation therein. Think back to where this discussion began, with the ancient Greeks. Several similarities emerge here regarding their ideas of citizenship and public participation and today's ideas about civic responsibility and engagement. Throughout history, citizens have been expected to be educated and able to express their opinions and make arguments to protect the good of the community or state. Though American democracy certainly requires public participation, this system has instituted representation as a form of governing rather than the unwieldy nature of Greek democracy, where thousands of people had to negotiate decision making. The evolution of such thought can be found in some milestones of U.S. history.

Rhetoric and the American Revolution

Many people articulated the ideals of democracy during colonial times in the early development of the United States. One of the most eloquent and effective writers was Thomas Paine (1737–1809). Born in England, Paine immigrated to the American colonies in 1774 and became a journalist and patriot. His pamphlet *Common Sense* stirred people at all levels of society, from farmers to intellectuals, arguing for the Revolution and American freedom. Paine's pamphlet emphasized many of the ideals of Enlightenment thinking, such as individual autonomy, reasonable action and thinking, and ethical involvement in public action.

Common Sense—the source of the well-known quotation, "These are the times that try men's souls"—is credited with helping to instigate the American Revolution. The 48-page pamphlet, published in 1776, argued vehemently for independence from British rule, attacked the British Monarchy, and persuasively listed the benefits of economic as well as governmental independence. Paine also believed in the equal distribution of rights among citizens. The pamphlet was a bestseller, both in the American colonies and in Europe, and demonstrates the power of words to inspire people to action. You can see from this example how important rhetoric can be as an instigator or propellant of social transformation.

We can turn to one of the first founding documents of the United States of America, the Declaration of Independence, to understand the importance of rhetoric in the formation of our government. Interestingly, Thomas Paine's ideas about freedom and the moral responsibility of America to model freedom for other nations inspired the spirit of the Declaration.

In this foundational document, Thomas Jefferson, its primary author, articulated grievances against the British king on behalf of the American colonies and put forth a call to arms demanding separation from British rule. The document's wording frames the American Revolution as necessary and unavoidable—an almost natural phenomenon. Thus, the Declaration of Independence, widely regarded as one of the most politically and philosophically significant documents of Western civilization, foreshadowed the American Revolutionary War and led to the eventual establishment of the United States Constitution, another example of rhetoric in action.

> Starting in the 1600s into the 20th century, people used **broadsides** to communicate with the public. A broadside, sometimes called a "broadsheet," was posted for public viewing and often contained both images and text. Broadsides were a tool for sharing ideas by providing information, sending out proclamations or even making political statements with the public. Broadsides were even used to publish poetry and songs. Today, you see the idea of broadsides being used in full page newspaper advertisements or proclamations, as well as in billboards that line the United States' highways.

The Declaration of Independence offers a unique perspective on information dissemination and social change. Upon completing and initially signing the Declaration, the 1776 Congress ordered the document printed and distributed to each colony, to various newspapers, and to the commanding officers of army troops. Two hundred copies, or "broadsides," were printed on July 4, 1776, and sent to members of Congress for distribution. The news of the colonies' separation from Britain was read out loud in the streets, from church pulpits, and to troops assembled close to fields of battle (for the colonists had been skirmishing with the British for nearly a year by this point).

When Congressional delegates returned to their home territories, they decided whether to publish the Declaration in newspapers or have official copies printed for broad distribution (many colonists could not afford to buy newspapers). Clearly, it was important that all citizens of the newly forming country be made aware of the news. Especially interesting about this process is that the Declaration was circulated in its entirety, so that citizens could read each and every word of the document. Thus, everyone who read the Declaration of Independence had the opportunity to understand all of the arguments put forth and agreed to by their Congressional delegates. It's hard to imagine today's Congress circulating all of their bills to the public, given their size and complexity.

The United States as a democratic nation thus came together as a result of ideals, practices, and documents that trace their heritage and strategies to ancient Greece. Further, we can look at the history of this democracy and identify the emergence of publics (the people who read Thomas Paine's *Common Sense* and debated its merits, for example, or the people who shaped the Declaration of Independence through debate and dialogue), as well as the development of various public spheres wherein deliberation occurred as to the shape of the rhetorical documents (the Continental Congress, for example), that molded the political landscape of the nation.

Rhetoric and the Nineteenth Century

Another important and interesting document from our history is the Declaration of Sentiments, written in 1848. Modeled upon the Declaration of Independence, the Declaration of Sentiments was drafted by Elizabeth Cady Stanton and presented at the first Woman's Rights Convention in Seneca Falls, New York. At that point in U.S. history, women had very few rights. Several activists, including Elizabeth Cady Stanton, Susan B. Anthony, and Lucretia Coffin Mott, organized the 1848 convention to mobilize women into a social movement to seek the right to vote as well as general equality with men. At the convention in Seneca Falls, the women discussed, debated, and voted upon the Declaration of Sentiments.

The Declaration of Sentiments is notable because its wording and rhythm echo the Declaration of Independence. The Declaration of Sentiments presents a message of the moral rightness of equality, a key Enlightenment value, similar to the Declaration of Independence's sense of the moral rightness of independence from Great Britain. However, the Declaration of Sentiments seeks a more modest goal than the overturning of a government sought by the Declaration of Independence. Basically, the women wanted admission to the governmental process, not a revolutionary transition from one government to another.

Although much of society frowned upon the early women's movement, the activists were determined to pursue their goals. The belief system and the system of government instituted by the new democracy offered Stanton, Anthony, Mott, and their fellow activists a forum for expressing their views. At that time, women were barred from speaking in public, so public appearances were difficult. However, these women spoke, wrote, and spread their messages of women's equality, regardless of the difficulties. They used rhetoric—they analyzed their audiences and situations, determined the resources available to them, and planned their messages

Student Voices

The Declaration of Independence and Declaration of Sentiments both greatly reflected thoughts of the Enlightenment period. They represented a major transition in thought as traditional concerns were overlooked by matters of style and delivery.

Rationality was used as a main truth instead of authority (much like the British) to reach solutions to the problems of society. Writing achieved new prominence as newspapers and periodicals dominated the time period and provided an outlet to be heard. Ordinary people could now be heard and could express ideas or opinions in a variety of new settings.

A rise of nationalism led to increased education and awareness. Citizens were starting to realize that it was no longer about winning arguments by any means necessary. Rhetoric was used to forcefully communicate one's reasoned arguments, which was the case with both of these historical texts.

—Derek

carefully. By strategizing carefully, woman suffrage activists reached and motivated sympathetic audiences of men and women who joined the cause for equality.

These rhetorical strategies clearly paid off because women can now vote, go to school, earn as much money (or more) as men, and participate fully in citizenship in the United States, including running for president.

The examples discussed so far—Paine's *Common Sense*, the Declaration of Independence, and the Declaration of Sentiments—illustrate how rhetoric shapes culture and changes history. History moves, in large part because people:

- Practice rhetoric
- Come together into publics
- Engage with social questions, and, in turn,
- Shape and reshape the public sphere and the culture

Historically significant rhetoric does not occur only in the political or governmental arena. For example, upon its publication in 1851–1852 in serial form, *Uncle Tom's Cabin*, the novel by Harriet Beecher Stowe, inflamed public opinion on slavery. In fact, legend has it that President Abraham Lincoln met Stowe and said, "So, this is the little lady who started this big war."

Of course, the U.S. Civil War was not instigated solely by one book. Yet within the context of the debate over slavery, the power of that book, which described the injustices and abuses of the system, was immense. The story made slavery real to people who otherwise might not have thought very much about the topic. *Uncle Tom's Cabin* illustrates some of the ways in which discourse *other than* political or policy-oriented writing or speaking came to be considered rhetorical.

Rhetoric and the Twentieth Century

Creative works, including visual messages, can also fulfill the definition of rhetorical communication. Originally published in 1916 for a magazine cover, the Uncle Sam "I Want You" poster was used during World War I as a military recruiting poster. It was so popular that the image was adapted for use in World War II. The U.S. Congress adopted Uncle Sam as a national symbol in 1961.

Before considering what it means to be a national symbol, let's explore the rhetorical significance of the Uncle Sam poster. What about this very simple message is so powerful that it helped motivate two war efforts in the United States? Look first at the colors. Red, white, and blue are associated with American patriotism. Uncle Sam's hatband sports large white stars, just as the U.S. flag does. And look at Uncle Sam's facial expression. His face is stern, serious, and authoritative. His finger points directly at the viewer, emphasizing the "YOU" in the worded message as well as the seriousness of his expression. Sometimes the simplest message carries the most weight. People seeing this poster during the world war years would need no explanation for *why* Uncle Sam sought their services. Uncle Sam thus became an icon in U.S. history—a national symbol.

Uncle Sam joins a long list of national symbols. What does it mean to be a national symbol? Ultimately, the designation means that the image or location is rhetorical because it evokes a response in those who see it, it has symbolic power, and it brings to mind qualities of the United States. Other national symbols of the United States include the White House, the bald eagle, the U.S. flag, the Statue of Liberty, and Mount Rushmore.

National (and other) symbols can provoke discussion, motivate people to action, or help make a point. Obviously, the government needed people to join the military during the world wars. Uncle Sam, with his stern face, white hair, and authoritative finger, helped encourage potential soldiers to join. In addition, his image reminded average citizens of the war effort and the need to sacrifice at home.

Rosie the Riveter was another important motivational image that appeared during World War II. As you know, the poster was created by the War Advertising Council as part of the campaign to fill jobs left empty by men gone to war. Rosie's image helped recruit more than two million women to the workforce between 1942 and 1945. These jobs were located in war production plants building airplanes and other equipment, and in civilian services jobs making sure that the country continued to function and the troops overseas were supplied.

The campaign was significant because so many women in the United States had never worked outside the home. The idea of going to work violated social norms at the time, particularly given the nature of the jobs. Some women were horrified at the idea of doing production labor, as hard, dirty, work was viewed as unfeminine. That attitude explains Rosie's appearance. Notice her clean,

National Archives (NWDNS-44-PA-71)

Image © William Milner, 2010. Used under license from Shutterstock, Inc.

National Archives (NWDNS-179-WP-1563)

made-up face. And although she is showing us her muscle, there is nothing manly about her. Rosie's image appeared on posters, postage stamps, and magazines. Going to work was promoted to women as a patriotic responsibility, and those images of Rosie the Riveter made that responsibility palatable. The campaign to encourage women to join the workforce changed how women participated in their communities and their democracy, thus changing the public sphere and the culture.

The Civil Rights Movement

Through time, the effect of rhetorical actions have created and changed history. Moving closer to the current historical moment, one of the most significant social movements in history—the movement to gain civil rights for African Americans—offers many examples of the powerful forces of rhetoric to lift up and tear down communities.

Several legal decisions contributed to the shaping of the Civil Rights Movement:

- The *Brown v. Board of Education* decision in 1954 declaring school segregation illegal
- The Civil Rights Act of 1964, which barred discrimination based on race, color, religion, or national origin in public facilities—such as restaurants, theaters, or hotels—as well as discriminatory hiring practices

Citizenship Schools

In 1954, in response to literacy tests being implemented to bar African Americans from voting in the South, the Highlander School instituted Citizenship Schools. The Highlander School operated in rural Tennessee and was created to educate citizens to become leaders in the labor force. From its work with the labor unions in the South, Highlander moved the focus of its work to civil rights in 1953. The citizenship schools exemplified a successful voter education program, teaching people to read in order to pass the literacy tests and enable them to vote.

- The Voting Rights Act of 1965, which removed barriers to voting

In a movement replete with significant rhetorical action, from demonstrations to speeches to various methods of civil disobedience, it is difficult to choose one outstanding example. However, for the purposes of this discussion, one of the most famous speeches of the movement—Dr. Martin Luther King Jr.'s "I Have a Dream" speech—is illuminative.

Dr. King, one of the key leaders of the Civil Rights Movement, gave the famous "I have a dream" speech on August 28, 1963, as part of the enormous March on Washington for Jobs

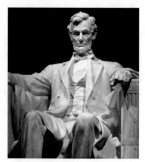

Image © Dave Wetzel, 2010. Used under license from Shutterstock, Inc.

and Freedom. With more than 250,000 demonstrators, the march was one of the largest human rights events ever, bringing together people from all walks of life. Dr. King's speech was given toward the end of the program, which began with a rally at the Washington Monument and ended a mile away at the Lincoln Memorial.

The "I Have a Dream" speech is a notable piece of rhetoric for many reasons. Among those reasons is the skillful use of metaphor and language, which brings the speech to life by sparking the imaginations and emotions of listeners. The speech is also noteworthy because it stands as a testament to life-changing events and the role played by words and rhetoric in changing history. Dr. King's dream, as articulated in the speech, was shared with those in Washington that day, as well as many people watching on television. Through his use of imagery and emotion-arousing language, Dr. King invites listeners to identify with the frustration and anger expressed in the opening words:

> Five score years ago, a great American, in whose symbolic shadow we stand today, signed the Emancipation Proclamation. This momentous decree came as a great beacon light of hope to millions of Negro slaves who had been seared in the flames of withering injustice. It came as a joyous daybreak to end the long night of their captivity.

> But one hundred years later, the Negro still is not free. One hundred years later, the life of the Negro is still sadly crippled by the manacles of segregation and the chains of discrimination. One hundred years later, the Negro lives on a lonely island of poverty in the midst of a vast ocean of material prosperity. One hundred years later, the Negro is still languishing in the corners of American society and finds himself an exile in his own land. So we have come here today to dramatize a shameful condition.

The opening lines resonate because they also follow the parallel structure of Lincoln's Gettysburg Address. This similarity to Lincoln's address lends credence to King's speech. Yet, beyond sharing the essence of oppression in these opening lines, King reaches out to his audience:

> I am not unmindful that some of you have come here out of great trials and tribulations. Some of you have come fresh from narrow jail cells. Some of you have come from areas where your quest for freedom left you battered by the storms of persecution and staggered by the winds of police brutality. You have been the veterans of creative suffering. Continue to work with the faith that unearned suffering is redemptive.

Go back to Mississippi, go back to Alabama, go back to South Carolina, go back to Georgia, go back to Louisiana, go back to the slums and ghettos of our northern cities, knowing that somehow this situation can and will be changed. Let us not wallow in the valley of despair.

I say to you today, my friends, so even though we face the difficulties of today and tomorrow, I still have a dream. It is a dream deeply rooted in the American dream.

The speech gathers momentum with King's dream. He shares vivid images of the South and its troubled path of racism, his hopes for his children, and the need for hope and faith in each other. He closes the speech in ringing tones of hope:

And if America is to be a great nation this must become true. So let freedom ring from the prodigious hilltops of New Hampshire. Let freedom ring from the mighty mountains of New York. Let freedom ring from the heightening Alleghenies of Pennsylvania!

Let freedom ring from the snowcapped Rockies of Colorado!

Let freedom ring from the curvaceous slopes of California!

But not only that; let freedom ring from Stone Mountain of Georgia!

Let freedom ring from Lookout Mountain of Tennessee!

Let freedom ring from every hill and molehill of Mississippi. From every mountainside, let freedom ring.

And when this happens, When we allow freedom to ring, when we let it ring from every village and every hamlet, from every state and every city, we will be able to speed up that day when all of God's children, black men and white men, Jews and Gentiles, Protestants and Catholics, will be able to join hands and sing in the words of the old Negro spiritual, "Free at last! free at last! thank God Almighty, we are free at last!"

King could simply have said "Let freedom ring from coast to coast!" In our modern age of text messages and abbreviated styles of communicating, it might be hard to understand why someone would spend so many words saying something simple. But, if you compare the impact of the seven-word, simple version of the sentence to the imagery and rhythm used by Dr. King, you can easily see why this speech is powerful, even today. It is hard to ignore the repetition of "Let freedom ring." In addition, Dr. King's descriptive language and use of vivid adjectives bring his message to life. For example, the hilltops in New Hampshire are "prodigious," the slopes of California are "curvaceous." The mountains and vast landscape of the United States leap to life through descriptions that create sensations and mental pictures in the minds of his audience.

Dr. King's speech on that day is credited by some to have mobilized advocates of desegregation and hastened the passage of the Civil Rights Act of 1964. Great and necessary changes have occurred in the United States because of events like the March on Washington, the Montgomery Bus Boycott, and the Freedom Rides. This speech is an example of very public rhetoric, rhetoric that fostered identification between people and transformed public understandings and procedures.

Rhetoric and Everyday Citizenship

Does every important piece of rhetoric have to occur on the scale of Dr. Martin Luther King's "I Have a Dream" speech, or be circulated as widely as Rosie the Riveter posters? In a word, no. Your words, actions, and participation are important to your rhetorical world. As a student in today's world, your opportunities to learn about and practice citizenship are numerous. In fact, getting an education can be considered a form of citizenship. Why? Bettering yourself and improving your own prospects not only makes your life better, but also improves your community and social in general. How? When people learn, they think. When people think, they are more likely to pay attention to what's happening around them and to understand how society works.

Furthermore, people who are educated are also more likely to be able to attend to their communities' issues and problems on some level, whether that means participating in parent–teacher organizations in schools, voting locally and nationally, writing letters to the editor of the local paper, or otherwise being involved in the community. On a more immediate level, schools, colleges, and universities are places of community and opportunity. You can join organizations like student government or sports teams. You might live in the dorms or be a resident assistant, if your school has a residential campus. There are social organizations as well as activist organizations.

Just as an example, try an Internet search for "student activism." You will likely come across many interesting sites, from lists of organizations to reports from other countries about what students are doing for social change. Some activist groups at schools around the United States and abroad include:

- A Cleaner Earth
- Access Sudan
- Central Park Conservancy Youth Leadership
- Las Vegas 20 Million Loud
- Movement for the Advancement of Student Power

In addition to opportunities to practice citizenship and rhetorical communication at your school, you can look around you for evidence of democratic practices. For example, popular music is often rhetoric in action. Do a web search for "Katrina song." You might be surprised at what you find. You can also explore:

- Newspapers
- Blogs
- College classrooms
- Textbooks
- Radio talk shows
- Television newscasts

Throughout various media, we can find spaces of public debate across the political spectrum. Citizens are engaging in rhetoric, and thus in citizenship, on a host of levels right now. What will be your next expression of your citizenship?

A Brief Review

- **The public sphere**
  - We all exist in different public spheres depending on our interests and beliefs. A public sphere is where public deliberation about public issues occurs. Remember, as we've discussed, we form publics when we respond to rhetorical messages such as a speech, a new law, or a policy that raises issues for debate. A public may consist of a small number of people at its inception and may grow over time; at the same time, as an issue is resolved, some publics might dissipate and, in fact, even disappear.

- **Rhetorical actions in history**
  - Rhetorical actions in history shape our communities and what we believe and think. We covered a number of examples, ranging from the Declaration of Independence to the Declaration of Sentiments, the emergence of Uncle Sam on World War I posters, and the civil rights speeches of Dr. Martin Luther King. These are only some of the many examples that exist in American history that demonstrate how rhetoric has helped not just to shape our communities, but also to maintain the democratic process.
  - You, too, exist in history and have the power to engage in rhetorical practices and communities that lead to public discussion and social changes. Democratic practices exist all around us in various forms, ranging from music to blogs to news reports to political speeches to governmental policies and more. Where do you see rhetoric in action?

The Declaration of Independence

Written in 1776, the Declaration of Independence's primary author was Thomas Jefferson. He was assisted by a committee that included John Adams, Benjamin Franklin, Robert R. Livingston, and Roger Sherman.

Prereading: When was the last time you read the Declaration of Independence? What do you remember about it?

IN CONGRESS, July 4, 1776.

The unanimous Declaration of the thirteen united States of America,

When in the Course of human events, it becomes necessary for one people to dissolve the political bands which have connected them with another, and to assume among the powers of the earth, the separate and equal station to which the Laws of Nature and of Nature's God entitle them, a decent respect to the opinions of mankind requires that they should declare the causes which impel them to the separation.

We hold these truths to be self-evident, that all men are created equal, that they are endowed by their Creator with certain unalienable Rights, that among these are Life, Liberty and the pursuit of Happiness.—That to secure these rights, Governments are instituted among Men, deriving their just powers from the consent of the governed, —That whenever any Form of Government becomes destructive of these ends, it is the Right of the People to alter or to abolish it, and to institute new Government, laying its foundation on such principles and organizing its powers in such form, as to them shall seem most likely to effect their Safety and Happiness. Prudence, indeed, will dictate that Governments long established should not be changed for light and transient causes; and accordingly all experience hath shewn, that mankind are more disposed to suffer, while evils are sufferable, than to right themselves by abolishing the forms to which they are accustomed. But when a long train of abuses and usurpations, pursuing invariably the same Object evinces a design to reduce them under absolute Despotism, it is their right, it is their duty, to throw off such Government, and to provide new Guards for their future security.—Such has been the patient sufferance of these Colonies; and such is now the necessity which constrains them to alter their former Systems of Government. The history of the present King of Great Britain is a history of repeated injuries and

National Archives, http://www.archives.gov/national-archives-experience/charters/declaration_transcript.html usurpations, all having in direct object the establishment of an absolute Tyranny over these States. To prove this, let Facts be submitted to a candid world.

He has refused his Assent to Laws, the most wholesome and necessary for the public good.

He has forbidden his Governors to pass Laws of immediate and pressing importance, unless suspended in their operation till his Assent should be obtained; and when so suspended, he has utterly neglected to attend to them.

He has refused to pass other Laws for the accommodation of large districts of people, unless those people would relinquish the right of Representation in the Legislature, a right inestimable to them and formidable to tyrants only.

He has called together legislative bodies at places unusual, uncomfortable, and distant from the depository of their public Records, for the sole purpose of fatiguing them into compliance with his measures.

He has dissolved Representative Houses repeatedly, for opposing with manly firmness his invasions on the rights of the people.

He has refused for a long time, after such dissolutions, to cause others to be elected; whereby the Legislative powers, incapable of Annihilation, have returned to the People at large for their exercise; the State remaining in the mean time exposed to all the dangers of invasion from without, and convulsions within.

He has endeavoured to prevent the population of these States; for that purpose obstructing the Laws for Naturalization of Foreigners; refusing to pass others to encourage their migrations hither, and raising the conditions of new Appropriations of Lands.

He has obstructed the Administration of Justice, by refusing his Assent to Laws for establishing Judiciary powers.

He has made Judges dependent on his Will alone, for the tenure of their offices, and the amount and payment of their salaries.

He has erected a multitude of New Offices, and sent hither swarms of Officers to harrass our people, and eat out their substance.

He has kept among us, in times of peace, Standing Armies without the Consent of our legislatures.

He has affected to render the Military independent of and superior to the Civil power.

He has combined with others to subject us to a jurisdiction foreign to our constitution, and unacknowledged by our laws; giving his Assent to their Acts of pretended Legislation:

For Quartering large bodies of armed troops among us:

For protecting them, by a mock Trial, from punishment for any Murders which they should commit on the Inhabitants of these States:

For cutting off our Trade with all parts of the world:

For imposing Taxes on us without our Consent:

For depriving us in many cases, of the benefits of Trial by Jury:

For transporting us beyond Seas to be tried for pretended offences

For abolishing the free System of English Laws in a neighbouring Province, establishing therein an Arbitrary government, and enlarging its Boundaries so as to render it at once an example and fit instrument for introducing the same absolute rule into these Colonies:

For taking away our Charters, abolishing our most valuable Laws, and altering fundamentally the Forms of our Governments:

For suspending our own Legislatures, and declaring themselves invested with power to legislate for us in all cases whatsoever.

He has abdicated Government here, by declaring us out of his Protection and waging War against us.

He has plundered our seas, ravaged our Coasts, burnt our towns, and destroyed the lives of our people.

He is at this time transporting large Armies of foreign Mercenaries to compleat the works of death, desolation and tyranny, already begun with circumstances of Cruelty & perfidy scarcely paralleled in the most barbarous ages, and totally unworthy the Head of a civilized nation.

He has constrained our fellow Citizens taken Captive on the high Seas to bear Arms against their Country, to become the executioners of their friends and Brethren, or to fall themselves by their Hands.

He has excited domestic insurrections amongst us, and has endeavoured to bring on the inhabitants of our frontiers, the merciless Indian Savages, whose known rule of warfare, is an undistinguished destruction of all ages, sexes and conditions.

In every stage of these Oppressions We have Petitioned for Redress in the most humble terms: Our repeated Petitions have been answered only by repeated injury. A Prince whose character is thus marked by every act which may define a Tyrant, is unfit to be the ruler of a free people.

Nor have We been wanting in attentions to our Brittish brethren. We have warned them from time to time of attempts by their legislature to extend an unwarrantable jurisdiction over us. We have reminded them of the circumstances of our emigration and settlement here. We have appealed to their native justice and magnanimity, and we have conjured them by the ties of our common kindred to disavow these usurpations, which, would inevitably interrupt our connections and correspondence. They too have been deaf to the voice of justice and of consanguinity. We must, therefore, acquiesce in the necessity, which denounces our Separation, and hold them, as we hold the rest of mankind, Enemies in War, in Peace Friends.

We, therefore, the Representatives of the united States of America, in General Congress, Assembled, appealing to the Supreme Judge of the world for the rectitude of our intentions, do, in the Name, and by Authority of the good People of these Colonies, solemnly publish and declare, That these United Colonies are, and of Right ought to be Free and Independent States; that they are Absolved from all Allegiance to the British Crown, and that all political connection between them and the State of Great Britain, is and ought to be totally dissolved; and that as Free and Independent States, they have full Power to levy War, conclude Peace, contract Alliances, establish Commerce, and to do all other Acts and Things which Independent States may of right do. And for the support of this Declaration, with a firm reliance on the protection of divine Providence, we mutually pledge to each other our Lives, our Fortunes and our sacred Honor.

The 56 signatures on the Declaration appear in the positions indicated:

Column 1	Georgia:	Button Gwinnett
		Lyman Hall
		George Walton
Column 2	North Carolina:	William Hooper
		Joseph Hewes
		John Penn
	South Carolina:	Edward Rutledge
		Thomas Heyward, Jr.
		Thomas Lynch, Jr.
		Arthur Middleton
Column 3	Massachusetts:	John Hancock
	Maryland:	Samuel Chase
		William Paca
		Thomas Stone
		Charles Carroll of Carrollton
	Virginia:	George Wythe
		Richard Henry Lee
		Thomas Jefferson
		Benjamin Harrison
		Thomas Nelson, Jr.
		Francis Lightfoot Lee
		Carter Braxton

Column 4	Pennsylvania:	Robert Morris
		Benjamin Ruhs
		Benjamin Franklin
		John Morton
		George Clymer
		James Smith
		George Taylor
		James Wilson
		George Ross
	Delaware:	Caesar Rodney
		George Read
		Thomas McKean
Column 5	New York:	William Floyd
		Philip Livingston
		Francis Lewis
		Lewis Morris
	New Jersey:	Richard Stockton
		John Witherspoon
		Francis Hopkinson
		John Hart
		Abraham Clark
Column 6	New Hampshire:	Josiah Bartlett
		William Whipple
	Massachusetts:	Samuel Adams
		John Adams
		Robert Treat Paine
		Elbridge Gerry
	Rhode Island:	Stephen Hopkins
		William Ellery
	Connecticut:	Roger Sherman
		Samuel Huntington
		William Williams
		Oliver Wolcott
	New Hampshire:	Matthew Thornton

1. What are the three main principles underlying the Declaration of Independence?

2. The writers of the Declaration are making a request to the British government. What is that request?

3. How do the writers of the Declaration organize the document?

Analyzing the Text

1. Think about the time period in which the Declaration of Independence was written. What "public" do you think the writers were addressing? Think about gender, race, and economic status.

2. Think about how the Declaration is viewed today. Has the "public" it addresses changed? To whom does this document have meaning today?

3. When written, the Declaration of Independence was viewed as a call to arms. Why do you think this is so?

The Declaration of Sentiments (1848)

For the Seneca Falls Convention, the first women's rights convention in the United States, Elizabeth Cady Stanton wrote the Declaration of Sentiments. This document outlines areas of grievance on behalf of the women of the United States.

Prereading: What do you know about women's suffrage in the nineteenth century? Take a few minutes to write down some thoughts before reading this document.

The Declaration of Sentiments

When, in the course of human events, it becomes necessary for one portion of the family of man to assume among the people of the earth a position different from that which they have hitherto occupied, but one to which the laws of nature and of nature's God entitle them, a decent respect to the opinions of mankind requires that they should declare the causes that impel them to such a course.

We hold these truths to be self-evident: that all men and women are created equal; that they are endowed by their Creator with certain inalienable rights; that among these are life, liberty, and the pursuit of happiness; that to secure these rights governments are instituted, deriving their just powers from the consent of the governed. Whenever any form of government becomes destructive of these ends, it is the right of those who suffer from it to refuse allegiance to it, and to insist upon the institution of a new government, laying its foundation on such principles, and organizing its powers in such form, as to them shall seem most likely to effect their safety and happiness. Prudence, indeed, will dictate that governments long established should not be changed for light and transient causes; and accordingly all experience hath shown that mankind are more disposed to suffer, while evils are sufferable, than to right themselves by abolishing the forms to which they are accustomed. But when a long train of abuses and usurpations, pursuing invariably the same object, evinces a design to reduce them under absolute despotism, it is their duty to throw off such government, and to provide new guards for their future security. Such has been the patient sufferance of the women under this government, and such is now the necessity which constrains them to demand the equal station to which they are entitled.

The history of mankind is a history of repeated injuries and usurpations on the part of man toward woman, having in direct object the establishment of an absolute tyranny over her. To prove this, let facts be submitted to a candid world.

He has never permitted her to exercise her inalienable right to the elective franchise.

He has compelled her to submit to laws, in the formation of which she had no voice.

He has withheld from her rights which are given to the most ignorant and degraded men—both natives and foreigners.

Having deprived her of this first right of a citizen, the elective franchise, thereby leaving her without representation in the halls of legislation, he has oppressed her on all sides.

He has made her, if married, in the eye of the law, civilly dead.

He has taken from her all right in property, even to the wages she earns.

He has made her, morally, an irresponsible being, as she can commit many crimes with impunity, provided they be done in the presence of her husband. In the covenant of marriage, she is compelled to promise obedience to her husband, he becoming, to all intents and purposes, her master—the law giving him power to deprive her of her liberty, and to administer chastisement.

He has so framed the laws of divorce, as to what shall be the proper causes, and in case of separation, to whom the guardianship of the children shall be given, as to be wholly regardless of the happiness of women—the law, in all cases, going upon a false supposition of the supremacy of man, and giving all power into his hands.

After depriving her of all rights as a married woman, if single, and the owner of property, he has taxed her to support a government which recognizes her only when her property can be made profitable to it.

He has monopolized nearly all the profitable employments, and from those she is permitted to follow, she receives but a scanty remuneration. He closes against her all the avenues to wealth and distinction which he considers most honorable to himself. As a teacher of theology, medicine, or law, she is not known.

He has denied her the facilities for obtaining a thorough education, all colleges being closed against her.

He allows her in church, as well as state, but a subordinate position, claiming apostolic authority for her exclusion from the ministry, and, with some exceptions, from any public participation in the affairs of the church.

He has created a false public sentiment by giving to the world a different code of morals for men and women, by which moral delinquencies which exclude women from society, are not only tolerated, but deemed of little account in man.

He has usurped the prerogative of Jehovah himself, claiming it as his right to assign for her a sphere of action, when that belongs to her conscience and to her God.

He has endeavored, in every way that he could, to destroy her confidence in her own powers, to lessen her self-respect, and to make her willing to lead a dependent and abject life.

Now, in view of this entire disfranchisement of one-half the people of this country, their social and religious degradation—in view of the unjust laws above mentioned, and because women do feel themselves aggrieved, oppressed, and fraudulently deprived of their most sacred rights, we insist that they have immediate admission to all the rights and privileges which belong to them as citizens of the United States.

In entering upon the great work before us, we anticipate no small amount of misconception, misrepresentation, and ridicule; but we shall use every instrumentality within our power to effect our object. We shall employ agents, circulate tracts, petition the state and national legislatures, and endeavor to enlist the pulpit and the press in our behalf. We hope this Convention will be followed by a series of conventions embracing every part of the country.

Seneca Falls Resolutions

Whereas, the great precept of nature is conceded to be that "man shall pursue his own true and substantial happiness." Blackstone in his Commentaries remarks that this law of nature, being coeval with mankind and dictated by God himself, is, of course, superior in obligation to any other. It is binding over all the globe, in all countries and at all times; no human laws are of any validity if contrary to this, and such of them as are valid derive all their force, and all their validity, and all their authority, mediately and immediately, from this original; therefore,

Resolved, That such laws as conflict, in any way, with the true and substantial happiness of woman, are contrary to the great precept of nature and of no validity, for this is "superior in obligation to any other."

Resolved, That all laws which prevent woman from occupying such a station in society as her conscience shall dictate, or which place her in a position inferior to that of man, are contrary to the great precept of nature and therefore of no force or authority.

Resolved, That woman is man's equal, was intended to be so by the Creator, and the highest good of the race demands that she should be recognized as such.

Resolved, That the women of this country ought to be enlightened in regard to the laws under which they live, that they may no longer publish their degradation by declaring themselves satisfied with their present position, nor their ignorance, by asserting that they have all the rights they want.

Resolved, That inasmuch as man, while claiming for himself intellectual superiority, does accord to woman moral superiority, it is preeminently his duty to encourage her to speak and teach, as she has an opportunity, in all religious assemblies.

Resolved, That the same amount of virtue, delicacy, and refinement of behavior that is required of woman in the social state also be required of man, and the same transgressions should be visited with equal severity on both man and woman.

Resolved, That the objection of indelicacy and impropriety, which is so often brought against woman when she addresses a public audience, comes with a very ill grace from those who encourage, by their attendance, her appearance on the stage, in the concert, or in feats of the circus.

Resolved, That woman has too long rested satisfied in the circumscribed limits which corrupt customs and a perverted application of the Scriptures have marked out for her, and that it is time she should move in the enlarged sphere which her great Creator has assigned her.

Resolved, That it is the duty of the women of this country to secure to themselves their sacred right to the elective franchise.

Resolved, That the equality of human rights results necessarily from the fact of the identity of the race in capabilities and responsibilities.

Resolved, That the speedy success of our cause depends upon the zealous and untiring efforts of both men and women for the overthrow of the monopoly of the pulpit, and for the securing to woman an equal participation with men in the various trades, professions, and commerce.

Resolved, therefore, That, being invested by the Creator with the same capabilities and same consciousness of responsibility for their exercise, it is demonstrably the right and duty of woman, equally with man, to promote every righteous cause by every righteous means; and especially in regard to the great subjects of morals and religion, it is self-evidently her right to participate with her brother in teaching them, both in private and in public, by writing and by speaking, by any instrumentalities proper to be used, and in any assemblies proper to be held; and this being a self-evident truth growing out of the divinely implanted principles of human nature, any custom or authority adverse to it, whether modern or wearing the hoary sanction of antiquity, is to be regarded as a self-evident falsehood, and at war with mankind.

Comprehending the Text

1. Identify three requests made by the writers of the Declaration of Sentiments.

2. What resolution stands out the most to you and why?

3. What does the Declaration of Sentiments ultimately ask for?

Analyzing the Text

1. How does the Declaration of Sentiments model the Declaration of Independence? Why might the writer decide to follow the strategies of the Declaration of Independence?

2. In what ways does the Declaration of Sentiments rely upon the writing strategy of definition, which we discussed in Chapter 2? What issues or events are defined? Do definitions like these help to shape the publics affected by this document? How does this act of definition help create a sense of a public?

3. What types of people will not be included in the publics for the Declaration of Sentiments?

Developing Your Skills: Responding to Texts

The discussion has asked you to contemplate the role of the rhetorical tradition in creating a democracy. Take some time to review the Declaration of Independence and the Declaration of Sentiments, as well as the Bill of Rights, which is located in Chapter 2. Then, develop a response in which you explain how these documents create a foundation for democracy and citizenship in the United States.

Looking Ahead

Within this chapter, you have been learning about the concept of publics, as well as how rhetorical actions have taken place in U.S. history that have contributed to the foundation of our democracy. You might have noticed that often rhetorical actions in history have a cause; that is, something that creates a community and brings it to engage with an issue. This public movement, then, has an effect on society. The Declaration of Independence and the Declaration of Sentiments are two famous documents in American history that demonstrate this pattern of cause and effect. Another writing strategy that may be useful to you is **process analysis**. We use process analysis when giving directions about how to do something or providing information on how and why something happened. For example, you might be asked to write a paper explaining how women in the United States earned the right to vote in 1920. As part of your explanation, you would discuss the Declaration of Sentiments and the work of Elizabeth Cady Stanton, among others, in the fight for suffrage. Next, you would turn to developing your own skills in using cause and effect and process analysis in your writing. These writing strategies will benefit you not just in your future classes, but also in how you engage in your own rhetorical actions.

Your Writer's Toolkit

Writing Strategies: Cause and Effect and Causal Analysis

As you consider the long history of rhetoric and its impact on your world today, you might be wondering about the relationship between rhetoric and democracy. What is that cause-and-effect relationship? When working out complex concepts and relationships, or analyzing historical events, learning the thought processes for logically determining cause and effect can be a valuable tool in your writer's toolbox.

> Consider the movie *An Inconvenient Truth*. The movie connects the cause, human actions (for example, car emissions that lead to increased carbon dioxide levels that trap solar heat in the ozone layer), to the effect: global warming (which has the further effects of rising sea levels, higher temperatures, unpredictable and changing weather patterns, among other things).

When you're trying to answer the question "why?", working through cause-and-effect relationships will help you answer that question, regardless of your subject matter. As a strategy for organizing your writing, cause and effect—also called **casual analysis**—is the method by which writers analyze events. It is a method they choose when trying to discover, or argue for, order in a reality that appears to be in disorder. Journalists use the casual analysis strategy routinely, as do doctors, lawyers, law enforcement officers, politicians, and even movie makers to explain a series of events that resulted in a particular outcome.

Cause and effect are correlative terms—in other words, one term implies the other:

- A **cause** is a force or influence that produces an effect.
- An **effect** is anything that has been caused; it is the result of a force or an action.

But it is not always easy to determine cause-and-effect relationships, so you have to look for ways to further define your terms in order to be more accurate in your thinking and writing:

- A **necessary cause** is exactly that: a contributing factor necessary for the effect to occur. A necessary cause is always associated with the resulting action or effect. We find these clear distinctions often in biology and medicine. For example, the human papillomavirus is a necessary cause for invasive cervical cancer, which is to say that it is present in every case of cervical cancer. With that kind of clear cause-and-effect relationship, researchers have been able to develop a vaccine that can help prevents females from contracting that virus, therefore helping prevent cervical cancer.

- A **sufficient cause** is one that *could* be present to produce an effect. A given effect may have many sufficient causes, any one of which could produce the effect. For example, though a particular virus may be the necessary cause of disease, an overall weakened immune system could present a sufficient cause for someone contracting the virus. Often there are a number of sufficient causes that will result in a particular effect.

Because events are often the results of a series of causes, you also need to distinguish between **immediate** causes and **remote** causes. Knowing the immediate cause of an event will give you a limited cause-and-effect relationship, but also knowing the remote cause will provide you with a deeper understanding of that relationship.

For example, in the aftermath of Hurricane Katrina in New Orleans, where many homeowners had flood insurance but not hurricane protection, many insurance companies denied homeowners' claims of damage to their houses because the insurance company considered the cause of the damage to be the result of winds from the hurricane. The winds, in fact, could be considered the immediate cause—a hurricane blew through the area—but the remote cause of much of the damage left in the wake of Katrina was a result of the storm surge and the flooding in the area. The effect is the same—total destruction of the homeowners' property—but the actual cause is still up for debate. You can see that knowing how to effectively understand and argue cause and effect can be a useful tool.

In Exploring Cause and Effect Relationships, You Might Ask These Questions:

- What is the cause of X?
- Is there more than one cause of X?
- Which causes of X are necessary and which causes are sufficient?
- Which causes are immediate cause of X and which are remote?
- What are the effects of X?
- What comes before X? Are these causes?
- What comes after X? Are these effects?

Continuing with the Hurricane Katrina example, if you were the insurance adjuster determining the validity of claims in the aftermath of the hurricane and you were trying to limit the financial impact on your company, you might argue that the cause of the destruction of homes in New Orleans (X) was the wind from the hurricane. Remember, most homeowners had flood insurance, but not hurricane insurance. However, it is logical to claim that only wind caused X, the storm damage to homes? Not really. Anyone who saw the news reports of the hurricane, much less lived through it, witnessed wind *and* water from the storm surge and the flood. So the causal connection here is not clearly evident. Whether the damage to homes was an immediate effect of wind or water is difficult to determine. Thus, to write clearly about an event like Hurricane Katrina and its aftermath, the possibilities must be analyzed thoroughly so that your argument makes sense. You can see how thinking clearly and logically through a series of events will help you understand and write about cause-and-effect relationships.

As you construct your cause-and-effect argument, paying attention to the logic becomes very important. As demonstrated with the example of Hurricane Katrina, indicating the appropriate causal relationship can be difficult. Making choices too hastily can make your argument sound overly simple or even wrong. Therefore, watching for some potential pitfalls, such as logical fallacies, as you work will help build your ethos. **Logical fallacies** involve faulty or mistaken reasoning that essentially invalidate or falsify your argument. Interestingly, logical fallacies are sometimes used intentionally to mislead or confuse a reader or listener, especially in a debate situation.

The word "fallacy" in this situation simply means incorrect reasoning or belief. In other words, the reasoning—or the route from the claim to the conclusion—just doesn't make sense. Logical fallacies take a variety of forms. One of the most common is mistaking correlation for causation. Correlation is not necessarily causation. Remember, cause and effect are correlative terms—one term implies the other—but correlation is not automatically proof of causation. This relationship is so tricky it has a formal Latin name: ***cum hoc ergo propter hoc*** ("with this, therefore because of this"). Think of this concept as the act of asserting that one thing is the cause of another because that thing is often accompanied by the presumed cause. For example, "Every time I put on a new shirt, I drop food on it." The recent best-selling book *Freakonomics,* written by Steven D. Levitt and Stephen J. Dubner, explores this concept in depth as it questions the cause-and-effect relationships of such things as crime and violence:

> A correlation simply means that a relationship exists between two factors . . . [and] tells you nothing about the direction of that relationship. It's possible that X causes Y; it's also possible that Y causes X; and it may be that X and Y are both being caused by some other factor, Z (2005, p. 10).

In other words, you need to analyze your situation carefully to ensure that you are not assuming a correlation between things or that the relationship is easily understood.

It is also important to not mistake the chronology of an event as the causation for an event. The Latin term for this logical fallacy is ***post hoc ego propter hoc*** ("after this, therefore because of this"). Think of this concept as asserting one thing is the cause of another thing simply because it precedes the other thing in time. It's easy to assume that because Y follows X, that X caused Y, but that's not necessarily true. For example, "I'm not

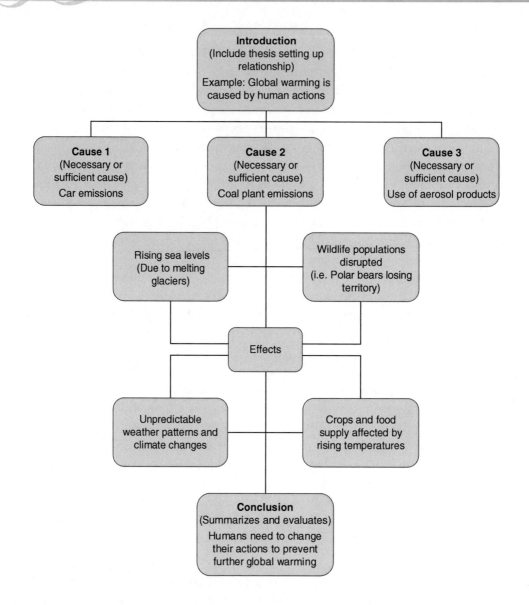

going to wash the car anymore because it rains every time I do." Be careful of making such assumptions and instead look for reliable evidence for those causal relationships.

After you have logically reasoned your way through your situational cause and effect, you need to think about organizing that information for your piece of writing. Whether it is an essay for your composition class or a biology report, you want to consider how you can best take your audience through your cause-and-effect relationship. Consider the following options:

- Arguing from cause to effect will let you take your reader from a known cause to a probable effect. For example, Hurricane Katrina brought sustained winds of over 125 miles per hour to the city of New Orleans, causing massive damage.
- Arguing from effect to cause will allow you to move from a known result to the event that caused it. This process of reasoning is often found in medical diagnosis. For example, a patient comes in with a sore throat—the effect—and the doctor speculates as to the cause, which could be anything from yelling too much at the basketball game to strep throat to throat cancer.
- Arguing from effect to effect will lead you to reason that whatever produced one effect will also routinely produce another effect. For example, hurricanes bring high winds that often result in damage, but they also bring storm surge and rainfall that may also result in damage.

Here's an example of how you might structure an essay that argues cause to effect: When you think about arranging your cause and effect essay, consider these options: **Arguing from cause to effect (keep in mind that these are structural suggestions, not necessarily paradigms for paragraphing your essay):**

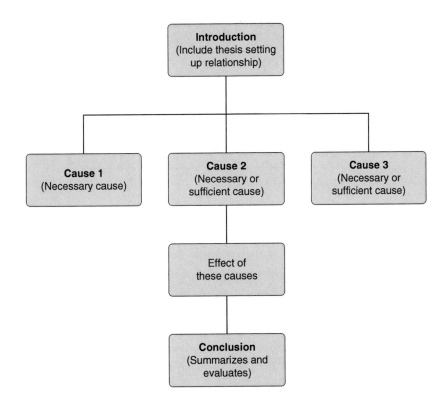

Or consider this structural strategy:

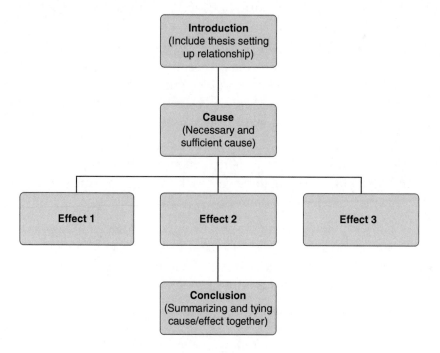

When you want to argue from effect to cause:

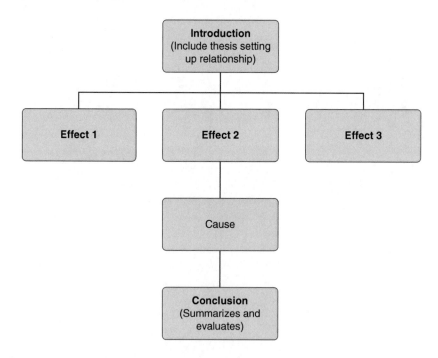

Or consider this structural strategy:

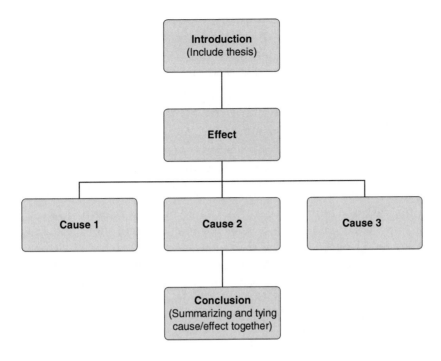

Developing Your Skills: Cause and Effect

Think about your "media diet" at this moment. What are you consuming—newspapers, movies, television, magazines, radio, podcasts, blogs, social networking sites? How do the communities you belong to (family, school, clubs, social media groups) dictate your media diet? Describe those relationships in cause-and-effect terms as you assess your media diet and its impact on your life and various communities.

Writing Strategies: Process Analysis

When thinking about your audience and how you might affect them, the writing strategy of process analysis can be useful. How did that happen? How did you do that? These are the questions that **process analysis** answers. Process analysis, one of the modes of exposition, either gives directions about how to do something (*directive*) or provides information on how and why something happened (*informative*). For example, a process analysis that is more directive would be an essay on how to lose weight or how to program your cell phone. An example of an informative process analysis would be an explanation of how the Twin Towers fell or how predatory lending led to the mortgage crisis in the American economy. In other words, process analysis is one of the strategies you can use to organize and focus your writing. You'll elect to use process analysis based on your purpose and audience.

Although the primary objective of process analysis is to instruct or inform, it can also be used to persuade. You will find examples of persuasive process analysis on topics such as global warming, the war on terrorism, and even child rearing. Typically, you will find process analysis in technical writing, scientific essays, cookbooks, instruction manuals, and the like. To see how process analysis works in essay form, look at this excerpt, "Serving in Florida" from Barbara Ehrenreich's *Nickel and Dimed: On (Not) Getting By in America*. Ehrenreich, a successful author and culture critic, spent a year working as a maid, a waitress, and a house cleaner in various cities in America in an effort to understand what life is like for low-wage workers. Here, in this "process analysis," she describes part of her experience:

> My first task is to find a place to live. I figure that if I can earn $7 an hour—which, from the want ads, seems doable—I can afford to spend $500 on rent or maybe, with severe economies, $600 and still have $400 or $500 left over for food and gas. In the Key West area, this pretty much confines me to flophouses and trailer homes—like the one, a pleasing fifteen minute drive from town, that has no air-conditioning, so screens, no fans, no television, and, by way of diversion, only the challenge of evading the landlord's Doberman pinscher. The big problem with this place, though, is the rent, which at $675 a month is well beyond my reach. All right, Key West is expensive. But so is New York City, or the Bay Area, or Jackson, Wyoming, or Telluride, or Boston, or any other place where tourists and the wealthy compete for living space with the people who clean their toilets and fry their hash browns. Still, it is a shock to realize that "trailer trash" has become, for me, a demographic category to aspire to.

Notice how she explains the "how" and "why" of her experience. We see her thought process as a means of informing her audience about where she begins in this pursuit of a place to live. You can see her looking at the ads, getting a sense of average wages for the jobs she is looking for, then guessing at what rents might be. But then she qualifies the process by noting this is happening in Key West, a tourist destination. In the full essay, she continues the process as she takes us on a drive to this decrepit place she can barely afford to rent and ends the paragraph with a new understanding of her current state of affairs.

Because process analysis answers the basic questions: "how does it work?" and "how or why did it happen?", it suggests there is some kind of movement or continuous action involved. So you have to focus your attention on that action or movement. You need to notice the changes, a sequence of actions, or a series of operations or procedures. It's about observing and recording your observations as you analyze a process.

Barbara Ehrenreich, *Nickled and Dimed: On (Not) Getting By in America*, New York: Henry Holt and Company, 2008.

Structure of Process Analysis

In writing process analysis essays, you should focus on the stages or phases of activity you are explaining. If the process you're writing about involves giving directions or making something, your introduction will usually contain a description of the material and the tools or implements to be used. If your process analysis does not involve directions, as in explaining the greenhouse effect, your introduction may include an explanation of the principles involved in the process. Then in the essay, you'll follow the chronological order for analyzing the process. Here's an example of how a process analysis essay might develop:

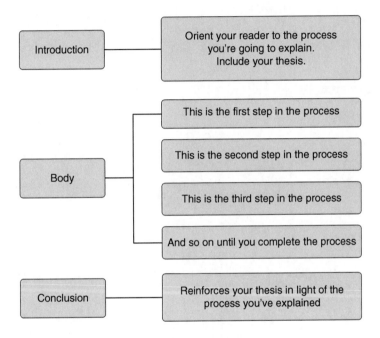

Developing Your Skills: Process Analysis

Describe the process you went through to select the college or university you attend. Was it a process of elimination (some accepted you; some did not)? Was it a process that included financial considerations as the deciding factor? Location? Sport opportunities? The opportunity to study abroad? It's likely that several elements went into your decision to attend this school. Describe that process.

YOUR TURN: Creating Your Ideas

1. Examine this employee poster from the Pocasset Mill in Fall River, Massachusetts in 1916. This poster, photographed by American photographer Lewis Hines, represents rhetoric in action and is modeled on the broadsides that were developed in the 1600s in the United States to communicate with the

public. Here, the poster communicates with a specific public—the Pocasset Mill workers. Write an essay in which you explain how the poster communicates with this public. Do you think the poster affected the workers' actions? Does the poster contribute to how the workers might see themselves as a public/community? Why or why not? What strategies of *ethos*, *pathos*, and/or *logos* do you see in action in the poster?

2. Imagine you have met someone who does not understand how a democratic culture is created or how such a culture is sustained. Write an essay in which you demonstrate how rhetorical practices, and the communities that form out of those practices, play an important role in the development and maintenance of a democracy. Think about the construction of laws, policies, and social customs. How do social agreements like community standards of decency or town councils, for example, contribute to or cause democracy? Your essay should include examples that you see in your community today.

3. If you were to create your own personal Declaration of Independence and Declaration of Sentiments, what would it be? Write a brief list of your own in keeping with the tone and style of these declarations.

TECH TALK: Spellchecking and Grammar Tools

A key element of *ethos*, which you learned about in Chapter 3, is accuracy and clarity in your written work. Fortunately, computers help us with this need through the use of the spellchecking and grammar tools.

To use the spellchecker, locate the "Tools" menu at the top of your word processing page. Click on the "Spelling and Grammar" link. The program will automatically begin checking your paper for errors. You should see the following box appear if you're using Microsoft Word:

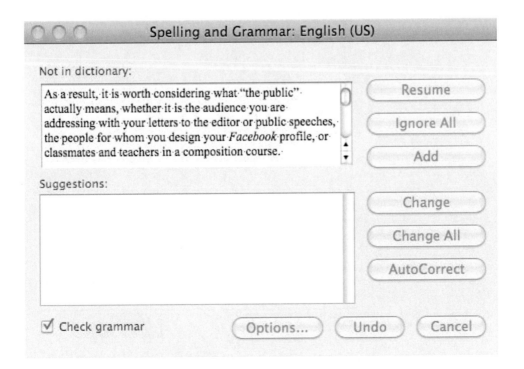

However, keep in mind that although it's important to use the technological capabilities in the computer, you need to be diligent and also *check your work yourself.* The spellchecker won't catch errors when you use homonyms (for example, "where" vs. "wear" or "weather" vs. "whether" or "effect" vs. "affect"). It's up to you, the writer, to go through your paper sentence by sentence and check for typos or spelling issues that the spellchecker misses.

In addition, you can take advantage of the grammar tool. Make sure the "check grammar" box is selected. As with the spellchecker, you need to be very careful about relying too much on the grammar tool. It will not catch all your errors; in fact, sometimes it might tell you something that is incorrect. It's up to you, the ethical writer, to proofread and edit your written work carefully.

Chapter 5

Making an Argument

The word "argument" often refers to two people screaming at each other, exchanging "Yes, you do" and "No, I don't" kinds of comments. However, a different understanding of the form and function of argument will help you develop your skills as a writer, citizen, and communicator. Once again, an idea from Aristotle will help clarify your understanding of argument.

In his important work *The Rhetoric*, Aristotle described an argument as consisting of two very essential components, **the claim and supporting data**:

- The **claim** is basically the point or points you want a person to understand or agree with. It's very similar to the thesis of a paper—it's the main idea you want to get across.

> Claim + data = argument

- The **data** completes Aristotle's notion of argument. Data consists of supporting material that will enable your audience to understand, agree with, be persuaded by, or otherwise buy into the main claim you wish to make. Anyone can claim anything; the data often makes or breaks an argument. Data can take the form of good reasons that are logical or emotional, statistics, facts, images, stories, credible testimony, or examples—almost anything can be used to support a claim.

It is critical for the person making an argument to consider whether the audience will respond to the choice of data. If your audience doesn't understand or react to the material you use in supporting your claim, the argument will fail. Some of the most critical decisions you make as a communicator will involve what data to include and how to use data in constructing arguments.

Claim: Smoking Cigarettes Can Cause Cancer.

Various types of data you might use:

- Pictures of cigarette smoke damaged lungs that are cancerous
- Testimony from the U.S. Surgeon General
- The story of a smoker, who died from cancer
- Scientific evidence and statistics that demonstrate the link between cigarette smoke and cancer
- Testimony from a person, a smoker, who currently has cancer or who has struggled with cancer in the past
- A list of the numerous cancer-causing chemical compounds found in cigarettes

Arguments surround you in both language and image. Advertising, political campaigns, opinion pages in newspapers and magazines, blogs, and chat rooms are all places full of persuasive arguments. This textbook is, in fact, a persuasive argument, as it takes the stance that being an engaged citizen of the world is a vital part of the human experience and tries to convince you of that while giving you ways—thinking and writing—to participate as a citizen of the world.

By the end of this chapter, you will have even more tools to help you make the important decisions that will enable you to communicate effectively. These tools include different kinds of claims, various forms of evidence or data, structuring arguments, and using logical reasoning as the glue that connects the data to the claim.

Claims

We will focus here on three kinds of claims:

- Claims of fact
- Claims of value
- Claims of policy

Just the facts, please!

A detective works from the "facts of a case" to determine what is actually true. The facts, then, are objectively verifiable.

It's important for you to think about the kind of claim you wish to present because that will determine the kind of argument you will make. Knowing your claims will also help you decide how much and what kinds of evidence you *must* provide in order to have a valid and more effective argument.

A **claim of fact** articulates ideas or events that can be objectively verified, but is not necessarily true. Now, you may ask, "How can a fact not be true?" A claim of fact is one that can be determined to be *true* or *false*. The claim, "Smoking cigarettes can cause cancer," is a claim of fact. Notice the key word "can." It is a claim of fact not because it is always true (for it is *not* always true), but because the truth or falsity of the statement can

Consider The Following Claim:

Recycling saves natural resources.

To support this claim, a writer or speaker requires data. The samples of data listed here are objective facts that can be proven. The list of data, or evidence of how recycling saves natural resources, thus supports the claim.

Samples of data:

- By recycling tons of steel, states like Pennsylvania can save million tons of iron ore, coal, and limestone.
- It takes a lot less energy to make an aluminum can from recycled aluminum cans rather than virgin resources. The leftover energy could run your TV!
- Much of the Earth's forests are gone, and the majority of the original forest area in the U.S. has been cut down.
- For every four-foot stack of paper you recycle, you save a tree.
- Recycling saves resources, decreases the use of toxic chemicals, cuts energy use, helps curb global warming, stems the flow of water and air pollution, and reduces the need for landfills and incinerators.

be determined and supported with evidence. If you do sufficient credible and effective research, you should be able to find evidence (or data) that will support the claim to the *satisfaction of the audience*, who will then agree with you. The validity of the data helps to demonstrate the truth of the claim that, in fact, smoking cigarettes can in many cases cause cancer.

> Claims of fact are objectively verifiable.

Now, someone could make the claim, "Abraham Lincoln is currently the president of the United States." Silly, perhaps, but that statement helps demonstrate the notion of objectively verifying a claim of fact. We know that Abraham Lincoln is not the *current* president, so the claim is false. However, it is a claim of fact—we can prove its truthfulness simply by going to www.whitehouse.gov or any U.S. news source to determine the current U.S. president. So, in other words, the words "fact" and "true" are not necessarily synonymous here.

Claims of fact, then, make objective statements that may or may not be true, but that can always be verified. We can determine whether the claim is actually true. Even if it is false, these claims are still "claims of fact." The data must include some basic information to prove or effectively support a claim of fact. If the claim contains any words that may be unclear or confusing to your audience, those terms should be *defined*. For example, in the recycling claim, you might want to explain very briefly what kind(s) of recycling you are promoting. You may also want to explain completely what sorts of natural resources you wish to save. The need to define your terminology is determined by the needs of your audience.

The second basic element of your data in support of your claim of fact is that you need to show that your claim makes sense to reasonable people. Sounds like overkill, doesn't it? In fact, by this criterion, our claim about Abraham Lincoln may fail simply because it's a ridiculous claim.

"I'm Not a Doctor, But I Play One on TV."

Is an expert necessarily a credible source? Only if she is an expert on the topic of discussion In other words, just because someone is a professor or doctor doesn't mean that he is credible sources in fields outside of his expertise. A writing professor, for example, may not be the best person to quote if your argument is about recycling, nuclear fission, or space walking.

Consider this claim: "The United States has plenty of landfill space."

This statement is a claim of fact because it can be objectively verified or denied. This claim would likely create controversy among many people. Part of the reason U.S. culture is so intent on recycling is that many folks believe that the United States is running out of places to put garbage. So if you want to make the claim that the United States has plenty of landfill space, you must be prepared to demonstrate that the statement makes sense.

How do you create that argument? You provide **evidence** that supports your viewpoint. For example, you might provide evidence in the form of statements like this: "Nationally, the U.S. Environmental Protection Agency says that landfill space is plentiful, according to the cofounder of Greenpeace in 2005." Or this: "Economist John Smith calculates that a single landfill 15 miles square could handle 1,000 years' worth of our present waste disposal needs." Both of these statements offer specific information in support of the claim about landfill space.

What else do these supporting statements do? They both cite credible sources of information. Rather than simply telling the audience that landfill space is plentiful, the EPA, the cofounder of Greenpeace (an international environmental organization), and an economist offer expertise in support of the claim. Such references to organizations or informed people increase the **credibility** or *ethos* of your argument as well as the likelihood that your audience will agree with you.

While we have defined an argument as a claim plus data, it is important to recognize that the data also consists of claims called sub-claims.

Claim of Value: Smoking Cigarettes is Bad for Your Health.

Data to support / prove the evaluation:

- Your lungs are directly exposed to the 4,000 toxic substances in cigarette smoke. These substances can *impair your lungs' ability to function* and interfere with the mechanisms that protect your lungs against disease.
- Smoking weakens your bones, which can cause you to develop a disease called *osteoporosis* as you grow older.
- Smoking increases a person's risk of several digestive tract diseases, and it can cause deadly *cancers* of the digestive organs.
- Smoking worsens a relatively common nervous system disease called *multiple sclerosis*.
- Smoking affects both your antibodies (a group of chemicals that circulate in the blood stream) and your cells that attack foreign substances.
- Smoking can also affect skin, especially on the face, and it can increase your chances of getting some types of skin diseases.

American Council on Science and Health. *The Scoop on Smoking.* 2010. Web. 17 June 2010.

Claims of value are very similar to claims of fact, with one key addition. Claims of value assert the **value** or how good or bad something seems. As a result, claims of value are **subjectively** verifiable. In other words, the claim can be determined to be credible or true only if you can prove or **support the evaluation** contained in the claim.

> Claims of value are subjectively verifiable.

Returning to the smoking issue, inserting a judgment or evaluation into the claim "Smoking cigarettes can cause cancer" can be done simply: "Smoking cigarettes is bad for your health." The difference between the two claims may seem minimal because most reasonable people will agree that cancer is bad. However, the statement that cigarette smoking can cause cancer does not state any explicit evaluation, and that is an important feature to keep in mind when making claims of value. The **claim of value explicitly states a judgment**, like in the statement "Smoking cigarettes is *bad* for your health." By the same token, the claim "Recycling saves natural resources" could be said to contain an implicit judgment that recycling is good. However, the claim does not actually say that recycling is good. To revise that claim to one of value, you might say, "Saving natural resources by recycling is valuable."

"The Scoop on Smoking," from www.thescooponsmoking.org. American Council on Science and Health. Used by permission.

Because claims of value rely on verifying your judgment or evaluation, they are a little bit harder to prove to the satisfaction of an audience. It's almost as though you must get your audience to see, understand, and agree with your opinion on a subject. That agreement can be made easier, though, by your providing good reasons and solid evidence verifying your position. After all, opinions should be smart and well supported. Expressing your opinion is making an argument. You must know what you want to claim, how you want to express that claim, and what you need to provide in terms of proof or evidence that will have an impact on your audience.

Here are some guidelines that will help prove the validity of your claim of value:

- Make sure that your audience understands the vocabulary you are using, which means defining your terms.

- Demonstrate the sensibility of the claim or that it is plausible to reasonable people in the real world.

- Make sure that your evaluation criteria are clear. What, for example, makes cigarette smoking bad? What makes recycling good? If you want to claim that a day is beautiful, what exactly makes it beautiful? Remember, just because a lot of people think a beautiful day is one full of sunshine and warm temperatures, there are other people whose idea of a great day is one with snow, cold temperatures, and howling wind. A claim of value, as you can see from these examples, is often rooted in abstract concepts such as "good," "bad," "love," "hate," and "beautiful." You may start with these abstractions, but make sure to push beyond the abstract term to get at how and why something is good or bad or lovable. A value argument needs to show the values driving the argument and define those abstract terms. Then the arguer must present his or her good reasons or data.

Claims of policy basically argue for a change in how things are done in virtually any venue. The different types of claims require varying levels of complex thinking to understand them and to prove them. Claims of policy operate on a "big-picture" level because most policy arguments require claims of value and fact as their building blocks.

For example, in your family, you may find policy claims made involving what should be served for dinner on Saturdays. Although such a policy may not have a monumental impact on a large community, it certainly affects the climate and behavior of your family. The policy claim would be something like, "The Smith family should enjoy spaghetti for dinner on Saturday." What makes this claim one of policy? Quite simply, the suggestion of a change in action and the word "should" qualifies the claim as one of policy. If a claim suggests a course of action, it is a claim of policy.

> **Policy claims** require sub-claims of fact and value for proof and support.

The Stock Issues of a Claim of Policy:

- **Problem:** What problem needs to be solved? How extensive is the problem? Who is being harmed?
- **Cause:** What is the cause of the problem?
- **Solution:** What is the complete set of procedures that will solve or lessen the problem?
- **Outcomes:** What are the possible positive **and** negative results of the solution? The advantages should outweigh the disadvantages.

Writing an argument based on a claim of policy requires you to prove very specific points:

- You will create what is called a ***prima facie*** ("on its face" or "at first view") **case**. In other words, the argument provides all the evidence that is needed to prove the claim.
- The specific points required for proving the claim are called **stock issues**. An effective argument must fulfill the stock issues, again satisfying the audience as to the validity, truthfulness, and credibility of the evidence and the arguer. The specific points you must cover for a claim of policy include:
  - Defining and explaining the problem
  - Pointing out the cause of the problem
  - Identifying a logical, reasonable and complete solution to the problem
  - Exploring the potential outcomes, both positive and negative, of your solution

A *prima facie* case is one of the most persuasive arguments possible, particularly if you want to suggest that something in the current system must change. This type of argument is persuasive because the evidence is complete, in part because you seriously consider what your audience knows, thinks, and believes about the current policy you wish to change. Even if you want to propose a regular Saturday night spaghetti supper for your family, you must think through the feelings and possible reactions of the rest of the family if you want to be successful. If there is a truly compelling reason to argue for Saturday night spaghetti (such as salvaging family relationships, addressing someone's food allergies or issues, or making sure all the kids in the family are in one place at the same time), there will be enough at stake to argue effectively. In a sense, providing sufficient and complete responses to each of the stock issues means that there is less opportunity for others to argue with you or to knock holes in the argument.

Consider an example of a policy claim and argument that you might read about in the newspaper from a politician or other concerned citizen.

Claim of Policy

Main Claim/ Proposition: **The U.S. government should subsidize health care.**

Problem: Many Americans have no health care because they can't afford insurance or doctors, which leads to more illness, time lost on the job, and higher child mortality.

Cause: High cost of insurance and medical care, high unemployment....What else?

Solution: Government subsidies of health insurance through employers (steps: establish a government agency to oversee, determine standards of employers (i.e., size of organization), determine budget constraints, determine who's in charge, etc.)

Possible Outcomes:

(+) greater equality of the health care system, healthier society, fewer epidemics, healthier kids, greater productivity in the workplace.

(–) high financial cost to the government, the unemployed are still left out, high cost to employers

What can you add to the argument?

Your exploration of the different claims of **fact, value**, and **policy** has provided important tools for your writer's toolkit. By remembering that argument has much to do with everything you write, you will be well prepared for creatively adapting claims and data to a variety of writing and communication challenges.

Data

A skillful communicator needs an array of resources in order to effectively support his or her claims. Once more, Aristotle's ideas offer useful insights about data, or supporting materials. Aristotle divided proof, or data, into two primary groups. He called the first **inartistic proof**, and the second **artistic proof**. **Inartistic proof** consists of supporting evidence that we find through research. Basically, the inartistic proofs are those you, the writer or arguer, must go out and find. Aristotle identified five types of inartistic proofs for his needs:

- Laws
- Witnesses
- Contracts
- Evidence of slaves taken under torture
- Oaths

Evidence: source materials external to us that are used to lend support or proof to a claim.

These sources of evidence are, according to Aristotle, outside the art of the communicator. In other words, the resources must be discovered and brought into our argument. For our twenty-first-century uses, we must revise this list to include:

- Facts
- Figures
- Statistics
- Quotations from important and relevant people
- Any other resources available to us through creative, credible, and thorough research

The **artistic proofs**, on the other hand, are within the decision-making control of the writer. In short, the communicator must decide how best to implement his or her data, or inartistic evidence, in support of the argument. Earlier, the artistic proofs were presented as tools to help you achieve your rhetorical goals. They are revisited briefly here in the form of proof, or data supporting your claims—again as tools for effective rhetorical communication and as integral elements of your arguments. As you know, the artistic proofs consist of:

- *Ethos:*
  - Good will—kindness and support
  - Good sense—practical skills and wisdom
  - Good character—virtue, goodness
- *Pathos:*
  - Arousing the emotions of the audience
- *Logos:*
  - Rationality, organization, "logic"

The artistic proofs mold and shape the research that you do, the examples you provide, and the stories you tell—all through the perceptions of the audience. If, for example, the audience trusts you, finds your evidence credible, and believes in your expertise on the topic, they will also find your argument credible. You have thus used *ethos* effectively.

When a communicator strives to make an audience feel a particular way, they are employing the proof of *pathos*. Pictures or stories of babies, families, kittens, puppies, tragedies, heartbreak, or tremendous joy are intended to arouse emotion in one's audience and provide support for their claims. Arousing feeling in your reader or audience **involves them** in the story or argument. When people get involved in the story, they become part of the narrative and thus are more likely to agree or be persuaded. Research shows that people viewing emotionally charged advertising are more likely to respond positively to those ads than logical ads, buying products, voting for candidates, or supporting courses of action.

The effective writer uses *pathos* cautiously. In other words, just because you can make a person laugh, cry, or get angry doesn't mean that you should go to any lengths to accomplish that result. Too much emotion can overshadow the message you are constructing.

Think of *logos* as the glue that holds together the communication process, or the logic, organization, rationality, and reasoning. Consider the challenge faced by U.S. presidents when responding to difficult situations such as space shuttle disasters, 9/11, or Hurricane Katrina. Regardless of the enormity of the tragedy, each president had to find words and an organizational structure for those words to give his listeners hope, a feeling of safety, and the sense that the president felt the pain of the nation, calling upon all of the artistic proofs.

For example, in the case of 9/11, President George W. Bush made a statement to the nation that day. In his speech, he said,

> The pictures of airplanes flying into buildings, fires burning, huge structures collapsing, have filled us with disbelief, terrible sadness, and a quiet, unyielding anger. These acts of mass murder were intended to frighten our nation into chaos and retreat. But they have failed; our country is strong.

These three sentences acknowledge the horrific and unbelievable images the American people saw on television that day, the great fear and sadness experienced by the entire nation, and the evil intent of those who committed terrorism. Yet the last sentence offers an important contrast to President Bush's recognition of the emotion of the day. He says, "But they have failed; our country is strong." His wording here is simple. He is not painting pictures of strength; rather, he simply tells his audience that the country is strong. Here we see a masterful combination of *pathos* and *logos*. Had President Bush focused solely on the fear, anguish, anger, and so on of that day, the result of his comments would have caused more panic on the part of his audience. Organizing his thoughts as a combination of *logos* and *pathos* helped to illustrate his *ethos* as well—he demonstrated his concern and goodwill, as well as his command of the moment.

Ethos, *pathos*, and *logos* provide valuable resources for constructing effective arguments. The artistic proofs enable you to present the evidence—your inartistic proof—to your audience in the most effective manner possible. By determining how to demonstrate your credibility and the reliability of your evidence, you also discover how best to appeal to your audience's emotions. And finally, your knowledge and skill of *logos* allows you to put together an effective essay, blog, PowerPoint or other type of slide presentation, or other form of rhetoric. Your writer's toolkit is becoming a powerful resource for you, the writer citizen.

Reasoning

Making an effective argument includes providing good reasons, in various forms, that will encourage your audience to accept and agree with the position you are arguing.

> **Reasoning** – looking for reasons on which to base one's actions, beliefs, or acceptance of a claim

Good reasons—whether a story, set of statistics, photograph, or other form of evidence—need to be woven together with your claim in order to establish the full understanding and awareness that your audience needs. The weaving, or connecting, involves **reasoning**—or looking for reasons on which to base one's actions, beliefs, or acceptance of a claim. You, the rhetorical communicator, must help your audience to see the connections between your claim and their actions and acceptance of your claim. Sometimes this will mean making your reasons very clear and explicit; other times you can rely on implicit, shared assumptions; and sometimes you need to choose from different forms of providing your argument. Two kinds of reasoning are inductive and deductive reasoning.

Inductive reasoning relies on a set of observations and experiences for evidence. The claim then addresses a larger population of similar observations, experiences, or populations. One way of putting together an argument in this way involves making a generalization, such as Steve does in the following example. Generalizations are easy to make, as you know.

Inductive reasoning: moves from the particular (an observation or set of experiences) to the general.

For example: Steve has seen four Hollywood movies in the past month. All four films contained numerous scenes of physical violence. Based on these four examples, Steve has concluded that Hollywood movies are too violent.

Claim: Hollywood movies are too violent.

Evidence: Four films exhibiting scenes of intense physical violence.

Reasoning: Inductive generalization. Steve has made a generalized claim about all Hollywood films based upon his experience of four films.

Further thought: From his experiences with these films, Steve has one building block of a **policy claim**. Is he working on detailing the problem, cause, solution, or outcomes? How might he phrase his policy claim?

You probably recognize that Steve's argument can be refuted or weakened simply by pointing out *one* Hollywood film that is *not* violent. When someone generalizes from a limited set of observations, making a claim about every other possible observation of the same sort is **invalid reasoning**. All that's necessary to destroy that argument is pointing out one example for which the claim is false. There are much better ways to phrase claims that make them reasonable and more realistic. You can modify or limit your claims by using qualifiers and reservations to make them easier to prove.

Qualifiers are words that limit the extent of the claim in a numerical fashion. Qualifiers use words such as "some," "many," "most," "often," "sometimes," "frequently," and "usually." The claim about Hollywood movies could be qualified in this way: "**Many** Hollywood movies are too violent." Reserved claims, on the other hand, indicate circumstances to which the claim does and does not apply. In other words, reservations indicate when the claim is not valid. Reserved claims feature words and phrases such as "unless," "in the case of," and "except." We might reserve his claim like this: "Hollywood films are too violent **unless** they have been specifically rated as R-17."

Limiting claims using qualifiers and reservations is important for inductive arguments because your claims will be more acceptable to your audience, and thus easier to support with sufficient credible evidence. Limiting your claims also increases your credibility, or *ethos*, as a communicator because your claims are reasonable, not ridiculous and unbelievable to your audience. Anticipating the objections of your audience will make your writing, blogging, speaking, or other form of arguing easier to understand and to support.

When reasoning deductively, limiting your claims is important as well. **Deductive reasoning**, in contrast to inductive reasoning, moves from the general to the specific. For example:

> **Major premise/broad assumption:** People who wear glasses are smart.
>
> **Minor premise/observation:** Steve wears glasses.
>
> **Claim/conclusion:** Therefore, Steve is smart.

The minor premise is the specific observation that works as evidence for the claim.

This form of logic is known as a **syllogism**. Yet most of the time people do not present their deductive arguments in this formal manner. On the one hand, the argument is silly because everyone knows that all people wearing glasses are not necessarily smart. On the other hand, working through the assumptions and observations to the conclusion is time-consuming and unnecessary most of the time. Therefore, you might consider limiting this argument like this:

> **People who wear glasses are often smart.**
>
> **Steve wears glasses.**
>
> **Therefore, Steve is probably smart.**

The argument is still faulty in its reasoning, but at least it doesn't sound completely ridiculous.

However, the problem remains of expressing the argument in ways that resemble real-life communication. One of Aristotle's enormous contributions to the field of argument was that he thought long and hard about practical communication and how people really express themselves. He considered how people reason, how they decide on their actions and beliefs, and importantly, how communities of people work together, resolve disputes, and get things done. Such communication practices, whether they take place in writing or orally, require flexibility, probability, and much common ground.

Aristotle's concept of the *enthymeme* takes into account the pragmatic realities that people face when creating legitimate arguments for audiences large and small. An **enthymeme** is a rhetorical syllogism. In other words, when reasoning using enthymemes:

- We use deductive logic, proceeding from a generally understood premise to our conclusion.
- One or more of the premises will be missing, letting the audience complete the argument.
- The argument begins with beliefs that are probable, rather than absolutely true because it is dealing with human issues—which are necessarily contingent.

This may sound complicated. However, if you think about the fact that we infuse argument into much of what we write, you're well on your way to getting a handle on enthymemes. Further, recognizing that advertisers and politicians use enthymemes in their communication all the time will help you grasp the overwhelming presence of this kind of reasoning in your world.

> **Enthymeme:** An enthymeme is a syllogism with one part of the argument missing. Thus one or more of the major premise, the minor premise or the conclusion is omitted.

Enthymemes are powerful forms of argument because they involve the audience. The audience is expected to fill in the missing pieces, often without explicitly having to put them into words. Those missing pieces come from culturally shared knowledge or attitudes, or other information shared between the writer or speaker and the audience. Read the following statement by Mark Twain quoted in *The National Paris* in 1850: "There is no law against composing music when one has no ideas whatsoever. The music of Wagner, therefore, is perfectly legal." Are you at all confused by the quotation? Or, somewhere in your mind, do you understand that Twain is implying that Wagner has no ideas? We believe that most people will get the quotation, even if they don't know who Wagner was or what kind of music he wrote. Here's how the enthymeme would break down in its deductive logic:

Major premise: There is no law against composing music when one has no ideas.

Minor premise (implied): Wagner (a famous German composer of the nineteenth century) has no ideas.

Conclusion or claim: The music of Wagner is perfectly legal.

Contemporary advertising relies heavily on the enthymeme as a form of persuasive reasoning. The Nike swoosh has become synonymous with Nike's various advertising campaigns, numerous well-known athletes, and,

---

Nike USA Inc.

to a certain extent, average people pushing themselves athletically. We could say that placing the Nike symbol on a golfer at the U.S. Open, a tennis player at Wimbledon, or a basketball player at the NCAA championship functions as an argument to those of us who watch such sporting events on television. For example:

- Nike gear works for great athletes.
- Serena Williams is a great athlete.
- Nike gear works for Serena Williams.
- Because Nike gear is sold at my local sporting goods store and online, I can buy Nike gear, which will probably work for me just as it works for people like Serena Williams. And I will be a more successful athlete.

Logically, this argument is a little suspect because it takes much more than a certain type of clothing or sporting gear to make someone a great athlete. However, what is interesting about this argument is that the argument is made without one word being written down or spoken. The entire argument takes place as a result of the image of the swoosh sparking a set of cultural assumptions and shared knowledge.

For example, consider this famous slogan from De Beers, a diamond company: "Diamonds Are Forever." This slogan is an enthymeme. Here is how:

> **Major premise (the cultural assumption is implied)**: Marriage is supposed to last forever.
>
> **Minor premise (the specific example is expressed)**: Diamonds are forever.
>
> **Claim (implied)**: A diamond engagement ring from De Beers will ensure that our marriage will last forever. This claim relies upon cultural knowledge of the longevity and preeminence of De Beers Diamond Jewellers Ltd.

Once again, the absolute truthfulness of this argument is weak. But the point is that three words, coupled with ads full of romantic imagery and sparkling gems, make a culturally compelling argument to the viewer. Through simple words that engage strong cultural beliefs, the argument gains rhetorical power and De Beers sells diamonds.

Advertisers, politicians, teachers, parents, you, and your friends all use enthymemes. Each of your communities shares values and assumptions that don't need to be spoken every time you refer to them. In your family, you don't need to repeat your values or beliefs when they function as reasons for your behaviors. For example:

- If your family has a tradition of having dinner together at least once a week, your argument for Saturday night's spaghetti supper doesn't necessarily require that tradition to be expressed as one of your reasons.
- The politician running for office does not have to restate his or her community's past record of historical preservation or crime prevention or educational reform.

- The person running for president is not required to prove her or his financial capacity for the campaign in every speech.
- The preacher or rabbi doesn't have to explain the significance of the rituals employed during services every week.

In other words, many of your everyday communication experiences occur through the use of enthymemes. Thus, the more you consciously employ enthymemes in your rhetorical communication, the more powerful your arguments will become. Spotting enthymemes and trying to verbalize the entire argument or syllogism when you see them in everyday life is great practice for your own enthymemes. Your audience will feel included because their beliefs and assumptions are included in the argument. In fact, they participate in your argument by filling in the missing premises and, as a result, will be more inclined to agree with your position. The enthymeme is an immensely valuable addition to your writing toolbox.

A Brief Review

- Claim + Data = Argument
- Claims of fact:
  - Make statements about the existence or truth of something
  - Are objectively verifiable (not necessarily true!)
- Claims of value:
  - Make statements about the goodness or badness of something
  - Make statements of judgment
  - Verifiable by proving/supporting the judgment of the claim
- Claims of policy:
  - Advocate changes to the status quo, courses of action
  - Require you to prove **stock issues**:
    - Problem
    - Cause
    - Solution
    - Outcomes
- Forms of data:
  - Inartistic proof: the evidence we go out and find
  - Artistic proofs:
    - *Ethos*—appeals to the credibility or character of the writer
    - *Pathos*—appeals to the emotions of the audience
    - *Logos*—appeals to reason, logic, using organization and good reasons

- Reasoning:
  - Inductive reasoning:
    - Moves from the specific to the general
    - Draws conclusions (sometimes generalizations) about a large group of situations based upon limited specific examples or experiences
  - Deductive reasoning:
    - Moves from the general (or broadly held assumptions) to the specific
    - Generally contains a major premise, minor premise, and conclusion
    - Uses enthymemes:
      - A rhetorical syllogism: a form of deductive reasoning that leaves out at least one of the premises, relying on the audience to complete the argument.

With this information, you are equipped to both make arguments effectively and to understand arguments that you run into in your everyday life. As citizens in today's world, the skills of making and understanding arguments are critical. They are critical skills for effective decision making, for engaging in public discussions, and for protecting our families and communities. Remember to make clear claims that consider and appeal to your audience, as it is the audience who will determine the success and effectiveness of your argument.

Rhetoric in Action

"The Moral Obligations of Living in a Democratic Society"

Cornel West (1953–) is an American author, critic, philosopher, and teacher. Currently the Class of 1943 Professor at Princeton University, West teaches in the Center for African American Studies. He is best known for his 1993 bestselling book *Race Matters*, and his focus on issues of race and class in the United States.

Prereading: Consider West's title to his essay. What do you think are the "moral obligations of living in a democratic society"? Make a list and then see how your list compares after reading the article.

One of the fundamental questions of our day is whether the tradition of struggle can be preserved and expanded. I refer to the struggle for decency and dignity, the struggle for freedom and democracy.

"The Moral Obligations of Living in a Democratic Society" by Cornell West, University Professor, Princeton University. Used with Permission.

In *Tradition and Individual Talent* (1919), T.S. Eliot claims that tradition is not something you inherit—if you want it, you must sacrifice for it. In other words, tradition must be fought for.

We live at the end of a century of unprecedented brutality and barbarity, a period when more than two hundred million fellow human beings have been murdered in the name of some pernicious ideology. Nazism was at the heart of a so-called civilized Europe. Stalinism was at the core of a so-called emancipator Soviet Union. European colonialism and imperialism in Africa, South America, and Asia have left palpable and lasting scars on fellow human begins. Patriarchal subordination of sisters of all colors and all regions and all countries is evident. The devaluation and degradation of gay brothers and lesbian sisters across race, region, and class, as well as the marginalization of the disabled and physically challenged.

What kind of species are we? What leads us to think that the tradition of struggle for decency and dignity can be preserved into the twenty-first century? Or will it be the case that we shall witness in the twenty-first century the unleashing of new, unnamable and indescribable forms of agony and anguish? At the moment, we are right to fear the emergence of ancient tribalisms that are revitalized under the aegis of an uncontested global capitalism, a movement accompanied by the "gangsterization" of community, nation, and the globe.

What attracts me to the Black-Jewish dialogue is the potential that is inherent to our respective traditions of struggle. It has nothing to do with skin pigmentation *per se*, nor with ethnicity in the abstract. Rather, it is because these two communities have developed a set of responses to combat the fundamental problem of evil.

The problem of evil refers to working out a response to undeserved suffering, unmerited pain, and unjustified harm. It is impossible to talk about Jews or Blacks, symbolically or literally, without discussing the problem of evil because these groups have been consistently devalued and subjugated, if not downright hated and despised. Indeed, the history of that treatment raises very alien dilemmas for America.

Henry James was correct when he declared America to be a "hotel civilization." In fact, this is the reason James left the country; he experienced American society as being too bland and culturally impoverished. At the turn of the twentieth century, America did not want to deal with the problem of evil, let alone the tragic and the comic—it was too preoccupied with the melodramatic and the sentimental.

A hotel—the fusion of a home and a market—is such a wonderful metaphor for America. The warmth, security, and motherhood of the home exists, as does that patriarchal tilt that burdens sisters of all colors, to caretake men who must forage in the marketplace. The men go forth into a heartless world, in a quest for mobility, liquidity, and profit-making. This fusion of home and market has its own distinct ethos: privatistic, individualistic, tribalisitc, ethnic-centered, racially subscribed, distrustful of the nation-state, distrustful of bureaucracy, and marginalizing of public interest and the common good.

It is no coincidence then, that the best of the Jewish and Black traditions has consistently infused a sense of the tragic and the comic in order to expand the precious traditions of their struggle. In my own case, I began to struggle with the problem of evil by grappling with the absurd, the absurd in America and the absurd *as* America. I did not have to read a book by Jean-Paul Sartre or see a play by Samuel Beckett to understand what the absurd was. I had a black body in a civilization deeply shaped by white supremacist perceptions, sensibilities, and institutional practices. When something as irrational and arbitrary as skin pigmentation is the benchmark of measuring one's humanity, then that state of affairs is totally absurd.

What is distinctive about this precious experiment in democracy called America is that it has always been inextricably interwoven with white supremacy and its legacy. Although some scholars call it an irony, I call it a hypocrisy. John J. Chapman described it accurately when he concluded that white supremacy was like a serpent wrapped around the legs of the table upon which the Declaration of Independence was signed by the founding fathers. It haunted America then and nearly 220 years later it still does. The challenge for America today is whether it will continue to deny, evade, and avoid various forms of evil in its midst.

In any discussion about race matters it is vital to situate yourself in a tradition, in a larger narrative that links the past to the present. When we think of Sojourner Truth, Harriet Tubman, Ida Buelle, Wells Barnett, A. Philip Randolph, Marcus Garvey, Ella Baker, James Baldwin, and so many nameless and anonymous ones, we cannot but be moved by their standards of vision and courage. They are wind at one's back.

The recovery of a tradition always begins at the existential level, with the experience of what it is to be human under a specific set of circumstances and conditions. It is very difficult to engage in a candid and frank critical discussion about race by assuming it is going to be a rational exchange. Race must be addressed in a form that can deal with its complexity and irrationality.

Perhaps no one understood the existential dimension of being human and African in America better than W.E.B. Du Bois. He recognized the absurd in American society and realized that being Black in America is to be a problem. Du Bois asserted that race in this country is the fetishization of a problem, black bodies in white space. He understood what it meant to be cast as part of a problem people rather than people with problems. Once the humanity of a people is problematized, they are called into question perennially. Their beauty is attacked: wrong hips, lips, noses, skin texture, skin pigmentation, and hair texture. Black intelligence is always guilty before proven innocent in the court of the life of the mind: *The Bell Curve* is just a manifestation of the cycle. Perhaps the gravest injustice is the image of the welfare queen. Looking at the history of black women in America, on the plantation taking care of white children in white households, how is it possible that they could become the symbol of laziness? All of the foregoing are signs of humanity that has been problematized.

Du Bois also underscored that to be part of a problem people is to be viewed as part of an undifferentiated blob, a monolithic block. Problem people become indistinguishable and interchangeable, which means that only one of them has to be asked to find out what all the rest of them think.

It is rare in human history, of course, that the notion of individuality and the civic are coupled so that a democratic project is generated. For most of history ordinary people have been viewed as "weeds and rain drops." as part of a mob, a rabble, all of which are ways of constituting them as an undifferentiated mob. Even the Greeks, despite their glorious yet truncated democratic experiment, would only apply the tragic to the elite. Ordinary people were limited to the idyllic and the comic, the assumption being that their lives were less complex and one-dimensional.

A democratic sensibility undeniably cuts against the grain of history. Most of human history is the history of elites, of kings, queens, princes, prelates, magistrates, potentates, knights, earls, and squires, all of whom subordinated and exploited everyday people.

This is why it becomes vital to talk about prevailing forms of oligarchy and plutocracy, and to some degree "pigmentocracy," in America. One percent of the population owns 48 percent of the total net financial wealth. The top 10 percent owns 86 percent of the wealth, while the top 20 percent owns 94 percent of the wealth. Meanwhile, 80 percent of the our population is experiencing stagnating and declining wages.

Corporations speak glibly about downsizing—bureaucratic language that simply means you do not have a job even though we have the highest profits we have had since 1948. And yet 25 percent of all of America's children live in poverty, and 42 percent of young brown brothers and sisters live in poverty, and 51 percent of young black brothers and sisters live in poverty in the richest nation in the history of the world. These sets of conditions are immoral.

When I examine the present state of American democracy, I believe we are living in one of the most terrifying moments in the history of this nation. We are experiencing a lethal and unprecedented linkage of relative economic decline (i.e., working class wage stagnation), cultural decay, and political lethargy. No democracy can survive with a middle class so insecure that it is willing to accept any authoritarian option in order to provide some sense of normalcy and security in their lives. It also opens the door for significant segments of that middle class to scapegoat those who are most vulnerable.

It is past time that we consider in our public discourse the civic responsibilities of corporations. There must be prescribed forms of public accountability for institutions that have a disproportionate amount of wealth, power, and influence. This is not a matter of demonizing corporations, but an issue of democratic survival.

We are all in the same boat, on the same turbulent sea. The boat has a huge leak in it and in the end, we go up and down together. A corporate executive recently said to me.

"We are not in the same boat. We're global." His response suggests why it is vital to inquire when corporate commercial interests must be subordinate to the public interest.

Democracy always raises the fundamental question: What is the role of the most disadvantaged in relation to the public interest? It is similar in some ways to the biblical question: What are you to do with the least of these? If we do not want to live in a democracy, we are not obliged to raise that question. In fact, the aristocracy does not address that question at all. Chekhov wrote in a play. "The Czar's police, they don't give a damn about raising that question. That's not the kind of society they are." But within a democratic society that question must be continually raises and pushed.

The conversation matters because the preservation of democracy is threatened by real economic decline. While it is not identical to moral and cultural decay, it is inseparable from it. Even though the pocketbook is important, many Americans are concerned more about the low quality of their lives, the constant fear of violent assault and cruel insult, the mean spiritedness and cold heartedness of social life, and the inability to experience deep levels of intimacy. These are the signs of a culturally decadent civilization.

By "decadent" I mean the relative erosion of systems of nurturing and caring, which affects each of us, but which has an especially devastating impact on young people. Any civilization that is unable to sustain its networks of caring and nurturing will generate enough anger and aggression to make communication near impossible. The result is a society in which we do not even respect each other enough to listen to each other. Dialogue is the lifeblood of democracy and is predicated on certain bonds of trust and respect. At this moment of cultural decay, it is difficult to find places where those ties of sympathy may be nurtured.

The roots of democracy are fundamentally grounded in mutual respect, personal responsibility, and social accountability. Yet democracy is also about giving each person a dignified voice in the decision-making processes in those institutions that guide and regulate their lives. These deeply moral suppositions have a certain spiritual dimension. John Dewey and Josiah Royce, among others, identified a spirituality of genuine questioning and dialogical exchange that allows us to transcend out egocentric predicaments, Spirituality requires an experience of something bigger than our individual selves that binds us to a community. It could be in an authoritarian bind, of course, which is why the kind of spiritual and moral awakening that is necessary for a democracy to function is based on a sense of the public—a sense of what it is to be a citizen among citizens.

Nurturing spirituality is so difficult today because we are bombarded by a market culture that evolves around buying and selling, promoting and advertising. The market tries to convince us that we are really alive only when we are addicted to stimulation and titillation. Given the fact that so much of American culture revolves around sexual foreplay and orgiastic intensity, for many people the good life might mean being hooked up to an orgasm machine and being perennially titillated.

The ultimate logic of a market culture is the gangsterization of culture: I want power now. I want pleasure now. I want property now. Your property. Give it to me.

Young black people call their block a "hood" now. I grew up in a neighborhood; it is a big difference. A neighborhood was a place not only for the nuclear family, but also included aunts and uncles, friends and neighbors, rabbis and priests, deacons and pastors, Little League coaches and dance teachers—all of whom served as a backdrop for socializing young people. This backdrop provided children with a sense of what it is to be human, with all its decency, integrity, and compassion. When those values are practiced, a neighborhood emerges.

Unfortunately, neighborhoods often took shape in my boyhood under patriarchal and homophobic conditions, and that history must be called into question. Still, we must recover its flow of nonmarket values and nonmarket activity.

These days we cannot even talk about love the way James Baldwin and Martin Luther King Jr. did. Nobody wants to hear that syrupy, mushy stuff. James Baldwin, however, said love is the most dangerous discourse in the world. It is daring and difficult because it makes you vulnerable, but if you experience it, it is the peak of human existence.

In our own time it is becoming extremely difficult for nonmarket values to gain a foothold. Parenting is a nonmarket activity; so much sacrifice and service goes into it without any assurance that the providers will get anything back. Mercy, justice; they are nonmarket. Care, service; nonmarket. Solidarity, fidelity; nonmarket. Sweetness and kindness and gentleness. All nonmarket.

Tragically, nonmarket values are relatively scarce, which is one of the reasons why it is so tough to mobilize and organize people in our society around just about any cause. It is hard to convince people that there are alternative options for which they ought to sacrifice. Ultimately, there can be no democratic tradition without nonmarket values.

In the last decade we have witnessed within popular culture wonderful innovation in forms of hip hop and rap. Compare that phenomenon to the 1960s when the Black Panther Party emerged and note the big difference between the two movements. One has to do with sacrifice, paying the price, dealing with the consequences as you bring power and pressure to bear on the prevailing status quo. The other has to do with marketing black rage. One movement had forty-seven local branches across the nation, the other sells millions of albums and CDs. The comparison is not a matter of patronizing this generation. Frankly, it is a critique of each us who has to deal with this market culture and through market mechanisms try to preserve some nonmarket values.

What then are we to do? There is no overnight solution or panacea, of course. We need to begin with something profoundly un-American, namely, recalling a sense of history, a very deep, tragic, and comic sense of history, a historical sensibility linked to empathy. Empathy is not simply a matter of trying to imagine what others are going through, but having the will to muster enough courage to do something about it. In a way, empathy is predicated upon hope.

Hope has nothing to do with optimism. I am in no way optimistic about America, nor am I optimistic about the plight of the human species on this globe. There is simply not enough evidence that allows me to infer that things are going to get better. That has been the perennial state and condition of not simply black people in America, but all self-conscious human beings who are sensitive to the forms of evil around them. We can be prisoners of hope even as we call optimism into question.

To be part of the democratic tradition is to be a prisoner of hope. And you cannot be a prisoner of hope without engaging in a form of struggle in the present moment that keeps the best of the past alive. To engage in that struggle means that one is always willing to acknowledge that there is no triumph around the corner, but that you persist because you believe it is right and just and moral. As T.S. Eliot said. "Ours is in the trying. The rest is not our business."

We are not going to save each other, ourselves, America, or the world. But we certainly can leave it a little bit better. As my grandmother used to say, "If the Kingdom of God is within you, then everywhere you go, you ought to leave a little Heave behind."

Comprehending the Text

1. What is West's main point in this essay?

2. How does West describe a "hotel civilization"? Why does he use this metaphor to describe America?

3. Why does West consider nurturing and caring to be important components of democratic society?

Analyzing the Text

1. How would you describe the tone of West's essay? How does reading it make you feel? What specific words, phrases, and/or metaphors does West use to create this tone?

2. West is making an argument in his essay about our moral obligation toward others in a democratic society. Is this an argument of fact, value, or policy?

3. Explore West's use of *ethos*, *pathos*, and *logos*. Find one example of each type of artistic proof and describe how he is using evidence.

Just like essays, visual images are rhetoric in action as well. As you look at these images, think about how they are making claims and providing evidence for those claims.

Prereading Consumer Freedom images: What are your first impressions when you see these ads?

YOU ARE TOO STUPID

…to make your own food choices. At least according to the food police and government bureaucrats who have proposed "fat taxes" on foods they don't want you to eat. Now the trial lawyers are threatening class-action lawsuits against restaurants for serving America's favorite foods and drinks.

We think they're going too far.

It's your food. It's your drink. It's your freedom.
Find out more about attacks on your favorite foods and drinks at:

ConsumerFreedom.com

Nutrition Warning

Center for Science in the Public Interest*
Serviing Size: Bloated

Amount Per Serving	% Daily Value
Junk Science	56%
Scare Tactics	41%
Sensationlism	28%
Sound Bites	92%
Doom and Gloom Prophecies	85%
Sanctimony	60%
Self-Righteousness	24%
Balance	0%
Objectivity	0%
Fairnes	0%

*CSPI bases its policy suggestions on the permise that people cannot make good decisions about to eat and drink wothout government intervention in the form of bans, taxes, lawsuits, and restrictions.
Caution: CSPI contains traces of nutsl.

WARNING!

Special interest with radical anti-choice agenda. Take recommandations with a grain of salt (just one, of course). Coution: Use of CSPI information may result in loss of common sense

The misnamed Center for Science in the Public Interest has issued hysterical warnings about everything from soup to nuts. Now they're calling for warning labels on soft drinks. The last time CSPI released a report on soda they had to admit their exaggerated figures were twice as high as they should have been.

The next thing you know, they'll be shouting about the evils of movie popcorn ...
Oh, wait, They've already done that.

Find out More About CSPI Hype and Hysteria at:

ConsumerFreedom.com

The center for Consumer fredom is a nonporfit organization dedicated to protecting consumer choices.
Help us place more ads like this one by donating online at ConsumerFreedom.com.

Nutrition Warning ad, The Center for Consumer Freedom, consumerfreedom.com. Used by permission.

Comprehending the Text

1. How does sarcasm play into the message of each these advertisements? Does sarcasm affect your perception of the ad?

2. What is the effect of using terms like "stupid," "junk science," and "scare tactics"?

3. Advertisements generally are designed to provoke some action on the part of the viewer. What actions are these advertisements designed to provoke? What type of argument is being made in these ads?

Analyzing the Text

1. Explain the significance of using the warning label in the first advertisement. Does the label function as evidence?

2. Explain the significance of the use of the images of donuts, sodas, pizzas, and so on in the second advertisement.

3. Which of these two advertisements is most effective? Why?

4. Identify examples of *ethos*, *pathos*, and *logos* in each ad if you can find them.

Developing Your Skills: Developing Arguments

Select one of these arguments—the West essay or one of the advertisements—and create a counterargument. Consider the *ethos*, *logos*, and *pathos* that would go into a counterargument. Would you use a claim of value or of policy? Consider the elements necessary to create a compelling counterargument and outline the details.

YOUR TURN: Creating Your Ideas

1. Identify a problem or issue on your campus (i.e., unsafe lighting, need for recycling, increasing tuition or fees), in your community (i.e., need for community policing, high taxes, potholes, feral cats), or at the state or federal level. Next, prepare to write an opinion piece about this issue. Here are some suggestions:

   - Based on the problem and its scope, choose a venue in which to publish an opinion piece. You may choose your school newspaper, your local paper, an e-zine, blog, or other Internet source, for example.
   - Take a stand on the problem or issue. Decide whether to argue a claim of fact, value, or policy. Do you have a creative solution to the problem? Do you want people to be informed? Get angry? Be very clear in presenting your point.
   - Provide credible and appropriate evidence to support your claims, taking into account the audience you are addressing.

Write an essay in which you express your opinion. Be sure that you know your audience. Who will care about or be motivated by your opinion? Think about the place in which your writing will appear. Use appropriate language and a tone that will fit well with the tone of the venue. Grab your audience's attention and use lively language to keep their attention, arouse their emotions, and generally get them to see and agree with your point. Be sure that you express your opinion clearly, using a claim of fact, value, or policy as your major point.

2. Take a stand on an issue related to the media, such as censorship, music lyrics, TV news, reality TV, the alleged link of media (e.g. film, music) to violence, entertainment programming vs. news programming, the V-chip, and so on. The possibilities are endless. Then, follow these steps:

   a. Write a *claim of fact* about this aspect of media. For example, if your topic is reality television, your claim of fact might be:

   There are many types of reality television programming.

   Write a response that supports this claim. Think about the decisions you must make to create an effective argument: addressing your audience, defining your terms, explaining the real-world significance of the claim. You should look up at least one outside source to use as evidence to help you craft this short argument.

   b. Write a *claim of value* about this topic. Using reality television again, we could make the following value claim:

   Reality television shows like *Survivor* offer viewers mind-numbing entertainment.

   Write a response that supports this claim. In addition to the decisions you made in your argument of fact, you must also remember to support the judgment being made in your claim. Think about using strategies of *ethos*, *pathos*, and *logos* to support your claim.

   c. Write a *claim of policy* about your topic. If we are interested in the topic of reality TV, we might propose the following course of action:

   Producers of reality television programming should avoid the use of violence in their shows.

   Write a response in support of your policy claim. Be sure to focus on the key, or stock, issues: prove there is a problem, identify the cause, propose a full solution, and identify the positive and negative outcomes of your proposal.

3. Analyze an editorial. Find an editorial in print on any topic that interests you. The topic can be local, national, or global. Write an essay of 750–1200 words that analyzes the arguments presented in this editorial. Your essay should:
   - Identify the essay's main claim or conclusion. What is the thesis?
   - Identify the arguments advanced in support of the essay's thesis.
   - Explain how the author uses those arguments to support his or her point. In other words, how does the argument develop?
   - Evaluate the editorial in terms of the arguments and the evidence. In other words, does the essay make sense? Is the evidence logical? Why or why not? (You are making an argument of your own as you evaluate the editorial!)

Be sure that the editorial:
   - Expresses a clear opinion
   - Is between 400–600 words in length
   - Was published within the last six months

The best choice for this assignment will be an editorial that makes clear claims of fact, value, and/or policy, and that uses a variety of evidence in support of its position.

TECH TALK: The World of Wikis

A **wiki** is a software program that easily allows users to create web page content. Wikis are an exciting Internet tool because not only do they make web page development accessible to anyone with computer access, but they also encourage group collaboration. Multiple people can edit a wiki page, and the software tracks who has contributed. Giving everyday users access to the Web and the power to create a page or to edit any page is one of the ways in which the Web builds democracy as it gives everyone with access to a computer the ability to contribute to the multitude of conversations and issues on the Web, or even to set up their own wiki page and start their own conversation. You can start your own wiki today by going to a free software provider like www.pbwiki.com. And don't be surprised if you see a wiki assignment show up in your classroom, as instructors are recognizing the value of this tool for group projects.

In addition, you've probably had some experience with wikis if you've used *Wikipedia* (www.wikipedia.org). Wikipedia is a free encyclopedia on the Web that anyone can edit. Of course, you need to be careful using Wikipedia because you need to evaluate the information provided there. Although Wikipedia has content editors who oversee additions and deletions to pages, you never know who is adding information or whether that information is completely objective. So take some time to evaluate your web source. We talk more about evaluating Internet sources in Chapter 7.

Chapter 6

Expanding Your Writer's Toolkit

A s a writer, choosing the shape of your message is one of the most critical decisions you face. Clearly, effectively communicating with an audience requires several complicated judgments. In this chapter, we cover only a few of these broad categories: letter writing, informative report writing, web writing, and presentational writing. It is important that you understand, however, that the forms or genres available to you run the gamut from poetry to proposals, reviews, and technical writing. It is up to you to make the appropriate choice of form, dependent on the rhetorical situation you face.

Letter Writing

Some of the most important rhetoric in history has come by way of a letter. For example, six years before the first atomic bomb was dropped on Japan, hastening the end of the Second World War, Albert Einstein wrote to President Franklin Roosevelt, imploring him to help speed up the development of this new, extraordinarily powerful bomb, which at that point had yet to be called the "atomic bomb." Einstein sought to preempt Germany's development of the same weapon by securing high-quality uranium from various sources.

Influential letters similar to Einstein's appear across the path of history. Though Einstein's letter to President Roosevelt was a private correspondence, some letters are written with a dual audience in mind—the person the letter is addressed to and also a broader audience. These "public" letters, called **open letters**, are often published with the writer knowing his or her writing is designed to reach a wider, more diverse audience. Martin Luther King, Jr.'s "Letter from Birmingham Jail," which is included as a reading in this chapter, is one example of this sort of open letter.

Though he was responding to a statement written by clergy and published in the *Birmingham News* asking him to not demonstrate for civil rights, King's response was written with more than just that small group of clergy in mind. King most certainly knew this letter, or at least parts of it, would be published; he wisely adopted the second-person perspective in that letter, suggesting an intimate communication with the clergy by addressing them as "My dear fellow clergymen" and referring to his audience there as "you." But by employing the second person "you," he invites *everyone* into the conversation, including especially those who would read the letter in the newspaper. Once it was published, the private letter to the clergy became a public call for individuals to protest in the streets of Birmingham.

The Opening of Dr. King's Letter:

While confined here in the Birmingham city jail, I came across **your** recent statement calling my present activities "unwise and untimely." Seldom do I pause to answer criticism of my work and ideas. If I sought to answer all the criticisms that cross my desk, my secretaries would have little time for anything other than such correspondence in the course of the day, and I would have no time for constructive work. But since I feel that you are men of genuine good will and that your criticisms are sincerely set forth, I want to try to answer **your** statements in what I hope will be patient and reasonable terms.

—Martin Luther King, Jr.

Public letters are often a call to action. You can find examples of powerful and influential people writing to other powerful and influential people in an effort to change the course of history. Dr. King's letter provides an interesting example of calls to action directed toward different audiences as a result of his open letter. On the one hand, Dr. King is writing to Birmingham's clergy. He calls directly to them in that capacity when he says,

> I hope the church as a whole will meet the challenge of this decisive hour. But even if the church does not come to the aid of justice, I have no despair about the future. I have no fear about the outcome of our struggle in Birmingham, even if our motives are at present misunderstood. We will reach the goal of freedom in Birmingham, here and all over the nation, because the goal of America is freedom. Abused and scorned though we may be, our destiny is tied up with America's destiny.

On the other hand, the fact that Dr. King's letter to the clergy was published indicates that another call to action is embedded within. His secondary audience included organizers and civil rights sympathizers. The action he seeks is the fight for and granting of civil rights for African Americans. His letter contains motivational strategies as well as strong reasoning on behalf of those rights. Consider this excerpt:

> We have waited for more than 340 years for our constitutional and God-given rights. The nations of Asia and Africa are moving with jetlike speed toward gaining political independence, but we still creep at horse-and-buggy pace toward gaining a cup of coffee at a lunch counter. Perhaps it is easy for those who have never felt the stinging dark of segregation to say, "Wait." But when you have seen vicious mobs lynch your mothers and fathers at will and drown your sisters and brothers at whim; when you have seen hate-filled policemen curse, kick and even kill your black brothers and sisters; when you see the vast majority of your twenty million Negro brothers smothering in an airtight cage of poverty in the midst of an affluent society; when you suddenly find your tongue twisted and your speech stammering as you seek to explain to your six-year-old daughter why she can't go to the public amusement park that has just been advertised on television, and see tears welling up in her eyes when she is told that Funtown is closed to colored children . . . then you will understand why we find it difficult to wait.

Though Dr. King directly addresses the clergymen of Birmingham here, the examples resonate with pathos and connect directly to the experiences and motives of activists and oppressed citizens.

Since the era of the 1960s, the practice of letter writing as an act of citizenship has remained a very common strategy. The presidential campaign of 2008, which ultimately pitted Barack Obama against John McCain in the race for the presidency, set a new standard in the use of letter writing—or in the digital age, e-mail blasts. In particular, then-Senator Obama's campaign used daily e-mails to an ever-growing e-mail list to communicate information about the campaign and/or to simply generate interest and awareness. This use of daily e-mails that appeared to come directly from the candidate had the effect of creating a feeling of inclusion among the general population. People who received these e-mails felt they were a part of the campaign and not simply spectators.

You may not be a nuclear physicist or a political activist, but the letters that you write during the course of your life will likely be some of the most important writing you will ever do and have just as much impact on the course of your own personal history. For example, the cover letter you include with your resume is your first introduction to a potential employer and can make or break your chances for landing a good job. The

What is a citizen action plan?

Ordinary citizens come together to share common concerns—about noise, crime, pollution, unfair taxes, DWI's—in their community or country. They develop a plan for combating or solving the problem. CAPs address national issues as well as local problems and take a wide variety of rhetorical forms. Letter writing is a common rhetorical strategy with CAPs.

"Dear John (or Jill)" letter, or e-mail, or tweet that you might write to break up with a romantic partner will certainly shape your future. Letters, because they tend to convey personal values and information, can be an extremely powerful form of rhetoric.

As in any other writing, your letter writing needs to start with the two key ingredients of effective communication: audience and purpose. Letters allow, even sometimes require, you to get very specific about both. You are writing to someone specific, or many specific people, about something in particular. In many ways, it makes your process much more simple and straightforward, though the same principles of good writing—clear ideas supported with concise examples—still hold true.

Letters often begin with the impulse: *I want something.*

- You may want more money from your parents while you're in college, so you write a letter to your parents conveying the hardships you've encountered living on your limited resources.

- You may want a job, so you write a cover letter to go with your resume.

- You may want to dispute a credit card charge, so you write a letter to the credit card company explaining the problem.

- You may want to express your opinion on recycling projects in your town, so you write a letter to the editor of your local newspaper.

- You may want to try to start an after-school art program for teenagers, so you write a letter to the school committee proposing your program.

Remember your **ethos**, **pathos**, and **logos** strategies for approaching a rhetorical situation? Consider your audience and purpose and label which of those strategies would be most effective in the following situations:

- An e-mail to your professor asking for an extension on the due date for your paper
- A letter to your parents asking for money
- A cover letter for a job on Wall Street
- A cover letter for a job as a nanny
- A letter to the Board of Trustees for your college asking them to not raise tuition this year
- A letter to the editor expressing your views on tax increases

What you want becomes your purpose. And notice that in each of these examples, you have a particular person (or group of people) that you need to persuade to give you what you want. That person or those people form your audience.

As with most of your writing, adopting a style and tone that fits the particular audience you're addressing in your letter aids in your ethos and in your ultimate success. Consider the style and tone of the open letter written by Martin Luther King, Jr. King's style employs a righteous anger in a gentle and restrained way as he calls people to non-violent action. **Style** (how you choose to say something, the language and structure of your writing) and **tone** (the feeling behind your words, your attitude toward the writing and the audience) can be as important as the message itself.

Beyond style and tone of the language you choose to use, there are some key strategies for writing a compelling letter that persuades your audience to give you what you want.

Engage your audience right away. There is no time in a letter for a long windup or an introductory paragraph like you might have in an essay. But you also do not want to just jump out in the first line asking for what you want, as that may shut your reader off immediately. Remember, you are writing to a specific audience and you know who it is, even if you may not know them personally. You want the audience engaged with your topic so that they will keep reading.

Find common ground on which you and your audience can agree. Here is where you want to establish your respect for your audience's position, even if you ultimately disagree with it. Look at "Letter from Birmingham Jail." Even though he fundamentally disagrees with what the clergy are suggesting, King respectfully writes, "But since I feel that you are men of genuine good will and that your criticisms are sincerely set forth, I want to try to answer your statements in what I hope will be patient and reasonable terms." He uses that tone of respect throughout the letter, again, despite the fact that he is advocating the very actions they are cautioning against. You want your audience to read your letter all the way through, so taking a hostile approach at any point is not going to serve your purpose.

Anticipate counterarguments to your position. In King's letter, he uses this strategy several times, the first coming early in the letter so as to demonstrate to the clergy (his initial audience) that he is fully aware of their concerns and objections to what he's proposing:

> You deplore the demonstrations taking place in Birmingham. But your statement, I am sorry to say, fails to express a similar concern for the conditions that brought about the demonstrations. I am sure that none of you would want to rest content with the superficial kind of social analysis that deals merely with effects and does not grapple with underlying causes. It is unfortunate that demonstrations are taking place in Birmingham, but it is even more unfortunate that the city's white power structure left the Negro community with no alternative.

A more current letter addressing copyright infringement on college campuses from students illegally downloading music might includes this strategy, as well, although in a very different tone. The letter from attorneys representing the music industry could state, "We have evidence that you have been violating copyrights owned by various record labels." Clearly, the attorneys are anticipating the counterargument from students saying, "But I didn't download!" and they have countered that response in advance by noting that they have "evidence" of such activity.

Suggest, do not demand, a specific action for your audience to take. Of course, if you are a lawyer trying to persuade a group of people that their actions are illegal, as in the letter from the lawyers regarding illegal music downloading, you probably will demand action because a lack of response on the part of the audience will result in legal sanctions. The following statement emphasizes the seriousness of the letter regarding student downloading:

> YOU HAVE THIRTY (30) DAYS FROM THE DATE OF THIS LETTER TO RESPOND. IF WE DO NOT HEAR FROM YOU, WE WILL FILE SUIT AGAINST YOU IN COURT.

But even beyond the threatening tone of this paragraph, the letter goes on to suggest, in a slightly more friendly way, how individuals should go about responding to this issue.

> We encourage you to meet with a lawyer to discuss your rights and responsibilities. Please note we are not providing you with legal advice.

In a far less threatening tone, though still emphatic and clear, Martin Luther King, Jr. in his "Letter from Birmingham Jail," lays out, step by step, the course of action he's advocating:

> In any nonviolent campaign there are four basic steps: collection of the facts to determine whether injustices exist; negotiation; self-purification; and direct action.

Later, as a way of closing his letter and reemphasizing his respect for his opponent, King, without saying it outright, makes clear what action he hopes to engender in the clergy (and the wider audience who would soon read the published letter):

> I wish you had commended the Negro sit-inners and demonstrators of Birmingham for their sublime courage, their willingness to suffer and their amazing discipline in the midst of great provocation. One day the South will recognize its real heroes.

So, you see, you don't have to come out and bang your reader over the head with your demands, but rather you can suggest actions and, in this case, imagine what the world would be like if what you were asking for actually came true.

Of course, today's method of letter writing often comes in the form of an e-mail. You may hear your grandparents lament, "No one writes letters anymore," but that simply isn't true. In some ways, technological advances have so simplified the process of producing a letter that there are activist groups that use group letter-writing campaigns as a strategy for changing the world. For example, such disparate groups as Amnesty International and Focus on the Family routinely run national and worldwide letter-writing campaigns that focus on various social and political issues. And, as noted earlier, the impact of the email blasting of the political campaign of 2008 has more than likely changed political communication forever.

Developing Your Skills: Letter Writing

Imagine that your professor will let you determine your own final grade for this course. All you have to do is write a letter convincing your professor you deserve the grade you're requesting. Quickly note down some reasons backing up your request. Write down everything that comes to mind. Then, take a look at your list. Did you make appeals to *logos*? *Ethos*? *Pathos*? Then, write the letter.

Informative Report Writing

If you're writing an informative report, it's likely because someone—your instructor, your boss, the school committee, your town planning board—has asked you to answer a question, give an account of an incident, or offer a solution to a problem. Informative reports are a routine part of business and government. Police officers, sales managers, people in marketing, financial administrators, administrators in education, and so on all write reports.

Informative report writing is about as simple and straightforward as it gets, as the structure of the report serves as a guide for organizing your information. In fact, most of the real work of an informative report is the research necessary to sufficiently address or understand the problem or question. However, hard work is also involved in synthesizing the information and wording the report succinctly and in appropriate language and form.

As with most other writing, a report begins with audience and purpose—who has requested the report and what issue is the report supposed to address? An effective informative report:

- Addresses audience concerns directly
- Focuses on purpose
- Delivers accurate information in clear, logical ways
- Is organized with clear, informative section headings

Informative reports follow a standardized format. Your rhetorical flair and your personal writing style are less important here. The success of this type of writing comes from your ability to convey information concisely in a logically organized way. Here is the standard format for organizing the sections of an informative report:

1. Title page
2. Table of contents

3. Abstract or executive summary

4. Introduction

5. Discussion of subject matter (body paragraphs)

6. Conclusions based on discussion

7. Recommendations

8. Bibliography or works cited

Because informative reports are designed to convey factual information, not just your take on a subject, you'll have to begin with research on the subject matter. Typically, as these reports are usually requested by someone or some group and often used in broader projects or efforts, you want to start your research with audience and purpose—make sure that you understand what your audience is asking for and the purpose and scope of the report—what questions they want answers to, what proposals they are seeking, what level of detail they are requesting. Once you understand these elements of the report, you can hit the road to research, which may include interviews, surveys, data research, library resources, and Internet sources. As you begin gathering your research and collecting your data, be careful to record information accurately, whether you're taking down statistics, quotations, or general information. As always, there are several questions you may want to ask during your research:

- Is this information relevant to your audience and purpose?
- Is this information factual and correct?
- Is this information from a credible source?
- Is this information timely (i.e., is it current and not based on outdated data)?

Once you've completed your research and gathered all of your information, your next task is to structure your report, following the format that we have discussed. As you begin writing, consider the functions of different parts of the report:

- *Introduction:* This section establishes the subject of your report, briefly gives relevant background, lays out the scope of the research, addresses the audiences' concerns with regard to the purpose of the report, and leads the reader to the discussion of the issue coming up in the body paragraphs.

- *Discussion (body paragraphs):* Your discussion paragraphs describe, analyze, interpret, and evaluate the data in your report. Keep in mind, as always, that you'll want to adopt the appropriate tone with your use of language and give clear, concrete examples to illustrate your points. You might consider using headings to logically guide your reader through your research.

- *Conclusions:* Your conclusions are drawn from the evidence and analysis that you presented in your discussion. You'll restate your key points and main findings here.

Writer Citizen

- *Recommendations:* If your audience has requested you answer a question or suggest a solution to a problem, you'll include those recommendations at the end of your report. You should make recommendations for action based on your discussion and conclusions. Be rational and straightforward—they've requested this report from you for a reason, so give them your recommendations honestly and clearly.

After you've written the report, you'll need to write the **abstract**. (You have to write the report first to know what you need to summarize and encapsulate in an abstract or executive summary.) This is a concise summary of your report following the same structure as the report itself. This is not a bulleted list; instead, it should contain complete sentences and paragraphs. You should try to restrict the abstract to one page.

Your **title page** and **table of contents** are formatted after you've completed your report, as is your **works cited** (your list of interviews and works consulted in your research).

Any process can be improved with a checklist, whether you're packing for vacation or writing an informative report. The following checklist will help you ensure that you have covered the basics necessary for a successful, credible report.

Informative Report Checklist

Ask yourself:
- Did I fulfill the purpose of the report?
- Is it written with the audience in mind?
- Are my facts and research correct?
- Have I covered all of the elements implied in my purpose?
- Is the information included relevant and current?
- Is the information organized in a logical way?
- Did I use appropriate headings to guide my audience through the text?
- Is the style clear and concise and professional?
- Does my introduction effectively lay the groundwork for the report?
- Do my discussion paragraphs include concrete and relevant examples?
- Does the conclusion effectively analyze and evaluate the evidence?
- Are my recommendations reasonable and rational?
- Does the table of contents correspond to the actual contents of my report?
- Have I correctly documented information and acknowledged sources?
- Have I spellchecked and proofread my final document carefully?

Developing Your Skills: Report Writing

Recently, the Federal Trade Commission (FTC) studied the epidemic of identity theft. The result of their research was published in an informative report entitled "Combating Identity Theft: A Strategic Plan." The plan takes a detailed look at the problem and offers conclusions based on the research and recommendations for addressing the problem. You can find the report here: http://www.idtheft.gov/reports/StrategicPlan.pdf. Take a look at the report and note the format. Based upon your understanding of the process of informative report writing, write a short evaluation of the report. How did the FTC do? What works well in the report and why?

Writing for the Web

You have explored a number of approaches to rhetoric. Classically, rhetoric is about argument—about proving a particular point. Much of that classical tradition is based on a linear format; we tend to move from one point to the next, adding in our evidence, as we build our point. We typically move from introduction and statement of thesis to supporting evidence, to considering the counterarguments, to concluding, all in a fairly straight line.

Writing for the Web expands and extends the process of writing based in the classical tradition. Through the use of hypertext (those are the highlighted links on a web page that, when clicked on, lead you to another web page), we are no longer moving linearly through a piece of writing. The rhetorician Kenneth Burke, writing 40 years before the Internet was invented, uses the "unending conversation" metaphor to explain this type of rhetoric:

> Imagine that you enter a parlor. You come late. When you arrive, others have long preceded you, and they are engaged in a heated discussion, a discussion too heated for them to pause and tell you exactly what it is about. In fact, the discussion had already begun long before any of them got there, so that no one present is qualified to retrace for you all the steps that had gone before. You listen for a while, until you decide that you have caught the tenor of the argument; then you put in your oar. Someone answers; you answer him; another comes to your defense; another aligns himself against you, to either the embarrassment or gratification of your opponent, depending upon the quality of your ally's assistance. However, the discussion is interminable. The hour grows late, you must depart. And you do depart, with the discussion still vigorously in progress (Burke, 1974, p. 110).

The metaphor of a parlor conversation aptly describes what happens on a web page where hyperlinks are embedded. You continually merge with and leave the interaction and, if you choose to comment, you become part of the conversation. Furthermore, when you exit the web page, you know the conversation or debate continues without you.

Kenneth Burke, *The Philosophy of Literary Form 3e*, Berkeley, CA: California, University of California Press, 1973.

You need to distinguish among the wide variety of types of writing you find on the Internet. You can search university, college, and public libraries and find full online texts or PDFs (which stands for Portable Document Format) of articles and books that have been published in hard copy. Those, of course, are likely to be more linear forms of rhetoric. Or you may find web pages or blogs of businesses, colleges, political movements, or other groups or individuals that have been created exclusively for the Internet. It's this kind of writing that requires you to think differently about audience and purpose, particularly when it comes to presentation of material. You may have the same audience and purpose, but you have to think about approaching them in an exclusively electronic environment and tailoring your writing to that genre.

There are a number of "do it yourself" web page software packages that will allow you to quickly create and post your own web page on the Internet. Adobe and Microsoft offer simple software to handle the nuts and bolts of web publishing. In addition, several sites offer free website hosting with built in formats and layouts, making the designing of a quality web page much easier. Google and other sites offer these sorts of services.

The focus here is on what happens once you have the mechanism in place for publishing a web page. What's required of writers on the Internet? In terms of content and format, you want to think about how people read a web page. Rather than writing in the standard essay format—introduction, thesis, evidence, conclusion—you want to consider both the limitations of the screen and the attention span of a web surfer. Here are some tips:

- *Keep your content interesting, easy to navigate, catchy, and relevant.*

  Web page readers are looking for information; give it to them cleanly, simply, and directly. Think in terms of visual appeal and efficiency, as well as accessibility of your content.

- *Begin with the essentials.*

  In an essay, you want to engage your reader and pull him or her into your essay while you try to persuade him or her of your point of view. On the Internet, you don't have that luxury. You need to connect with your points immediately. Get to the point, then expand as you go on, as though you're writing in the form of a pyramid. Remember, your audience is looking for information. Give it to them.

- *Use action verbs.*

  Engage your audience with your language. Active, vivid language will keep your audience interested and engaged. Remember what you learned about description and narration in the earlier chapters? Use it.

- *Use one idea per paragraph.*

  Keep your paragraphs short, concise, and specific. It's more difficult to read words on the screen than it is to read on paper. When using vivid language, work to make your sentences readable and short.

- *Use lists and subheadings.*

  If you have key points or elements you want your reader to remember, using bulleted lists helps visually accent that information. Subheadings are also a way of visually organizing your information and directing your reader.

- *Integrate your links.*

  If a web page presents rhetoric as exploration, make sure your links to other information, web pages, or documents are imbedded in your text. Those links should provide more information or broaden or deepen your discussion.

- *Proofread, proofread, and proofread again.*

  You lose all credibility as a writer when you post material on the Internet that is riddled with errors. Check spelling and punctuation. Then check again once the page is online.

Another common and popular form of web writing can be found in the **blog**, or web log. Blogs continue to grow in presence and popularity on the Internet. However, before 1999, fewer than 30 blogs existed on the Internet. Since then, the number of blogs has exploded across the Internet. Blogs are essentially online journals that can be public or private and can be constructed by groups or individuals. Businesses, television shows, political campaigns, and social movements, university departments, and student groups, as well as everyday people like you, have blogs. In a matter of minutes, anyone can have his or her own blog by going to any one of a number of blog-hosting sites. You may even be asked to keep a blog online for a class you're taking.

Even though blogging takes place in an electronic medium, the fundamentals of writing and the writing process should guide your work. If you are going to write a blog, consider your audience and your purpose. Who are you trying to reach with your words and thoughts? Keep in mind that your potential audience is unlimited—once your blog appears on the Web, it's there for everyone to read. If you're writing just to vent, you might just keep a journal in a word document on your computer. A blog is public. What is it you want to write for broad public consumption? What ideas do you want to express? What experiences do you want to relate to a broader audience? Maybe you are a cancer patient and you want to document the chemotherapy process for others who may have to go through it. Maybe you are a sports fan and you want to document your reaction to every game—maybe even while the game is happening. No matter your interests, you still need to consider who you're trying to reach (audience) and why (purpose).

Some things to consider when creating a blog:

- The templates provided by free sites are usually simple and straightforward. You might want to try making adjustments so that your blog reflects your individual style, but, as with all other forms of written communication, keep the visual

Writer Citizen

aspects in mind. The message needs to be readable, not overwhelming with graphics, wildly varied fonts, animation, or clashing colors. Remember, you are writing to be read, so do not let the design take over.

- Pick a general focus and stay with it. You may choose a topic (your favorite sports team, favorite author, or social issue, for example) or a broad focus (your daily life). This is where you want to seriously consider your reasons for starting a blog and whether you have enough to say about your topic to maintain a blog. Blogs are living documents, as writers add to them regularly, either on a daily or weekly basis.

- Be informative with your blog. Remember, people perusing the Internet are most likely there for information or entertainment. Be predictable in order to gain a following. If you are hysterically funny about a lot of things, you can afford to write a humorous blog that riffs on whatever strikes you. But, typically, you want to think of your blog as offering information with a specific focus.

- Keep it current. Blogs are about what's happening, not what has happened (that's already archived in the blog's archive). You will lose readers quickly if you don't stay current. Why would they check your blog day after day if there's nothing new there?

- If you want to attract readers to your blog and get search engines to direct people to your blog, you will need to use keywords in the headlines of your entries so that those words get picked up in a search.

- Don't post anything on your blog that you would not want an employer or potential employer to read.

- Expand your reach. Link to other blogs and ask them to link to yours. Syndicate yourself. RSS (which stands for Real Simple Syndication) will expand the reach of your blog.

Developing Your Skills: Writing for the Web

Do you blog? If so, create a list of blogs you read and/or participate in. If not, brainstorm a list of topics you'd be interested in reading, then brainstorm a list of topics you'd be interested in blogging about. Now do a search on the Internet and see if there are blogs covering your interests to see how other people are writing about these interests. Then, develop a blog posting on your interest, keeping in mind web writing strategies for effective communication.

Presentation Writing

There are going to be many times, especially in your life beyond the college classroom, where you will have to adapt your writing to fit other forms. Presentations, whether they are a simple PowerPoint slideshow or a multimedia production, are a common feature in all kinds of businesses, including advertising, marketing, banking, investing, human resource management, and many other ventures. In the classroom, your presentation skills will come into play in collaborative projects across the curriculum.

Just like your essay or letter writing, presentation writing starts with audience and purpose. Often the success of any piece of writing, or communication in general, is dependent upon how accurately you can identify your audience and purpose. What is your point and who are you trying to convince to see the issue your way? Starting there, compiling your information and writing with those objectives in mind should come naturally.

When you write an essay, you evaluate your audience and purpose and then brainstorm your ideas for meeting the requirements of that particular objective. Once you have your ideas established, your essay begins to take shape around your thesis, which is the artful articulation of your argument. Of course, you are not going to say, "My purpose in this essay is . . . " but instead, you will construct a thesis that embodies that purpose and expresses it indirectly rather than coming out and saying expressly what your purpose is. After creating your thesis and introduction, your essay builds your argument and illustrates your points as you move smoothly from paragraph to paragraph with effective transitions that serve to connect your ideas.

Presentation writing differs from essay writing. When writing a presentation, your writing is less verbose; that is, it does not use as much language to communicate the essential point of your writing. Therefore, a presentation doesn't always communicate the subtleties and nuances of a complex piece of essay writing. At the same time, presentations can provide a laser focus on your purpose and more directly convey your point because you are presenting small chunks of information, slide by slide, for your audience.

Presentation writing actually refers to a wide variety of forms of communication, from **formal speeches**, to **slide presentations**, **small skits**, **video**, and **documentary films**. However, this discussion focuses on Microsoft PowerPoint as possibly the most typical and accessible form of presentational communication. PowerPoint is the standard presentation tool used across education, business, industry, and other enterprises. PowerPoint, a software program, makes creating slides to convey information almost effortless as you work your way through the points you want to make in your presentation.

Presentations of all kinds are, by design, both reductive and expansive; they require you to reduce your writing to key words or phrases, but also allow you to expand on

> ### Caution   Caution   Caution
> When you get into the PowerPoint program or any other presentation software, it's like getting into a candy store, all the pretty colors and shapes grab your attention and you want one of each. But here is where good presentations go terribly wrong. Don't be distracted by all of the options you have in a presentation program. Keep your design clean and simple and don't let it overwhelm your message.

information in a more graphic way through pictures, graphs, charts, flash media, video, and sound. As the culture becomes more visually oriented and time-compressed, the ability to convey information concisely and in a visually appealing way will become even more important. The popularity of Internet sites like YouTube and the online presence of publications like the *New York Times* and the *Washington Post*, each of which rely heavily on graphic presentation, are evidence of this trend. One of the most well-known Power-Point presentations is the one that is the central focus of former Vice President Al Gore's 2006 documentary *An Inconvenient Truth*. The documentary features Mr. Gore standing in front of a PowerPoint slide presentation making his case about global warming. The film is enhanced with cutaways to compelling video, but the central focus of the film is the PowerPoint presentation.

Again, this form of communicating is not unlike essay writing in terms of the process necessary to get to the material you need to include in your presentation. First, consider that an organization has asked you to give a presentation, so they don't want your essay on the screen; furthermore, they don't want you reading your notes and they don't want you silently showing slides. If they wanted just the information, they would have requested a written document. Before you start creating slides, work out your presentation on paper, at least in outline form, so that you can see exactly what information you need for your slides. Addressing the following familiar elements will help you organize your presentation.

- *Audience:* Who is your audience? (In this example, if you have been asked to give a presentation, you will probably be able to develop an audience profile easily.)

- *Purpose:* What do they want from you? Why did they ask you to present this information? The purpose will help shape your presentation.

- *Logical structure:* You're there to convey information, but if you have ever sat through a presentation that just conveys information, you know how boring that can be. Instead, think of telling a story with your presentation—one with a clear beginning, middle, and end. Use your skills of narration and description.

- *Take away:* What 3–5 things do you want to make sure that your audience takes away from this presentation? Shape your presentation with those points in mind.

Once you have your information organized, you can begin thinking about what kinds of slides you will need to shape the presentation. How much oral information will you present, and what kind of visual information will support you? Is the oral portion of the presentation in person or recorded? Here's where it gets tricky, as the decision making you do at this point as to what information goes on those slides can make or break your presentation:

- *Keep it simple:* The visuals (PowerPoint slides, charts, or whiteboard) are there to support your presentation; they are not the center of the presentation.

The information you include on them should enhance or emphasize your audience's understanding of what you are saying in your oral presentation.

- *Less is more:* The effective use of white space in your slides will add to the clarity of your presentation. Often, it is tempting to transfer all the information from a paper to a slide or a bulleted list so that there are one hundred words on one slide. Not only will that clutter the slide and make it impossible to read, the slide becomes an ineffective form of communication, as your audience can't absorb that much material at once. Rather than run the entire bulleted list, ask "What's the key point here that I want my audience to remember?" Put that *one key point* on your slide. In all likelihood, your oral presentation will include the detailed information from your bulleted list. Keep in mind the "take away"—what do you want them to take away from this presentation?

- *Limits:* The presence of numerous options on your presentation software does not require you to use all of them. In fact, your presentation will be much stronger if you limit yourself to one or two fonts, one or two colors, and one transition mode. (Having one slide fly away and another dissolve into bits might look cool, but it is very distracting for your audience.) Also keep your selections of other images— clip art, photos, and so on—to a minimum. Remember: the slides are there to support your point, not to distract your audience from what you're saying.

Developing Your Skills: Creating Presentations

Go here to see an online presentation that makes its argument in a series of words and quick cuts: **http://www.girleffect.org/-/home/**. Select the link "Play the Girl Effect Video" in the lower right hand corner of the page. Evaluate the effectiveness of this presentation based on what you just learned. What is the message? How is the argument achieved? How does this presentation use *ethos, logos,* and *pathos* to present its ideas? Does it need someone to deliver this message or does the message work as is? Create your own PowerPoint presentation on a current public issue to share with your class.

A Brief Review

In this chapter, we have focused on some of the many decisions you must make as an effective writer and communicator when shaping your message. The basic categories of writing covered here were letter writing, informative report writing, web writing, and presentation writing. Understand that these categories, or genres, are but a few that you have at your disposal, and your choice of strategies utterly depends upon your audience and purpose:

- Letter writing has a long history of important rhetorical action.
  - Public letters are often a call to action and contain evidence of *ethos, pathos,* and *logos.*

- Letters often begin with the impulse: *I want something*. What you want becomes your purpose.
- Your style and tone also depend upon your audience and your purpose.
- Informative report writing answers a question, gives an account, or offers a solution to a problem.
  - Informative reports follow a standard format.
  - Research for an informative report may include interviews, surveys, data research, library resources, and Internet sources.
  - An informative report contains an introduction, discussion, conclusion, and recommendations.
- Web writing extends classical approaches to rhetoric by moving into more dimensions.
  - Web writing may include web pages or blogs.
  - Audience and purpose are key in web writing.
- Presentation writing occurs in the classroom, but also in business and community communication.
  - Writing for presentations requires specific, concise use of language and information.
  - Power Point is an accessible form of presentation software that allows the writer to compose slides.
  - Keep it simple: too much animation, color, or verbiage can be confusing and distracting to your audience.

Rhetoric in Action

"A First Look at Gobbledygook"

John O'Hayre (b. 1946) was an employee of the United States Department of the Interior when he wrote a short book, *Gobbledygook Had Gotta Go*. In this 1966 publication, O'Hayre rails against the "officialese" of government documents. He argues for clear, concise language to communicate information directly.

Prereading: Where, in your experience, have you encountered the worst writing? What about it qualifies as "the worst?"

A disgruntled State Director tossed a copy of a memo on our desk some time back. "Here's a lusty sample of what good writing ain't," he said. "Maybe you can use it to show some of our staff how not to write."

He picked up the memo and rattled it, saying: "All I did was write this solicitor a short memo. I told him I thought we could solve a nasty trespass case we'd both been working on. We suggested we give this trespasser a special-use permit and make him legal. That way we'd all get off the hook. All I asked the solicitor was, "is this okay with you?"'

He threw the memo on the desk and scowled. "Cripes! All he had to do was say 'yes' or 'no'. But look what he sends me!"

Properly meek by this time, I asked: "Did the solicitor say 'yes' or 'no'?"

The state director whirled: "How the heck do I know! I've only read it twice!"

There was no doubt about it, that state director had a problem; he simply couldn't get readable writing out of his staff, or, more important this day, his solicitor.

Our distressed state director wasn't alone in his sweat over unreadable writing. Leaders in government, business, and industry have had the same feverish feeling for years. One chemical company executive put it this way: "If our antifreeze had the same quality as our writing, we'd rust out half the radiators in the country in six months."

A study showed executives in one company used 200 words to write 125-word memos, eight paragraphs for four-paragraph letters, and nearly 200 pages for 100-page reports. Another corporation finally got so frustrated it quit trying to hire writers and started training the ones it already had. Most big corporations are doing this now; they have to. This way they get good writing and save good money-lots of it. An average letter's cost varies from $6 for top executives to $2 at lower levels.

Let's read the memo that shook up the state director:

> To: State Director
> From: John Lawbook, Solicitor
> Subject: Roland Occupancy Trespass
>
> This responds to your memorandum dated February 21, 1964, requesting that we review and comment concerning the subject Roland trespass on certain lands under reclamation withdrawal.
>
> We appreciate your apprising us of this matter and we certainly concur that appropriate action is in order to project the interests of the United States.
>
> We readily recognize the difficult problem presented by this situation, and if it can be otherwise satisfactorily resolved, we would prefer to avoid trespass action. If you determine it permissible to legalize the Roland occupancy and hay production by issuance of a special use permit, as suggested in your memorandum, we have no objection to that procedure.

Any such permit should be subject to cancellation when the lands are actively required for reclamation purposes and should provide for the right of the officers, agents, and employees of the Unites States at all times to have unrestricted access and ingress to, passage over, and egress from all said lands, to make investigations of all kinds, dig test pits and drill test holes, to survey for reclamation and irrigation works, and to perform any and all necessary soil and moisture conservation work.

If we can be of any further assistance in this matter, please advise. We would appreciate being informed of the disposition of this problem.

Before we edit the solicitor's memo, let's look at two of its weak points:

1. *False Opening*: The solicitor starts his memo by telling the state director: "This is my memo to you, answering your memo to me." Who could care less? Openings like this tell nobody nothing. Yet many memos and letters start in this word-wasteful manner.

2. *Writer's Grade*:* The solicitor's memo has 217 words, 44 difficult words, 3 syllables or over, and a writer's grade of 53; it should grade out at 70 or above to be reasonably readable. A high grade means that, even if you're not saying what you mean, you're saying it readably well. Your sentences are short, your constructions simple, and your words are not painfully syllabic. A high writer's grade is a guarantee of readable writing. With it you're in business as a writer; without it you're in trouble with the reader.

A basic rule for all writing is: Have something to say; say it simply; quit! The next rule is: After you've quit, go over it again with a harsh pencil and a vengeance, crossing out everything that isn't necessary.

Let's see if the solicitor's memo takes well to the pencil. On our first trip through, in order to be fair to the solicitor, we won't change any of his words or word order.

Let's start penciling out:

~~This responds to your memorandum dated February 21, 1964, requesting that we review and comment~~ concerning the ~~subject~~ Roland trespass ~~on certain lands under reclamation withdrawal~~.

~~We appreciate your apprising us of this matter, and~~ we ~~certainly~~ concur that ~~appropriate~~ action is in order ~~to project the interests of the United States~~.

~~We readily recognize the difficult problem presented by this situation, and if it can be otherwise satisfactorily resolved,~~ we would prefer to avoid trespass action. If you determine it permissible to legalize Roland occupancy ~~and hay production~~ by issuance of a special use permit, ~~as suggested in your memorandum,~~ we have no objection ~~to that procedure~~.

---

*Refers to the Lensear Write Formula, a system for grading effective writing used by this author.

Any such permit should be subject to cancellation ~~when the lands are actively required for reclamation purposes~~ and should provide for the right of ~~the officers, agents and employees of the~~ United States at all times ~~to have unrestricted access and ingress to, passage over, and egress from all said lands, to make investigations of all kinds, dig test pits and drill test holes, to survey for reclamation and irrigation works, and~~ to perform any ~~and all~~ necessary ~~soil and moisture conservation~~ work.

~~If we can be of any further assistance in this matter, please advise.~~ We would appreciate being informed of the disposition of this problem.

What did we accomplish in this quick trip? Well, let's see. We cut the number of words from 217 to 75, cut the difficult words from 44 to 10, and raised the writer's grade from 53 (difficult) to 60 (acceptable).

Can we cut more yet? Let's go over it again and see, still without changing the solicitor's words or word order.

First sentence: Concerning the Roland trespass case, we concur that action is in order.

We can throw this whole sentence out, because: (1) the subject heading of the memo clearly states what the memo concerns; and (2) both knew "action was in order." That's why they had been writing each other.

Second and third sentences: We would prefer to avoid trespass action. If you determine it permissible to legalize Roland's occupancy by issuance of a special use permit, we have no objection.

Let's leave this for now; it contains the essence of the memo; it's the answer.

Fourth sentence: Any such permit should be subject to cancellation and should provide for the right of the United States at all times to perform all necessary work.

Let's throw this out, too. The state director and his staff issue special use permits as a matter of routine. They know what cancellation clauses and special-use provisions these have to carry. Why tell them what they already know?

Fifth sentence: We would appreciate being informed of the disposition of this problem.

Let's leave this sentence as it is and see what we have left after two editings.

> We would prefer to avoid trespass action. If you determine it permissible to legalize Roland's occupancy by issuance of a special use permit, we have no objection.

> We would appreciate being informed of the disposition of the problem.

A recount shows we're now down to 38 words, 8 difficult words, and have a writer's grade of 68.

The question now is: Does the edited memo carry the essential message and does it read easily? It does both pretty well. However, it could have a little more clarity and a little less pretension if it said simply:

> We'd like to avoid trespass action, if possible. So, if you can settle this case by issuing Roland a special use permit, go ahead.

> Please keep us informed.

This is the way we would have written the memo had we been in the solicitor's seat. The memo now has 28 words, 2 difficult words, and a writer's grade of 70. That's good writing.

Let's go back to the original memo. What we did first was to concentrate on axing out empty words and phrases. Note how they strain to sound unnatural-and succeed. Note how they can be replaced with simple, direct words.

First and second sentences: This responds to your memorandum dated February 21, 1964, requesting that we review and comment concerning the subject Roland trespass on certain lands under reclamation withdrawal. We appreciate your apprising us of this matter, and we certainly concur that appropriate action is in order to project the interests of the United States.

How much better had he said: "Got your memo on the Roland trespass case. You're right; action is needed."

Third sentence: We readily recognize the difficult problem presented by this situation, and if it can be otherwise satisfactorily resolved, we would prefer to avoid trespass action.

Why didn't he just say, "The problem is tough, and we'd like to avoid trespass action if we can"?

Fourth sentence: If you determine it permissible to legalize Roland's occupancy by issuance of a special use permit, as suggested in your memorandum, we have no objection to that procedure.

It's a lot clearer this way: "If you can solve this problem by issuing Roland a special use permit, go ahead."

Fifth sentence: Any such permit should be subject to cancellation when the lands are actively required for reclamation purposes and should provide for the right of officers, agents and employees of the United States at all times to have unrestricted access and ingress to, passage over, and egress from all said lands, to make investigations of all kinds, dig test pits and drill test holes, to survey for reclamation and irrigation works, and to perform any and all necessary soil and moisture conservation work.

Such a lawyerish enumeration belongs, if it belongs at all, in a legal contract, not in an inter-office memo. If the solicitor felt an obligation to give the state director a reminder, he might have said: "Please spell out the Government's cancellation rights and right-to-use provisions in the permit."

Sixth and seventh sentences (adequate but somewhat high-blown): If we can be of any further assistance in this matter, please advise. We would appreciate being informed of the disposition of this problem.

It's somewhat better, at least shorter, this way: "If we can be of further help, please call. Keep us informed."

How does the whole, empty-word-less memo read now? Would it, too, be satisfactory? Let's look:

> Got your memo on the Roland trespass case. You're right; action is needed. The problem *is* tough, and we'd like to avoid trespass action if we can. So, if you can settle this case by issuing Roland a special-use permit, go ahead. Please spell out the Government's cancellation rights and right-to-use provisions in the permit.
>
> If we can be of further help, please call. Keep us informed.

In this version we have 70 words, only four difficult words, and a writer's grade of 69.

Moreover, we've said everything the solicitor said in his original memo, even the stuff that didn't need saying. The only difference is that we threw out the empty words, shortened the sentences, changed the passive to the active, and generally tried to say things simple, directly, and clearly. The gobbledygook is gone! ❧

Comprehending the Text

1. What is O'Hayre's point about writing?

2. Is shorter writing better writing?

3. What is a "false opening"?

Analyzing the Text

1. What is the difference between passive voice and active voice?

2. Make a list of "empty words" you routinely use.

3. Cite examples of the "difficult" words used in this piece and come up with your own, simpler alternatives to those difficult words.

Writer Citizen

Letter from Birmingham Jail, April 16, 1963

Martin Luther King (1929–1968), American clergyman and social activist for equal rights. King is most known for his nonviolent civil disobedience on behalf of the fight for equal rights for African Americans, as well as for his famous speeches and essays, including this one, titled "Letter from Birmingham Jail."

Prereading: Note down what you know or have heard about the Civil Rights Movement in the United States. As you read, annotate the text, noting elements of purpose, language use, audience, ethos, pathos, and logos—as well as anything else that stands out to you.

*AUTHOR'S NOTE: This response to a published statement by eight fellow clergymen from Alabama (Bishop C. C. J. Carpenter, Bishop Joseph A. Durick, Rabbi Hilton L. Grafman, Bishop Paul Hardin, Bishop Holan B. Harmon, the Reverend George M. Murray, the Reverend Edward V. Ramage, and the Reverend Earl Stallings) was composed under somewhat constricting circumstance. Begun on the margins of the newspaper in which the statement appeared while I was in jail, the letter was continued on scraps of writing paper supplied by a friendly Negro trusty, and concluded on a pad my attorneys were eventually permitted to leave me. Although the text remains in substance unaltered, I have indulged in the author's prerogative of polishing it for publication.

MY DEAR FELLOW CLERGYMEN:

While confined here in the Birmingham city jail, I came across your recent statement calling my present activities "unwise and untimely." Seldom do I pause to answer criticism of my work and ideas. If I sought to answer all the criticisms that cross my desk, my secretaries would have little time for anything other than such correspondence in the course of the day, and I would have no time for constructive work. But since I feel that you are men of genuine good will and that your criticisms are sincerely set forth, I want to try to answer your statements in what I hope will be patient and reasonable terms.

I think I should indicate why I am here in Birmingham, since you have been influenced by the view which argues against "outsiders coming in." I have the honor of serving as president of the Southern Christian Leadership Conference, an organization operating in every southern state, with headquarters in Atlanta, Georgia. We have some eighty-five affiliated organizations across the South, and one of them is the Alabama Christian Movement for Human Rights. Frequently we share staff, educational and financial resources with our affiliates. Several months ago the affiliate here in Birmingham asked us to be on call to engage in a nonviolent direct-action program if such were deemed necessary. We readily consented, and when the hour came we lived up to our promise. So I, along with several members of my staff, am here because I was invited here. I am here because I have organizational ties here.

But more basically, I am in Birmingham because injustice is here. Just as the prophets of the eighth century B.C. left their villages and carried their "thus saith the Lord" far beyond the boundaries of their home towns, and just as the Apostle Paul left his village of Tarsus and carried the gospel of Jesus Christ to the far corners of the Greco-Roman world, so am I compelled to carry the gospel of freedom beyond my own home town. Like Paul, I must constantly respond to the Macedonian call for aid.

Moreover, I am cognizant of the interrelatedness of all communities and states. I cannot sit idly by in Atlanta and not be concerned about what happens in Birmingham. Injustice anywhere is a threat to justice everywhere. We are caught in an inescapable network of mutuality, tied in a single garment of destiny. Whatever affects one directly, affects all indirectly. Never again can we afford to live with the narrow, provincial "outside agitator" idea. Anyone who lives inside the United States can never be considered an outsider anywhere within its bounds.

You deplore the demonstrations taking place in Birmingham. But your statement, I am sorry to say, fails to express a similar concern for the conditions that brought about the demonstrations. I am sure that none of you would want to rest content with the superficial kind of social analysis that deals merely with effects and does not grapple with underlying causes. It is unfortunate that demonstrations are taking place in Birmingham, but it is even more unfortunate that the city's white power structure left the Negro community with no alternative.

In any nonviolent campaign there are four basic steps: collection of the facts to determine whether injustices exist; negotiation; self-purification; and direct action. We have gone through all of these steps in Birmingham. There can be no gainsaying the fact that racial injustice engulfs this community. Birmingham is probably the most thoroughly segregated city in the United States. Its ugly record of brutality is widely known. Negroes have experienced grossly unjust treatment in the courts. There have been more unsolved bombings of Negro homes and churches in Birmingham than in any other city in the nation. These are the hard, brutal facts of the case. On the basis of these conditions, Negro leaders sought to negotiate with the city fathers. But the latter consistently refused to engage in good-faith negotiation.

Then, last September, came the opportunity to talk with leaders of Birmingham's economic community. In the course of the negotiations, certain promises were made by the merchants—for example, to remove the stores' humiliating racial signs. On the basis of these promises, the Reverend Fred Shuttlesworth and the leaders of the Alabama Christian Movement for Human Rights agreed to a moratorium on all demonstrations.

As the weeks and months went by, we realized that we were the victims of a broken promise. A few signs, briefly removed, returned; the others remained.

As in so many past experiences, our hopes had been blasted, and the shadow of deep disappointment settled upon us. We had no alternative except to prepare for direct action, whereby we would present our very bodies as a means of laying our case before the conscience of the local and the national community. Mindful of the difficulties involved, we decided to undertake a process of self-purification. We began a series of workshops on nonviolence, and we repeatedly asked ourselves: "Are you able to accept blows without retaliating?" "Are you able to endure the ordeal of jail?" We decided to schedule our direct-action program for the Easter season, realizing that except for Christmas, this is the main shopping period of the year. Knowing that a strong economic withdrawal program would be the by-product of direct action, we felt that this would be the best time to bring pressure to bear on the merchants for the needed change.

Then it occurred to us that Birmingham's mayoralty election was coming up in March, and we speedily decided to postpone action until after election day. When we discovered that the Commissioner of Public Safety, Eugene "Bull" Connor, had piled up enough votes to be in the run-off we decided again to postpone action until the day after the run-off so that the demonstrations could not be used to cloud the issues. Like many others, we waited to see Mr. Connor defeated, and to this end we endured postponement after postponement. Having aided in this community need, we felt that our direct-action program could be delayed no longer.

You may well ask: "Why direct action? Why sit-ins, marches and so forth? Isn't negotiation a better path?" You are quite right in calling for negotiation. Indeed, this is the very purpose of direct action. Nonviolent direct action seeks to create such a crisis and foster such a tension that a community which has constantly refused to negotiate is forced to confront the issue. It seeks to so dramatize the issue that it can no longer be ignored. My citing the creation of tension as part of the work of the nonviolent-resister may sound rather shocking. But I must confess that I am not afraid of the word "tension." I have earnestly opposed violent tension, but there is a type of constructive, nonviolent tension which is necessary for growth. Just as Socrates felt that it was necessary to create a tension in the mind so that individuals could rise from the bondage of myths and half-truths to the unfettered realm of creative analysis and objective appraisal, so must we see the need for nonviolent gadflies to create the kind of tension in society that will help men rise from the dark depths of prejudice and racism to the majestic heights of understanding and brotherhood.

The purpose of our direct-action program is to create a situation so crisis-packed that it will inevitably open the door to negotiation. I therefore concur with you in your call for negotiation. Too long has our beloved Southland been bogged down in a tragic effort to live in monologue rather than dialogue.

One of the basic points in your statement is that the action that I and my associates have taken in Birmingham is untimely. Some have asked: "Why didn't you give the new city administration time to act?" The only answer that I can give to this query is that the new Birmingham administration must be prodded about as much as the outgoing one, before it will act. We are sadly mistaken if we feel that the election of Albert Boutwell as mayor will bring the millennium to Birmingham. While Mr. Boutwell is a much more gentle person than Mr. Connor, they are both segregationists, dedicated to maintenance of the status quo. I have hope that Mr. Boutwell will be reasonable enough to see the futility of massive resistance to desegregation. But he will not see this without pressure from devotees of civil rights. My friends, I must say to you that we have not made a single gain in civil rights without determined legal and nonviolent pressure. Lamentably, it is an historical fact that privileged groups seldom give up their privileges voluntarily. Individuals may see the moral light and voluntarily give up their unjust posture; but, as Reinhold Niebuhr has reminded us, groups tend to be more immoral than individuals.

We know through painful experience that freedom is never voluntarily given by the oppressor; it must be demanded by the oppressed. Frankly, I have yet to engage in a direct-action campaign that was "well timed" in the view of those who have not suffered unduly from the disease of segregation. For years now I have heard the word "Wait!" It rings in the ear of every Negro with piercing familiarity. This "Wait" has almost always meant "Never." We must come to see, with one of our distinguished jurists, that "justice too long delayed is justice denied."

We have waited for more than 340 years for our constitutional and God-given rights. The nations of Asia and Africa are moving with jetlike speed toward gaining political independence, but we still creep at horse-and-buggy pace toward gaining a cup of coffee at a lunch counter. Perhaps it is easy for those who have never felt the stinging dark of segregation to say, "Wait." But when you have seen vicious mobs lynch your mothers and fathers at will and drown your sisters and brothers at whim; when you have seen hate-filled policemen curse, kick and even kill your black brothers and sisters; when you see the vast majority of your twenty million Negro brothers smothering in an airtight cage of poverty in the midst of an affluent society; when you suddenly find your tongue twisted and your speech stammering as you seek to explain to your six-year-old daughter why she can't go to the public amusement park that has just been advertised on television, and see tears welling up in her eyes when she is told that Funtown is closed to colored children, and see ominous clouds of inferiority beginning to form in her little mental sky, and see her beginning to distort her personality by developing an unconscious bitterness toward white people; when you have to concoct an answer for a five-year-old son who is asking: "Daddy, why do white people treat colored people so mean?"; when you take a cross-country drive and find it necessary to sleep night after night in the uncomfortable corners of your automobile because no motel will accept you; when you are humiliated day in and day out by nagging signs reading "white" and "colored"; when your first name becomes "nigger," your middle name becomes "boy" (however old you are) and your last name becomes "John," and your wife and mother are never given the respected title "Mrs."; when you are harried by day and haunted by night by the fact that you are a Negro, living constantly at tiptoe stance, never quite knowing what to expect next, and are plagued with inner fears and outer resentments; when you go forever fighting a degenerating sense of "nobodiness" then you will understand why we find it difficult to wait. There comes a time when the cup of endurance runs over, and men are no longer willing to be plunged into the abyss of despair. I hope, sirs, you can understand our legitimate and unavoidable impatience.

You express a great deal of anxiety over our willingness to break laws. This is certainly a legitimate concern. Since we so diligently urge people to obey the Supreme Court's decision of 1954 outlawing segregation in the public schools, at first glance it may seem rather paradoxical for us consciously to break laws. One may want to ask: "How can you advocate breaking some laws and obeying others?" The answer lies in the fact that there are two types of laws: just and unjust. I would be the first to advocate obeying just laws. One has not only a legal but a moral responsibility to obey just laws. Conversely, one has a moral responsibility to disobey unjust laws. I would agree with St. Augustine that "an unjust law is no law at all."

Now, what is the difference between the two? How does one determine whether a law is just or unjust? A just law is a man-made code that squares with the moral law or the law of God. An unjust law is a code that is out of harmony with the moral law. To put it in the terms of St. Thomas Aquinas: An unjust law is a human law that is not rooted in eternal law and natural law. Any law that uplifts human personality is just. Any law that degrades human personality is unjust. All segregation statutes are unjust because segregation distorts the soul and damages the personality. It gives the segregator a false sense of superiority and the segregated a false sense of inferiority. Segregation, to use the terminology of the Jewish philosopher Martin Buber, substitutes an "I-it" relationship for an "I-thou" relationship and ends up relegating persons to the status of things. Hence segregation is not only politically, economically and sociologically unsound, it is morally wrong and awful. Paul Tillich said that sin is separation. Is not segregation an existential expression of man's tragic separation, his awful estrangement, his terrible sinfulness? Thus it is that I can urge men to obey the 1954 decision of the Supreme Court, for it is morally right; and I can urge them to disobey segregation ordinances, for they are morally wrong.

Let us consider a more concrete example of just and unjust laws. An unjust law is a code that a numerical or power majority group compels a minority group to obey but does not make binding on itself. This is difference made legal. By the same token, a just law is a code that a majority compels a minority to follow and that it is willing to follow itself. This is sameness made legal.

Let me give another explanation. A law is unjust if it is inflicted on a minority that, as a result of being denied the right to vote, had no part in enacting or devising the law. Who can say that the legislature of Alabama which set up that state's segregation laws was democratically elected? Throughout Alabama all sorts of devious methods are used to prevent Negroes from becoming registered voters, and there are some counties in which, even though Negroes constitute a majority of the population, not a single Negro is registered. Can any law enacted under such circumstances be considered democratically structured?

Sometimes a law is just on its face and unjust in its application. For instance, I have been arrested on a charge of parading without a permit. Now, there is nothing wrong in having an ordinance which requires a permit for a parade. But such an ordinance becomes unjust when it is used to maintain segregation and to deny citizens the First Amendment privilege of peaceful assembly and protest.

I hope you are able to see the distinction I am trying to point out. In no sense do I advocate evading or defying the law, as would the rabid segregationist. That would lead to anarchy. One who breaks an unjust law must do so openly, lovingly, and with a willingness to accept the penalty. I submit that an individual who breaks a law that conscience tells him is unjust and who willingly accepts the penalty of imprisonment in order to arouse the conscience of the community over its injustice, is in reality expressing the highest respect for law.

Of course, there is nothing new about this kind of civil disobedience. It was evidenced sublimely in the refusal of Shadrach, Meshach and Abednego to obey the laws of Nebuchadnezzar, on the ground that a higher moral law was at stake. It was practiced superbly by the early Christians, who were willing to face hungry lions and the excruciating pain of chopping blocks rather than submit to certain unjust laws of the Roman Empire. To a degree, academic freedom is a reality today because Socrates practiced civil disobedience. In our own nation, the Boston Tea Party represented a massive act of civil disobedience.

We should never forget that everything Adolf Hitler did in Germany was "legal" and everything the Hungarian freedom fighters did in Hungary was "illegal." It was "illegal" to aid and comfort a Jew in Hitler's Germany. Even so, I am sure that, had I lived in Germany at the time, I would have aided and comforted my Jewish brothers. If today I lived in a Communist country where certain principles dear to the Christian faith are suppressed, I would openly advocate disobeying that country's antireligious laws.

I must make two honest confessions to you, my Christian and Jewish brothers. First, I must confess that over the past few years I have been gravely disappointed with the white moderate. I have almost reached the regrettable conclusion that the Negro's great stumbling block in his stride toward freedom is not the White Citizen's Counciler or the Ku Klux Klanner, but the white moderate, who is more devoted to "order" than to justice;

who prefers a negative peace which is the absence of tension to a positive peace which is the presence of justice; who constantly says: "I agree with you in the goal you seek, but I cannot agree with your methods of direct action"; who paternalistically believes he can set the timetable for another man's freedom; who lives by a mythical concept of time and who constantly advises the Negro to wait for a "more convenient season." Shallow understanding from people of good will is more frustrating than absolute misunderstanding from people of ill will. Lukewarm acceptance is much more bewildering than outright rejection.

I had hoped that the white moderate would understand that law and order exist for the purpose of establishing justice and that when they fail in this purpose they become the dangerously structured dams that block the flow of social progress. I had hoped that the white moderate would understand that the present tension in the South is a necessary phase of the transition from an obnoxious negative peace, in which the Negro passively accepted his unjust plight, to a substantive and positive peace, in which all men will respect the dignity and worth of human personality. Actually, we who engage in nonviolent direct action are not the creators of tension. We merely bring to the surface the hidden tension that is already alive. We bring it out in the open, where it can be seen and dealt with. Like a boil that can never be cured so long as it is covered up but must be opened with all its ugliness to the natural medicines of air and light, injustice must be exposed, with all the tension its exposure creates, to the light of human conscience and the air of national opinion before it can be cured.

In your statement you assert that our actions, even though peaceful, must be condemned because they precipitate violence. But is this a logical assertion? Isn't this like condemning a robbed man because his possession of money precipitated the evil act of robbery? Isn't this like condemning Socrates because his unswerving commitment to truth and his philosophical inquiries precipitated the act by the misguided populace in which they made him drink hemlock? Isn't this like condemning Jesus because his unique God-consciousness and never-ceasing devotion to God's will precipitated the evil act of crucifixion? We must come to see that, as the federal courts have consistently affirmed, it is wrong to urge an individual to cease his efforts to gain his basic constitutional rights because the quest may precipitate violence. Society must protect the robbed and punish the robber.

I had also hoped that the white moderate would reject the myth concerning time in relation to the struggle for freedom. I have just received a letter from a white brother in Texas. He writes: "All Christians know that the colored people will receive equal rights eventually, but it is possible that you are in too great a religious hurry. It has taken Christianity almost two thousand years to accomplish what it has. The teachings of Christ take time to come to earth." Such an attitude stems from a tragic misconception of time, from the strangely rational notion that there is something in the very flow of time that will inevitably cure all ills. Actually, time itself is neutral; it can be used either destructively or constructively. More and more I feel that the people of ill will have used time much more effectively than have the people of good will. We will have to repent in this generation not merely for the hateful words and actions of the bad people but for the appalling silence of the good people. Human progress never rolls in on wheels of inevitability; it comes through the tireless efforts of men willing to be co-workers with God, and without this hard work, time itself becomes an ally of the forces of social stagnation. We must use time creatively, in the knowledge that the time is always ripe to do right. Now is the time to make real the promise of democracy and transform our pending national elegy into a creative psalm of brotherhood. Now is the time to lift our national policy from the quicksand of racial injustice to the solid rock of human dignity.

You speak of our activity in Birmingham as extreme. At first I was rather disappointed that fellow clergymen would see my nonviolent efforts as those of an extremist. I began thinking about the fact that I stand in the middle of two opposing forces in the Negro community. One is a force of complacency, made up in part of Negroes who, as a result of long years of oppression, are so drained of self-respect and a sense of "somebodiness" that they have adjusted to segregation; and in part of a few middle class Negroes who, because of a degree of academic and economic security and because in some ways they profit by segregation, have become insensitive to the problems of the masses. The other force is one of bitterness and hatred, and it comes perilously close to advocating violence. It is expressed in the various black nationalist groups that are springing up across the nation, the largest and best-known being Elijah Muhammad's Muslim movement. Nourished by the Negro's frustration over the continued existence of racial discrimination, this movement is made up of people who have lost faith in America, who have absolutely repudiated Christianity, and who have concluded that the white man is an incorrigible "devil."

I have tried to stand between these two forces, saying that we need emulate neither the "do-nothingism" of the complacent nor the hatred and despair of the black nationalist. For there is the more excellent way of love and nonviolent protest. I am grateful to God that, through the influence of the Negro church, the way of nonviolence became an integral part of our struggle.

If this philosophy had not emerged, by now many streets of the South would, I am convinced, be flowing with blood. And I am further convinced that if our white brothers dismiss as "rabble-rousers" and "outside agitators" those of us who employ nonviolent direct action, and if they refuse to support our nonviolent efforts, millions of Negroes will, out of frustration and despair, seek solace and security in black-nationalist ideologies, a development that would inevitably lead to a frightening racial nightmare.

Oppressed people cannot remain oppressed forever. The yearning for freedom eventually manifests itself, and that is what has happened to the American Negro. Something within has reminded him of his birthright of freedom, and something without has reminded him that it can be gained. Consciously or unconsciously, he has been caught up by the Zeitgeist, and with his black brothers of Africa and his brown and yellow brothers of Asia, South America and the Caribbean, the United States Negro is moving with a sense of great urgency toward the promised land of racial justice. If one recognizes this vital urge that has engulfed the Negro community, one should readily understand why public demonstrations are taking place. The Negro has many pent-up resentments and latent frustrations, and he must release them. So let him march; let him make prayer pilgrimages to the city hall; let him go on freedom rides--and try to understand why he must do so. If his repressed emotions are not released in nonviolent ways, they will seek expression through violence; this is not a threat but a fact of history. So I have not said to my people: "Get rid of your discontent." Rather, I have tried to say that this normal and healthy discontent can be channeled into the creative outlet of nonviolent direct action. And now this approach is being termed extremist.

But though I was initially disappointed at being categorized as an extremist, as I continued to think about the matter I gradually gained a measure of satisfaction from the label. Was not Jesus an extremist for love: "Love your enemies, bless them that curse you, do good to them that hate you, and pray for them which despitefully use you, and persecute you." Was not Amos an extremist for justice: "Let justice roll down like waters and righteousness like an ever-flowing stream." Was not Paul an extremist for the Christian gospel: "I bear in my body the marks of the Lord Jesus." Was not Martin Luther an extremist: "Here I stand; I cannot do otherwise, so help me God." And John Bunyan: "I will stay in jail to the end of my days before I make a butchery of my conscience." And Abraham Lincoln: "This nation cannot survive half slave and half free." And Thomas Jefferson: "We hold these truths to be self-evident, that all men are created equal ..." So the question is not whether we will be extremists, but what kind of extremists we will be. Will we be extremists for hate or for love? Will we be extremists for the preservation of injustice or for the extension of justice? In that dramatic scene on Calvary's hill three men were crucified. We must never forget that all three were crucified for the same crime—the crime of extremism. Two were extremists for immorality, and thus fell below their environment. The other, Jesus Christ, was an extremist for love, truth and goodness, and thereby rose above his environment. Perhaps the South, the nation and the world are in dire need of creative extremists.

I had hoped that the white moderate would see this need. Perhaps I was too optimistic; perhaps I expected too much. I suppose I should have realized that few members of the oppressor race can understand the deep groans and passionate yearnings of the oppressed race, and still fewer have the vision to see that injustice must be rooted out by strong, persistent and determined action. I am thankful, however, that some of our white brothers in the South have grasped the meaning of this social revolution and committed themselves to it. They are still too few in quantity, but they are big in quality. Some—such as Ralph McGill, Lillian Smith, Harry Golden, James McBride Dabbs, Ann Braden and Sarah Patton Boyle—have written about our struggle in eloquent and prophetic terms. Others have marched with us down nameless streets of the South. They have languished in filthy, roach-infested jails, suffering the abuse and brutality of policemen who view them as "dirty nigger lovers." Unlike so many of their moderate brothers and sisters, they have recognized the urgency of the moment and sensed the need for powerful "action" antidotes to combat the disease of segregation.

Let me take note of my other major disappointment. I have been so greatly disappointed with the white church and its leadership. Of course, there are some notable exceptions. I am not unmindful of the fact that each of you has taken some significant stands on this issue. I commend you, Reverend Stallings, for your Christian stand on this past Sunday, in welcoming Negroes to your worship service on a non segregated basis. I commend the Catholic leaders of this state for integrating Spring Hill College several years ago.

But despite these notable exceptions, I must honestly reiterate that I have been disappointed with the church. I do not say this as one of those negative critics who can always find something wrong with the church. I say this as a minister of the gospel, who loves the church; who was nurtured in its bosom; who has been sustained by its spiritual blessings and who will remain true to it as long as the cord of life shall lengthen.

When I was suddenly catapulted into the leadership of the bus protest in Montgomery, Alabama, a few years ago, I felt we would be supported by the white church. I felt that the white ministers, priests and rabbis of the South would be among our strongest allies. Instead, some have been outright opponents, refusing to understand the freedom movement and misrepresenting its leaders; all too many others have been more cautious than courageous and have remained silent behind the anesthetizing security of stained-glass windows.

In spite of my shattered dreams, I came to Birmingham with the hope that the white religious leadership of this community would see the justice of our cause and, with deep moral concern, would serve as the channel through which our just grievances could reach the power structure. I had hoped that each of you would understand. But again I have been disappointed.

I have heard numerous southern religious leaders admonish their worshipers to comply with a desegregation decision because it is the law, but I have longed to hear white ministers declare: "Follow this decree because integration is morally right and because the Negro is your brother." In the midst of blatant injustices inflicted upon the Negro, I have watched white churchmen stand on the sideline and mouth pious irrelevancies and sanctimonious trivialities. In the midst of a mighty struggle to rid our nation of racial and economic injustice, I have heard many ministers say: "Those are social issues, with which the gospel has no real concern." And I have watched many churches commit themselves to a completely other worldly religion which makes a strange, un-Biblical distinction between body and soul, between the sacred and the secular.

I have traveled the length and breadth of Alabama, Mississippi and all the other southern states. On sweltering summer days and crisp autumn mornings I have looked at the South's beautiful churches with their lofty spires pointing heavenward. I have beheld the impressive outlines of her massive religious-education buildings. Over and over I have found myself asking: "What kind of people worship here? Who is their God? Where were their voices when the lips of Governor Barnett dripped with words of interposition and nullification? Where were they when Governor Wallace gave a clarion call for defiance and hatred? Where were their voices of support when bruised and weary Negro men and women decided to rise from the dark dungeons of complacency to the bright hills of creative protest?"

Yes, these questions are still in my mind. In deep disappointment I have wept over the laxity of the church. But be assured that my tears have been tears of love. There can be no deep disappointment where there is not deep love. Yes, I love the church. How could I do otherwise? I am in the rather unique position of being the son, the grandson and the great-grandson of preachers. Yes, I see the church as the body of Christ. But, oh! How we have blemished and scarred that body through social neglect and through fear of being nonconformists.

There was a time when the church was very powerful—in the time when the early Christians rejoiced at being deemed worthy to suffer for what they believed. In those days the church was not merely a thermometer that recorded the ideas and principles of popular opinion; it was a thermostat that transformed the mores of society. Whenever the early Christians entered a town, the people in power became disturbed and immediately sought to convict the Christians for being "disturbers of the peace" and "outside agitators." But the Christians pressed on, in the conviction that they were "a colony of heaven," called to obey God rather than man. Small in number, they were big in commitment. They were too God-intoxicated to be "astronomically intimidated." By their effort and example they brought an end to such ancient evils as infanticide. and gladiatorial contests.

Things are different now. So often the contemporary church is a weak, ineffectual voice with an uncertain sound. So often it is an archdefender of the status quo. Far from being disturbed by the presence of the church, the power structure of the average community is consoled by the church's silent and often even vocal sanction of things as they are.

But the judgment of God is upon the church as never before. If today's church does not recapture the sacrificial spirit of the early church, it will lose its authenticity, forfeit the loyalty of millions, and be dismissed as an irrelevant social club with no meaning for the twentieth century. Every day I meet young people whose disappointment with the church has turned into outright disgust.

Perhaps I have once again been too optimistic. Is organized religion too inextricably bound to the status quo to save our nation and the world? Perhaps I must turn my faith to the inner spiritual church, the church within the church, as the true ecclesia and the hope of the world. But again I am thankful to God that some noble souls from the ranks of organized religion have broken loose from the paralyzing chains of conformity and joined us as active partners in the struggle for freedom. They have left their secure congregations and walked the streets of Albany, Georgia, with us. They have gone down the highways of the South on tortuous rides for freedom. Yes, they have gone to jail with us. Some have been dismissed from their churches, have lost the support of their bishops and fellow ministers. But they have acted in the faith that right defeated is stronger than evil triumphant. Their witness has been the spiritual salt that has preserved the true meaning of the gospel in these troubled times. They have carved a tunnel of hope through the dark mountain of disappointment.

I hope the church as a whole will meet the challenge of this decisive hour. But even if the church does not come to the aid of justice, I have no despair about the future. I have no fear about the outcome of our struggle in Birmingham, even if our motives are at present misunderstood. We will reach the goal of freedom in Birmingham, and all over the nation, because the goal of America is freedom. Abused and scorned though we may be, our destiny is tied up with America's destiny. Before the pilgrims landed at Plymouth, we were here. Before the pen of Jefferson etched the majestic words of the Declaration of Independence across the pages of history, we were here. For more than two centuries our forebears labored in this country without wages; they made cotton king; they built the homes of their masters while suffering gross injustice and shameful humiliation-and yet out of a bottomless vitality they continued to thrive and develop. If the inexpressible cruelties of slavery could not stop us, the opposition we now face will surely fail. We will win our freedom because the sacred heritage of our nation and the eternal will of God are embodied in our echoing demands.

Before closing I feel impelled to mention one other point in your statement that has troubled me profoundly. You warmly commended the Birmingham police force for keeping "order" and "preventing violence." I doubt that you would have so warmly commended the police force if you had seen its dogs sinking their teeth into unarmed, nonviolent Negroes. I doubt that you would so quickly commend the policemen if you were to observe their ugly and inhumane treatment of Negroes here in the city jail; if you were to watch them push and curse old Negro women and young Negro girls; if you were to see them slap and kick old Negro men and young boys; if you were to observe them, as they did on two occasions, refuse to give us food because we wanted to sing our grace together. I cannot join you in your praise of the Birmingham police department.

It is true that the police have exercised a degree of discipline in handling the demonstrators. In this sense they have conducted themselves rather "nonviolently" in public. But for what purpose? To preserve the evil system of segregation. Over the past few years I have consistently preached that nonviolence demands that the means we use must be as pure as the ends we seek. I have tried to make clear that it is wrong to use immoral means to attain moral ends. But now I must affirm that it is just as wrong, or perhaps even more so, to use moral means to preserve immoral ends. Perhaps Mr. Connor and his policemen have been rather nonviolent in public, as was Chief Pritchett in Albany, Georgia but they have used the moral means of nonviolence to maintain the immoral end of racial injustice. As T. S. Eliot has said: "The last temptation is the greatest treason: To do the right deed for the wrong reason."

I wish you had commended the Negro sit-inners and demonstrators of Birmingham for their sublime courage, their willingness to suffer and their amazing discipline in the midst of great provocation. One day the South will recognize its real heroes. There will be the James Merediths, with the noble sense of purpose that enables them to face jeering and hostile mobs, and with the agonizing loneliness that characterizes the life of the pioneer. There will be the old, oppressed, battered Negro women, symbolized in a seventy-two-year-old woman in Montgomery, Alabama, who rose up with a sense of dignity and with her people decided not to ride segregated buses, and who responded with ungrammatical profundity to one who inquired about her weariness: "My feets is tired, but my soul is at rest." There will be the young high school and college students, the young ministers of the gospel and a host of their elders, courageously and nonviolently sitting in at lunch counters and willingly going to jail for conscience's sake. One day the South will know that when these disinherited children of God sat down at lunch counters, they were in reality standing up for what is best in the American dream and for the most sacred values in our Judaeo-Christian heritage, thereby bringing our nation back to those great wells of democracy which were dug deep by the founding fathers in their formulation of the Constitution and the Declaration of Independence.

Never before have I written so long a letter. I'm afraid it is much too long to take your precious time. I can assure you that it would have been much shorter if I had been writing from a comfortable desk, but what else can one do when he is alone in a narrow jail cell, other than write long letters, think long thoughts and pray long prayers?

If I have said anything in this letter that overstates the truth and indicates an unreasonable impatience, I beg you to forgive me. If I have said anything that understates the truth and indicates my having a patience that allows me to settle for anything less than brotherhood, I beg God to forgive me.

I hope this letter finds you strong in the faith. I also hope that circumstances will soon make it possible for me to meet each of you, not as an integrationist or a civil rights leader but as a fellow clergyman and a Christian brother. Let us all hope that the dark clouds of racial prejudice will soon pass away and the deep fog of misunderstanding will be lifted from our fear-drenched communities, and in some not too distant tomorrow the radiant stars of love and brotherhood will shine over our great nation with all their scintillating beauty.

Yours for the cause of Peace and Brotherhood,

Martin Luther King, Jr.

Comprehending the Text

1. What was Martin Luther King, Jr.'s purpose in writing this letter?

2. What is his point about nonviolent protest?

3. What does Martin Luther King, Jr. say about the "white moderate"?

Analyzing the Text

1. Identify exact passages where the writer appeals to *ethos*.

2. Identify exact passages where the writer appeals to *logos*.

3. Identify exact passages where the writer appeals to *pathos*.

Developing Your Skills: Identifying Effective Rhetoric

Dr. King's speech is considered to be one of the most powerful in American history. In a short response, analyze that speech in the following way:

- Write first about feelings: How do the words of this speech make you feel? What is your "gut level" response to the imagery, imagination, and persuasion?

- Write next about your analysis: How do the words, sentences, or other rhetorical strategies used by Dr. King work to bring about your feelings? What are the "inner workings" of his rhetoric?

YOUR TURN: Creating Your Ideas

1. Read the current edition of your campus newspaper and your local community newspaper. Pay particular attention to the editorial page and the letters to the editor section of the publication. There, you will find opinion pieces designed to argue a point and persuade readers on an issue. Select one of those opinions that you disagree with and write a letter in response. Write with that publication in mind—that's your audience. Your purpose is to argue the opposite point of

view. Remember, it's not enough to simply disagree; you need to assert your own ideas and give evidence to support them.

2. Imagine your college has just announced a 25 percent increase in tuition for next year. Imagine you are charged with creating a PowerPoint presentation for the Student Senate to present to the Board of Trustees to both object to the increase and recommend alternatives was to increase revenue rather than increasing tuition. Use this example and do the research relative to your own college. You will want to find out what your current tuition is, what a 25 percent increase would mean, and brainstorm some alternative ways for the administration to raise that revenue elsewhere. Then, create a PowerPoint presentation that addresses these issues and recommends alternatives.

3. Begin a blog today. Go to blogspot.com or blogger.com and set up a blog. Do it with a clear intent and with a clear audience in mind. For example, from this day forward, you may want to track your progress through college and your audience may be your parents, who may be paying your way, or it may be a group of friends who are majoring in another field. You are going to keep a record of your experiences and your reactions to your class and extracurricular activities. You may also want to post papers or excerpts of papers to illustrate your thoughts and feelings along the way. By the time you graduate, you will be a seasoned blogger and you'll have insight into your process as a college student.

4. "A First Look at Gobbledygook" shows how "official" messages tend to get weighed down with unnecessarily complex language. Find an example of "gobbledygook" writing in a published piece of nonfiction writing—editorials in newspapers or magazines, policy statements on government websites, or maybe even writing in your own textbooks. On a copy of the document, underline every unnecessary word or phrase. Rewrite the document in more clear and concise prose.

TECH TALK: Using PowerPoint

Not familiar with PowerPoint? If you know how to use a word processing program, you will find PowerPoint relatively easy to use. Here are some explanations of Power-Point to help you experiment with this presentation tool. The following image shows you a basic slide template page. This page, which is a title page, will appear when you open the PowerPoint program on the computer.

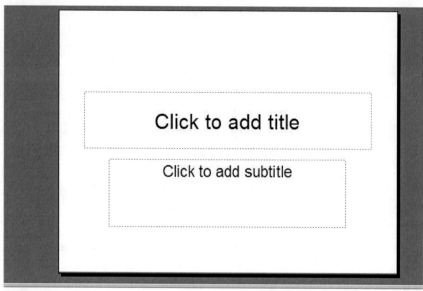

Note how the slide gives you directions. If you click in any of these areas, you can add the information you need. Then, to add another slide, go to Insert > New Slide. Following is an image of a **content** slide:

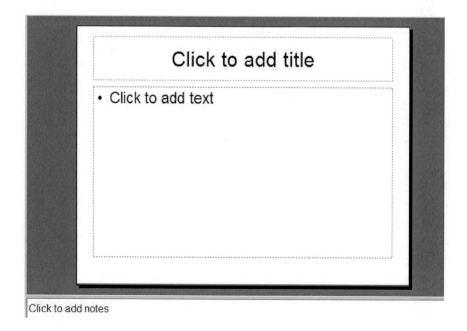

Note how there is a title area for the slide where you can add text in preformatted bullet points. Also, the "notes" area is an effective space for you to add additional information to your slides or to remind yourself of the comments you want to make for an oral presentation.

Finally, if you want to post your slide to a class website with audio added to it, follow these directions:

- Go to Insert > Movies and sounds > Record sound
- Click the "red" button and speak into a microphone. If you have a laptop, you can often just speak at your screen and the computer's microphone will pick up your voice. If you have a desktop computer, you may need to use a microphone that is attached to the tower. Microphones are under $20 at any office store.

Most importantly, remember when writing and using a PowerPoint presentation to keep your design clean and simple.

Chapter 7

Supporting Your Argument

n order to craft effective arguments, writers must often draw upon other sources, or **data,** to support their claims. In creating arguments, whether informative or persuasive, we begin with a **claim,** or a controversial or debatable statement with which we want our audience to agree, and support the claim with data, or evidence.

The focus here is on data—the evidence you need to locate and then effectively use in your writing to support your arguments. Effective writers make a claim, offer **evidence** to support that claim, consider the **opposition,** and come to a **conclusion.** By the end of this chapter, you will have learned and practiced several skills. You will be able to determine when and how to use outside sources (data) in your writing. You will practice effective research methods in order to obtain those sources. You will understand the differences between primary and secondary research, and scholarly and popular sources. Finally, you will know how to evaluate those sources for their credibility and usefulness for your purposes. All of these skills can be added to your writer's toolkit to make you a more powerful communicator.

Deciding on Evidence

Knowing when and how to use outside sources denotes a well-rounded writer. Once more, Aristotle's concepts of *artistic* and *inartistic* proofs come into play. As you know, the effective communicator understands that a strong argument contains a unique combination of the three artistic proofs of ethos (from the character of the writer), pathos (appeals to the emotions), and logos (appeals to rationality and reason). You, the writer, make strategic choices and decisions about how to use those appeals.

At the same time, you must also decide when to incorporate outside sources, or inartistic proofs, to support your claims. In Aristotle's time, the inartistic proofs included laws, witnesses, contracts, evidence taken from slaves under torture, and oaths, to name some. According to Aristotle, these are sources of evidence that are outside the art of the communicator. In other words, these sources are elements that a writer locates and then brings into the rhetorical process to support his or her ideas.

As discussed earlier, inartistic proofs have evolved over the last several thousand years. For the twenty-first century, the inartistic proofs include the following types of sources:

- Facts
- Figures
- Statistics
- Quotations from important and relevant people
- Other resources available to us through creative, credible, and thorough research

The key question that you need to ask yourself as you consider the types of sources available to you is:

What kinds of evidence (data) will help you make the most effective argument?

This is a decision that you, as the writer, are going to have to make every time you set out to write or communicate verbally. Once again, to answer the previous question, we need to return to our earlier chapters—specifically, to the discussions about the rhetorical situation and the definition of rhetoric itself. As we discussed, Aristotle defined rhetoric as "the faculty of discovering, in the given case, all the available means of persuasion." This statement breaks down in the following way:

- A "faculty" is an art or ability. So rhetoric involves some kind of ability to discover.
- "In the given case" simply means that one must look to the immediate situation. A given case then, is the situation at hand.
- "All of the available means of persuasion" means that any person is going to have access to a variety of ways to accomplish a persuasive goal, and must choose which persuasive (or rhetorical) tools to use.

Consequently, Aristotle's definition of rhetoric can be translated as "the ability to analyze a situation and choose the appropriate tool for accomplishing a persuasive goal."

When you choose to use rhetoric to accomplish a persuasive goal, you need to determine what rhetorical strategies to employ. Remember, there are three key elements to keep in mind with any rhetorical act:

- *Audience:* Any rhetorical act requires an audience that you need to identify. Your audience greatly affects the type of evidence you may decide to use.

- *Purpose:* You also need to consider your purpose. What is the ultimate goal of your rhetorical act? What do you hope to accomplish?

- *Situation:* Rhetorical acts occur in response to a situation or an exigence (as discussed in Chapter 3). The exigence may be an assignment in class, a social or community problem, or some other occasion that calls for a rhetorical response.

Each of these elements influences the others. In other words, the situation affects the purpose, as does the audience. It is virtually impossible to separate these three elements from each other. These three elements also influence the types of evidence you need, how much evidence is required, and how you will use that evidence.

For example, imagine that your school has banned free speech anywhere on campus except in a particular spot that they have labeled the "free speech zone." As a student, you believe anyone should be able to exercise free speech anywhere on campus. You decide to write a letter to the editor of your school newspaper protesting this new policy. This new policy has created your **situation.**

In making this decision, you have also determined your **purpose**—you'd like to demonstrate why the free speech zone policy is wrong. The next important step is to identify your **audience.** Do you want to persuade the administrators who made the policy? Or do you want to motivate your peers and/or faculty to get them to protest this policy?

Once you decide on your audience, you can then determine what type of evidence you need for your argument. For instance, let's assume you choose to address the administrators who created the policy. What do you think you need to do to prove to them that this policy is detrimental to the campus community? Perhaps it might make sense to research free speech policies at other schools, which could give you information about who has such a policy and what purpose it serves, as well as the reasons why some schools elect not to have such a policy. Or you might want to research the First Amendment so that you can base your argument on the right to free speech as it is documented in the U.S. Constitution.

Finally, once you have determined your audience, situation, and purpose, and if you have decided that bringing in outside sources will help substantiate your project, you then need to turn to the research process to locate the most compelling evidence for your project.

When locating evidence for support, writers need to understand the differences between primary sources and secondary sources.

- **Primary sources** fall into the following categories:
  - Original documents such as speeches, autobiographies, news footage, personal letters, blogs, email messages, and statistical surveys. For example, Martin Luther King, Jr.'s famous "Letter from Birmingham Jail" is a primary document relative to the U.S. Civil Rights Movement.

- Creative works like poems, novels, plays, memoirs, or essays. For example, Toni Morrison's novel *Beloved* is a creative work, as is Maxine Hong Kingston's essay "No Name Woman." In addition, original research can be a primary source, such as Barbara Ehrenreich's *Nickel and Dimed: On (Not) Getting By In America.*

Primary sources are documents or artifacts that were created during the time under study. Primary sources offer an inside look at an event or time period. You will find that you will often use primary sources in your courses and in your daily life. Primary sources exist in both print and digital formats. For instance, you will find primary sources in books, journals, on the Internet, and in audio and visual formats such as documentaries, television news reports, Internet news reports, and more.

For example, we can turn to the Internet to learn more about the current issue of global warming and find a large variety of information. One site, the Pew Center on Global Climate Change, offers Internet viewers fact sheets, such as the one titled "Coal and Climate Change," that lists statistics and facts (see http://www.pewclimate.org/global-warming-basics/coalfacts.cfm). This online document is a primary electronic source that could be used to develop a discussion on the causes of global warming and climate change.

- **Secondary sources** are typically writings about primary sources that interpret, analyze, and/or evaluate the primary source or offer information that relates to the primary source. For example, the King Center website (http://www.martinlutherking.org), which is focused on the work of Martin Luther King, Jr., is a secondary source because it provides a biography and chronology of his life and work. Full length books also serve as secondary sources, such as *The World Is Flat: A Brief History of the Twenty-First Century* by Thomas L. Friedman.

You will find that you also will often use secondary sources in your courses and in your daily life. Secondary sources, like primary sources, exist in print and electronic formats. These types of sources are most often found in books or journals, but they also can be documentaries or papers from scholarly conferences or even a website.

When searching for sources, another consideration to keep in mind is the difference between scholarly and popular sources:

- A **scholarly source** is one that has been peer-reviewed, which means the source has been reviewed by experts in the field and is considered to be well written and researched. Scholarly sources are typically found in books and journals and are usually written by people who have significant knowledge and experience in the subject matter being discussed for an audience of similarly knowledgeable people. Charles Darwin's *The Origin of the Species* (1859), for instance, is a scholarly source that offers a theory of evolution. Through research, Darwin created his theory of evolution, and then he published his ideas in a book. We also find scholarly sources in journals for specific disciplines such as *Professional Psychology: Research and Practice*, the *American Journal of Sociology*, or the *American Political Science Review.* Your campus library has databases that help you search for these types of sources.

- **Popular sources,** on the other hand, are sources we find around us every day in newspapers, magazines, on the Internet, the radio, and television. They are written for a broad, general audience in easily understandable language. Most popular articles tend to not cite sources or provide bibliographies; they also tend to be shorter than scholarly articles. Popular sources include magazines like *Time, Newsweek, Sports Illustrated*, and *BusinessWeek.*

Making Decisions: Which Types of Sources (Primary, Secondary, Scholarly, or Popular) to Use?

In deciding which types of sources to use, you have to consider your audience, purpose, and situation. To do this, think about a scenario used in Chapter 3, where your Introduction to Sociology class assignment was to create an informational brochure concerning recycling because your campus has no program. In order to inform faculty and students about the problems associated with this issue, and to motivate them to recycle on campus, you need to consider the types of evidence that will work most effectively to convince them to agree with your ideas. Remember that you need to include evidence to which your specific audiences will relate. Consider these possible types of evidence:

- Statistics that document how much a school may save financially
- Information about how a recycling program contributes to the local economy
- Evidence that recycling programs work
- Information about how recycling contributes to a sustainable future that may affect their families

As you consider the variety of evidence you can gather, think about the students and faculty you know on your campus. To create the informational brochure for this assignment, you need to decide which of these examples of evidence would work best to inform and motivate your audience.

Once you have your list of possible evidence, you then need to find that evidence. Where might you discover information about how recycling has benefited other schools, for instance? Some schools might advertise the success of recycling programs on their websites; others might have news articles published in local newspapers. These sources are considered popular sources because they are not peer-reviewed. On the other hand, you might locate some environmental journals that contain peer-reviewed articles written by scientists about the benefits of recycling. These articles are scholarly sources.

Given your audience, what types of sources do you think would be most effective? Or would using both types of sources provide you with the support you need to make your argument? These are the types of questions you need to ask yourself as you develop your brochure. You, the writer, are the decision maker, and it is up to you to shape your rhetorical communication by choosing from the various strategies and forms of evidence you have obtained through your research. As you locate evidence, remember that it is also important to evaluate those sources as you proceed.

Locating Your Sources

An effective researcher uses a number of different media to find sources. These media range from a library's book catalog to an electronic database to print journals to Internet search engines. Here are some tips for using each of these research areas.

Searching the Library Catalog or a Library Database

As with any search engine, you need to use subject words to search for sources related to your topic. For example, if you were searching for information to support the claims you make in your brochure, you might type in the word "recycling" and hit "search." When we searched for "recycling" in our library book database, we came up with 82 books. That's a lot of books to review.

Our next step was to narrow our search by being more specific with our keywords. We typed in "recycling college campuses." However, this search produced no hits. So, we revised our keywords to "recycling universities." This search located three books for us and provided the following information:

1. *Campus and Environmental Responsibility*/ David J. Eagan, David W. Orr, editors, 1992; location 3rd floor library; status: not checked out

2. *Encyclopedia of Accounting Systems*/ Tom M. Plank and Lois R. Plank, general editors, 1993; location: 2nd floor library, non-circulating; status: available

3. *Greening of Industrial Ecosystems*/ Braden R. Allenby and Deanna J. Richards, editors, 1994; location, 3rd floor library; status: not checked out

Once you have a list of sources in front of you, like the example list, you can scan the list quickly for the following information:

- *Book title:* The title might be interesting and draw you in further. Note that the second source in the example list is *Encyclopedia of Accounting Systems*. Because the title doesn't include anything about recycling, you might rule it out as potentially useful. On the other hand, it might be worth considering; it will be difficult to know without getting more information.

- *Date of publication:* The date of publication tells you how current the source is. Note that the three sources in the example list are all from the early 1990s. Considering that your assignment is to provide information to your college campus, recent sources might be more effective in accomplishing your goal.

- *Status:* Whether the source is available to you. Note that two of the sources listed in the example are available ("not checked out") and the other source is noncirculating. In other words, you must consult the *Encyclopedia of Accounting Systems* in the library only. You cannot check it out.

Next, we turned to a general database in search of scholarly and popular articles. There, we searched for "recycling college campus" and located the following possibilities:

1. Campus Recycling (college teaching; column). James M. Lang. *The Chronicle of Higher Education* 50.8 (Oct. 17, 2003): pNA (1392 words)

2. Composting joins recycling on college campuses. Jennifer Schoonover. *BioCycle* v35.n2 (Feb. 1994): pp56(2).

3. The use of posted feedback to promote recycling. Richard Katzev and Henry R. Mishima. *Psychological Reports* v71.n1 (August 1992): pp259(6).

4. Recycling the campus. (renovation of college buildings). Milton Jordan. *American Education* v14 (August-Sept 1978): pp19(5).

Once again, you need to scan the list to determine if you want to pursue any of these sources. Ask yourself the following questions:

- Is the title related to my purpose?

- When was the source written?

- Where is the source published? For example, the second source comes from *BioCycle*, a scientific journal, while the fourth source comes from *American Education*, another scholarly source.

- Can you access the source as full-text? In other words, is the full article available online in the database? Look below your source listing for links. You might see "full-text," indicating the source is available online, or you might see "abstract," indicating you can access a summary of the source. If the full-text is not available, you need to go to the library to find the source in a print version of the journal. Consider also that you can search for full-text articles using online databases such as Google Scholar as well.

Finally, we also turned to the Web to locate information. There, we went to a web search engine and searched for responses to the question "Why recycle on college campuses?" Our search located 939,000 sites related to our subject! However, a quick scan of the first few pages brought us to some useful sites as pictured here:

Marist **College**: **Campus** Life - Recycling
Recycle. Figure 1. Marist **College** solid waste categorization by mass as determined on 11 ... kg) obtained from 11 **campus** dumpsters. Dumpster Dive 1 vs. ...
www.marist.edu/campuslife/**recycle**/campusevents.html - 16k -
Cached - Similar pages - Note this

National Recycling Coalition - **College** and University Recycling ...
The **College** and University Recycling Council (CURC) was formed in 1992 and ... Residence hall move-in provides **campuses** with an opportunity to **recycle** and ...
www.nrc-**recycle**.org/curc.aspx - 19k - Cached - Similar pages - Note this

National Recycling Coalition - CURC Projects
Recycling and Beyond: A **College Campus** Primer provides an overview of strategies for implementation and program development of a **college campus** recycling ...
www.nrc-**recycle**.org/curcprojects.aspx - 18k - Cached - Similar pages - Note this

Recycling Mania Hits **College Campuses** | Resource Conservation ...
Recycle Mania Trophy created by Robin Kelly of Carpenter, Ohio. ... Kicked off in 2001 to address the wastefulness at **college campuses**, the ten week long, ...
www.epa.gov/epaoswer/osw/conserve/2004news/09-mania.htm - 18k -
Cached - Similar pages - Note this

How do you know whether these sites are useful? Consider who has written them. Note that the final site is an Environmental Protection Agency site. Above that, the link leads to the National Recycling Coalition, which provides information about college campus recycling efforts. You need to take time to review the links and evaluate the sites for what they offer to your research project, which you will learn more about next.

Last but not least, as you search for sources, make sure to have a balance of sources. In other words, you don't want all your sources to come from the Internet or all of your sources to be books. Finding a blend of print, electronic, and web sources is a good practice to follow, as is

What is a web search engine?

A web search engine is a site that allows you to type in keywords on any topic and it will search the www for you and create a list of possible sources. Keep in mind the web is a vast universe, and you need to evaluate any web source carefully, as we discuss below. Here are some web search engine sites:

Google: www.google.com

Yahoo: www.yahoo.com

Ask Jeeves: www.askjeeves.com or www.ask.com

a blend of scholarly and popular sources. Also, make sure to review your assignments carefully to identify what types of sources and the number of sources required.

Evaluating Your Sources

Keep in mind that once you have found your sources, you need to evaluate each source for its reliability. In other words, you need to evaluate the sources to determine whether each source is reliable and something that will help substantiate your argument. An effective way to interrogate your evidence is to ask these questions:

- Who is the author? An expert in the field? Someone writing a personal blog?
- Is the author or are the authors biased in anyway?
- Does the author consider other viewpoints?
- Where is the source published? A scholarly journal or publishing press? A popular magazine? A newspaper?
- When was the source published? Is it current enough for your purpose?
- What does the source cover? Is the information relevant to your purpose?
- Does the source and author depend on logical fallacies? (Remember, we discussed these in Chapter 5.)
- How does the author support his or her argument and claims?
- Is the evidence used in the source reliable?

Overall, your goal is to assess your sources to determine whether your audience will trust your source and therefore believe your argument more fully.

As we've discussed with our research examples, the Web has become a major part of our lives. We turn to the Internet to make travel plans, to find out the current news, to share information with friends via sites like MySpace and Facebook, and to locate information. With the ever-growing range of information and

Did you know that there are 13 top level domains on the Internet? Here are some of them

.com (commercial sites; the most common website domain for the public)

.edu (educational institutions)

.gov (a United States government website)

.mil (a United States military organization)

.net (a network resource)

.org (an organization that is typically not for profit)

.firm (businesses)

.web (web related organizations)

.arts (organizations to do with the arts)

.rec (organizations with emphasis on recreational events)

.info (organizations that provide info)

websites available, it is important for us to consider the following questions when we turn to the Internet to locate information for our writings:

- Is a source found on the Internet a reliable one?

- Is a website providing accurate, truthful information?

- Also, is the information provided (once you know it's accurate) useful to you in your writing project?

- How do we figure this all out?

There are no easy answers to these questions, as the Internet is overloaded with information. What is most important to realize is that the Internet is here to stay, and we are going to find ourselves using it more and more in schools and in the everyday work place. More importantly, we need to learn ways to evaluate sites from the Internet just as we evaluate print sources so that we know our sources are reliable.

The best way to evaluate a website is to ask the same questions you use for print material. However, with sources from the Web, some additional questions are crucial, such as:

- When was the website last updated?

- Are the links on the website current? (Active links show that someone is paying attention to the site and maintaining it for accuracy.)

- Do you know if the website presents the most up-to-date information on your topic?

- Are there any supporting materials, such as a list of works cited?

Using Your Sources Effectively

In Chapter 1, we discussed writing summaries and paraphrasing readings. Keep in mind these objectives when writing summaries:

- Summaries contain the main ideas and most important points of the text you are discussing.

- Summaries in your own writing are used to lead up to or extend your argument as you draw upon an outside source for support.

When you paraphrase, you provide a restatement of the original work *in your own words* that closely mirrors the original work. Summaries are short and concise; paraphrasing is often similar to the original work in terms of length and complexity. Typically, you will find yourself using both summary and paraphrasing interchangeably when working with outside sources in your writing.

Writing an effective summary often depends on your ability to paraphrase or quote from a source. When you paraphrase, your goal is to restate the ideas contained in the source in your own words. Here are some guidelines to follow when **paraphrasing:**

- Attribute the information to the source you are using by referencing the author or authors in your discussion when you first bring in the ideas from the source.
- Use your own words and phrases to explain what the source is saying.
- Be concise, as effective summaries are short and to the point.
- Conclude your passage by citing the source in parentheses. (Note: we'll discuss documentation formats more fully later in this chapter.)

When you **quote,** you copy the words from your selected text into your document just as they appear in the original. The words should be put inside quotation marks. For example, notice that quotation marks indicate quoted material in the following passage:

> In "Write Till You Drop," Annie Dillard describes how it feels to write a book, telling readers that the "sensation of writing a book is the sensation of spinning, blinded by love and daring." For Dillard, it is also the "sensation of a stunt pilot's turning barrel rolls, or an inchworm's blind rearing from a stem in search of a route. At its worst, it feels like alligator wrestling, at the level of the sentence."

The quotation marks indicate that we've quoted verbatim from Dillard's essay. Now, we also could choose to paraphrase Dillard. For instance, we could write:

> In "Write Till You Drop," Annie Dillard tells readers that writing a book is like spinning out of control as if you were a stunt pilot or as if you were exuberantly in love. At the same time, for Dillard, writing a book can also be like fighting with an alligator and struggling to write each sentence.

What's the difference? The actual quote from Dillard accurately captures her language and creates a much more vivid description of the sensation of writing a book; thus, the quoted passage helps readers actually envision what Dillard is talking about.

Once you've located your sources, evaluated them, and decided upon which sources are useful for your purpose, you then need to consider how best to employ these sources in your project. Sources are used for the following reasons:

- To support an argument
- To add description and imagery to your writing

What is Plagiarism?

Plagiarism is using the intellectual property of others with attributing it to them.

Put more simply, plagiarism is the use of another person's words and/or ideas from any communication medium such as print, broadcast or electronic sources.

To avoid plagiarism, familiarize yourself with your school's definition of and policies regarding plagiarism and cheating. Also, take time to familiarize yourself with how to cite your sources, which we discuss in more detail further on in this chapter.

- To use someone else's more eloquent or more effective point
- To bring in an opposing viewpoint

Most often, writers bring in sources by using summaries and paraphrasing. A summary provides the main ideas of the text, indicates how the ideas fit together, and is objective.

Using Quotations

Key words or phrases: Writers often quote specific words that help to develop their discussion. Notice how Joan Didion, in her essay "Why I Write," sets off certain words when she explains why she stole her title from George Orwell:

> I stole the title not only because the words sounded right but because they seemed to sum up, in a no-nonsense way, all I have to tell you. Like many writers I have only this one "subject," this one "area": the act of writing.

The quotation marks highlight the words "subject" and "area," thus alerting the reader to their importance for Didion. Writers also quote specific phrases that someone else has created for specific purposes. For example, consider the following passage:

> Barbara Kingsolver's novel *Prodigal Summer* makes use of the "Volterra Principle" and the "keystone predator concept," two scientific beliefs that explain how an ecosystem survives.

The quotation marks here identify the terms coined by other people.

Key sentences and passages: Writers also use passages from sources to develop their discussions. You need to determine when you think a passage quoted directly from a text might be more effective than paraphrasing that text. Notice how a passage is included in this example:

> In the 1950s, the concept of a "literary canon" developed in American literature. Paul Lauter, a scholar of American literature, defines and explains the influences of the term "canon" for us in Canons and Contexts (1991): "the set of literary works, the grouping of significant philosophical, political, and religious texts, the particular accounts of history generally accorded cultural weight within a society" (ix). As Lauter points out, how we define the literary canon not only "shapes collegiate curricula and research priorities, but it also helps to determine precisely whose experiences and ideas become central to academic study" (ix). According to Lauter, the canon has much to do with determining what we teach in the university.

Because the writer wanted to clearly define the term "canon," she relied upon the actual definition given by an expert in the field.

Notice in the examples that we have purposefully integrated our quotes into sentences. In other words, we've made sure that the quotes used are part of a sentence.

This practice of integrating quotes into your writing is an important one, and it is accomplished through the use of **signal phrases** or **verbs**. These phrases or verbs help connect your idea to a supporting quote or even to a paraphrase of your chosen source.

Here are some examples of how a signal phrase or verb works to integrate your chosen source into your writing:

Common Signal Verbs	
asserts	observes
answers	replies
claims	responds
concludes	says
declares	suggests
describes	thinks
discussions	writes
emphasizes	

> In New York City, officials are working to have residents use more tap water rather than purchasing water in plastic containers that contribute to landfill overflows. Specifically, as Bill Marsh reports in "A Battle Between the Bottle and the Faucet," city officials **assert** that the eight glasses of water that are supposed to create good health and cost only "49 cents a year—if you take it from a New York City tap" (*New York Times*, July 15, 2007). However, the same city officials **suggest**, "you could spend 2,900 times as much, roughly $1,400 yearly, by drinking bottled water," which gives you the "responsibility for piling on to the nation's waste heap and encouraging more of the industrial emissions that are heating up the planet" (Marsh).

In addition to using signal phrases, there are other stylistic strategies when using quotations. These strategies help you shorten or add information to a quotation:

- *Ellipses:* Ellipses (three periods with spaces between them) are used when you want to shorten a quotation by deleting part of the phrasing. The ellipsis marks where deleted words or phrases were in the original quotation. Ellipses should be used sparingly. If you trail on several sections connecting them with ellipses, you run the risk of actually distorting the intent of the author. You've seen that in advertisements for films where a reviewer is quoted as saying, "...absolutely outstanding..." when really what came before and after those two words might be, "This movie is an absolutely outstanding example of an awful movie." Here's an example of how to use ellipses effectively:

> In New York City, officials are working to have residents use more tap water rather than purchasing water in plastic containers that contribute to landfill overflows. Specifically, as Bill Marsh reports in "A Battle Between the Bottle and the Faucet," city officials assert that the eight glasses of water that are supposed to create good health will cost "49 cents a year—if you take it from a New York City tap" (*New York Times*, July 15, 2007). However, the same city officials suggest, "you could spend ... roughly $1,400 yearly, by drinking bottled water,"

which gives you the "responsibility for piling on to the nation's waste heap and encouraging ... industrial emissions that are heating up the planet" (Marsh).

Note that we have deleted the words "2,900 times as much" and "more of the." If you choose to use ellipses, keep these guidelines in mind:

- After omitting words or phrases from a quote, make sure that the quotation and your integration still create a grammatically correct sentence.
- Don't use ellipses at the beginning of a quotation. It's assumed that readers know that the quote is taken from a longer work.
- Use ellipses at the end of a quotation only if you drop the ending words of that sentence.

- *Brackets:* Brackets [ ] allow you to insert a word or a phrase into a quote. Often, this insertion helps make a grammatically correct sentence or explains a reference that is unclear to your readers. This, however, is not a place to insert your commentary. Consider this example:

> The Environmental Protection Agency claims that "In 2005, U.S. residents, businesses, and institutions produced more than 245 million tons of MSW [municipal solid waste], which is approximately 4.5 pounds of waste per person per day" (www.epa.gov/epaoswer/non-hw/muncpl/facts.htm).

Note that we added the words "municipal solid waste" to explain what the letters MSW mean.

Long Quotations

Sometimes, you will find yourself wanting to include a long quotation to develop and support your point. The Modern Language Association (MLA) defines a long quote as any quote that exceeds four lines of your text. The American Psychological Association (APA) defines a long quote as any quote that exceeds 40 words. Whatever documentation format you are following, you need to make sure to follow the guidelines for in-text citations. Typically, a long quote is integrated with a sentence that sets up the quote for readers; the quote is also indented to set it off from your regular text. Here is an example using Ellis Cose's essay "Why I Write," which you read in Chapter 2:

In "Why I Write," Ellis Cose explains the experiences of riots in the 1960s in his neighborhood that drew him to journalism. As he explains,

> After the riots of April, my interest in journalism grew. The more I read, the more convinced I became that I had something to contribute. In many news accounts, the 1968 Democratic National Convention, held in Chicago, was chronicled as a war between the forces of order and deranged hippies—with innocent newsmen

caught in the middle. I suspected the real story was much more complicated and regretted not being able to report on and tell the story myself. (Cose 49)

As a result of his experience, Cose devoted himself to the study of writing and journalism, eventually landing himself a job with the *Sun-Times* in Chicago with his own op-ed column at the young age of nineteen.

Note that there are no quotation marks when you indent the quote as the physical placement of the passage indicates that you have quoted directly from your source. Also note the parentheses with the author information is not included within the quote. The parentheses stand outside the period that punctuates the quotation.

Writing an Annotated Bibliography

A bibliography is a list of sources that you have used for any project that required research or evidence to support your points. A list might include books, journal articles, newspaper articles, websites, an email you received, and more. This list is most commonly known as the **works cited** list at the end of formal papers.

At times, you will be asked to complete an **annotated bibliography.** The key word here is "annotated." When we annotate a source, we summarize the source or evaluate a source or, at times, we do both. Thus, an annotated bibliography includes both a works cited list and summary and/or evaluation of the sources. What purposes does an annotated bibliography serve?

- To gain an understanding of the evidence you might use for a writing project
- To help you formulate an approach to a topic that is different from what others have done
- To help others learn about the research on a particular topic

It's here that your summary skills will be useful. After selecting your sources for a project and reading through them, annotating means summarizing the source concisely, often in two to four sentences. Then, if the assignment calls for it, you need to add one to two sentences evaluating the source. This paragraph, your annotation, is included with your source citation. It's important to remember that your source citation needs to follow the documentation format expected by your instructor. For example, if we were listing this textbook and annotating it using MLA format, it would look like this:

Houser, Catherine, Jeannette E. Riley, and Kathleen M. Torrens. *Writer/Citizen.* Dubuque, IA: Kendall Hunt Publishers, 2010. Print. *Writer/Citizen* works to help first-year college student to become engaged citizens through the process of writing in a variety of public spheres. Students learn to analyze the rhetorical moment—that nexus of challenge meeting opportunity where writers must astutely evaluate audience and purpose, critically assess information, and make an array of choices about genre, style, medium, and format.

Documenting Your Sources

There are several different documentation formats that are used in academic settings. Writers use these formats to create **in-text citations** and to develop works cited lists at the end of writing assignments or projects. This process, which is called **documenting** your sources, enables your audience know what sources you used, which in turn allows your audience to go look those sources up if they are interested in learning more about your subject matter.

The MLA designed a documentation format for scholars in the humanities, which means that people writing in the fields of English, history, and philosophy use it most often. We encourage you to use a writing handbook to familiarize yourself with the MLA format. In addition, we've outlined the most common formats for in-text citations and works cited lists in the following section.

MLA Style for In-Text Citations

1. **Author named in a signal phrase** (Signal phrases, which usually include the author's name, introduce material and cite the page number in parentheses.)

    Example: Gessner also describes a great blue heron as having a "funky seventies TV pimp strut" (7).

2. **Author named in a parenthetical reference** (Include the author's last name before the page number in parentheses when the author is not mentioned in the signal phrase.)

    Example: Nature writers discuss their dissatisfaction with the world "in order to recover a natural relation to it" (Warnock 308).

3. **Two or three authors** (Put the authors' last names in the signal phrase or in parentheses.)

    Example: It is clear that as Thoreau writes, he is, at times, trying to sort through feelings—"the filtering of experience," as Finch and Elder say (28).

Annotated Bibliography Writing Tips

- Familiarize yourself with the basic guidelines of the documentation format you need to use for this assignment before going to the library.
- If you use a source that cannot be checked out, you will need to make sure that you write down the necessary information for your citation. Remember that there is specific information you need to illustrate whether your source is a *print* source or an *electronic* source.
- Be very careful to proofread your bibliography for typographical errors. Such errors can make it seem like you are not following the proper format.

Pay close attention to the many different ways to cite journal articles (and books, for that matter); you'll need to use the citation format that is specifically designated for the kind of journal you are using.

4. **Author of two or more works** (When your list of works cited includes more than one work by the same author, use a shortened version of the work's title in the parentheses or in the signal phrase.)

Example: Gessner declares that he is sick of trees, birds and the ocean, and suggests that perhaps Thoreau retreated to Walden to have more time for "masturbatory binges" (*Sick* 5).

5. **Literary work** (Cite the page number(s) from the edition you use followed by a semicolon and other identifying information about the passage. For a novel, note the part or chapter; for a play, the act or scene; for a poem, note the part and line(s) separated by a period.)

Example: Thoreau's enthusiasm for the small beast and the sense of wildness it arouses in him is quite evident as he speaks of "a strange thrill of savage delight" and his temptation to "seize and devour him raw" (189; ch. 13).

6. **Work without page numbers or a one-page article** (Cite the work in the text and omit page number. If the work uses paragraph numbers, use the abbreviation **par(s).**)

Example: Milton regarded Shakespeare's work as "honorable, brilliant and creative" in the words of Smith (par. 12).

7. **Electronic or nonprint source** (Provide enough information in the signal phrase or parenthetical reference for readers to find the source in your works cited list. Note the author or title under which the source is listed. Also note the page, section, paragraph or screen numbers, if given, in parentheses.)

Example: Explaining how language is always evolving, McWhorter compares it to a lava lamp, and notes that new versions of English words and phrases "should not be considered lazy or sloppy speech" (Smith, sec. 2).

MLA Style for Works Cited Lists

In this section, you will find explanations of how to use MLA formatting for your works cited lists for the most common types of sources that you will encounter in your classes. Keep in mind that you don't indent the first line of each entry; rather, you indent subsequent lines five spaces or one-half inch. Also, the entire list should be double-spaced and the sources listed alphabetically by the author's or editor's last names or the title of the work if there is not an author.

Books

1. **One author**

Tyson, Lois. *Critical Theory Today: A User-Friendly Guide.* New York: Routledge, 2006. Print.

2. Two or three authors

Thomas, Lee and Stephen Tchudi. *The English Language: An Owner's Manual.* Boston: Allyn and Bacon, 1999. Print.

3. Editor(s)

Brock, Bernard L., Robert L. Scott, and James W. Chesebro, Eds. *Methods of Rhetorical Criticism.* Detroit: Wayne State University Press, 1990. Print.

4. Anthology

Root, Robert L., Jr. and Michael Steinberg, eds. *The Fourth Genre: Contemporary Writers of/on Creative Nonfiction.* 3rd ed. New York: Pearson Longman, 2005. Print.

5. Work in an anthology or chapter in a book with an editor

Schwartz, Mimi. "My Father Always Said." *The Fourth Genre: Contemporary Writers of/on Creative Nonfiction.* Eds. Robert L. Root, Jr. and Michael Steinberg. 3rd ed. New York: Pearson Longman, 2005. 215–222. Print.

6. Entry in a reference work

"Abolitionist Movement." The Dorling Kindersley Children's Illustrated Encyclopedia. 2000 ed. Print.

7. Government publication

United States. Centers for Disease Control and Prevention. *State of the CDC: Protecting Health for Life.* Atlanta: CDC, 2004. Print.

Periodicals

8. Article in a journal paginated by volume (Follow the journal title with the volume number in Arabic numerals.)

Rhein, Henry and Abrams, Jake. "The Significance of Speech to Preschoolers." *Psychology* 16 (1980): 397–403. Print.

9. Article in a journal paginated by issue (If each issue begins with page 1, follow the volume number with a period and the issue number.)

Brooks, Barbara. "Grace Paley's Place in the Writing Sisterhood." *The Writer's Chronicle* 37.2 (2004): 17–23. Print.

10. Article in a weekly magazine

Reilly, Rick. "Old-timer's Game." *Sports Illustrated* 21 Feb. 2005: 82. Print.

11. Article in a newspaper

Paulson, Michael. "A Natural Devotion: Robert F. Kennedy Jr.'s Faith Inspired His Children's Book." I 15 Mar. 2005, C1+. Print.

12. Review (List reviewer's name and review title, then "Rev. of" and the title and author or director of the work reviewed. Add publication information for the periodical where the review appears.)

Haigh, Jennifer. "A Wicked Thirst." Rev. of *Paradise*, by A.L. Kennedy. *Boston Globe* Mar. 13 2005: D6. Print.

Electronic Sources

13. Article from an online database or subscription service (Follow the directions for a print article in a journal and then add at the end of the citation: title of the database you used; the medium of the publication (Web); and the date you accessed the source.)

Welch, Laine. "Disney characters soon to star on a dinner plate near you." *Alaska Journal of Commerce* 29.4 (2005): A4. ProQuest. Web. 17 Mar. 2005.

14. Work found on the Web only (List the author, title of work, title of the overall website italicized if different from the title of the work, version or edition used, publisher or sponsor of the website (if not available, write n.p.), date of publication (if not available, write n.d.), medium of publication (Web), date you accessed the site.)

Herszenhorn, David M. And Tamar Lewin. "Student Loan Overhaul Approved by Congress." *New York Times*. New York Times, 25 Mar. 2010. Web. 19 April 2010.

15. Work from a professional website (List the author, if available; document title; name of the website, underlined or italicized; date of publication or last update; name of organization associated with the site; name of editor, if applicable; access date; and URL.)

"What is MLA Style?" *mla.org*. Modern Language Association, 13 Jan. 2009. Web. 19 April 2010.

16. Work from personal website (Name the creator of the site, its title underlined or italicized; if there is no title, use a description, such as "Home page." Then list the date of the last update, access information, and the URL.)

Gessner, David. Home page. 8 Aug. 2009. Web. 15 March 2010.

APA Documentation

The APA designed a documentation format for scholars and researchers in the social sciences, which means people writing in the fields of psychology, sociology,

Useful Websites on MLA Format
Modern Language Association Website on Documenting Sources from the World Wide Web
http://www.mla.org/handbook_faq
The Purdue OWL [Online Writing Lab at Purdue]
http://owl.english.purdue.edu/owl/section/2/11/

anthropology, and others. If you are a social science major, you will take classes that require you to use APA documentation. With APA documentation formatting, you include in-text citations and a full listing of your sources in a reference list at the end of your paper.

APA Style for In-text Citations

1. **Author named in a signal phrase** (Put the author's name in the signal phrase, which introduces the cited material, followed by the date in parentheses. When a quotation is involved, put the page number, preceded by **p.**, in parentheses after the quote. For quotes that are set off and have more than 40 words, put the page reference in parentheses one space after the sentence and its final punctuation.)

Examples

Citing source while paraphrasing: Another consideration for educators attempting this kind of classroom setup, as Yee (1988) points out, is that while students can be evaluated on their production, they can't be graded on their cooperation—or lack thereof (p. 33).

Citing source while quoting directly from a text: As Blackmore (1999) explains, "memes spread themselves around indiscriminately without regard to whether they are useful, neutral, or positively harmful to us" (p. 7).

2. **Author named in a parenthetical reference** (When the author isn't noted in the signal phrase, put the author's name and the date, separated by a comma, in parentheses at the end of the cited material.)

Examples

Parenthetical reference while paraphrasing: Not only are the students account-able to themselves, but they also need to treat one another responsibly in the class-room, as well as act responsibly with the subject matter (Shrewsbury, 1998, p. 167).

Parenthetical reference when quoting directly from the text: However, the reality of the context of the university classroom is such that "there cannot really be any genuine equality between student and teacher" (Broughton and Potts, 2001, p. 378).

3. **Citing source when quoting directly from the text**

4. **Two authors** (Both names go in all citations, with **and** used in the signal phrase but the **ampersand** (&) used in parentheses.)

Examples

Millis and Cottell (1998) argue that "the power of cooperative learning lies in its ability to promote what is known as deep learning. Deep learning does not occur simply because students are placed in groups. It emerges from careful, sequenced assignments and activities "orchestrated" by a teacher committed to student learning" (p. 37).

Creating classroom activities that involve students in discussions, questioning, clarifying and writing about the subject matter enables them to retain the subject matter more effectively (Meyers & Jones, 1993, p. xii).

Three to five authors (All of the authors' names are listed in the first reference. In subsequent references, note only the first author's name with **et al.**)

Example

Golen, Powers, and Titkemeyer (1983) use Pearce's work to illustrate the need for studying ethics and to advocate for the use of basic ethical principles in the classroom.

5. **Website or web text** (To note an entire website, put the URL in parentheses in the text. Do not include it in your references list. To cite only a portion of web text, note the chapter or figure. Include page or paragraph numbers for a quotation.)

Example

New reports are showing that global warming is creating changes in the Arctic regions (www.msnbc.msn.com/id/21347288/).

APA Style for a List of References

In this section, you will find explanations for APA documentation for sources you will often encounter in your classes. Keep in mind that you don't indent the first line of each entry; rather, you indent subsequent lines five spaces or one-half inch. Also, the entire list should be double-spaced and the sources listed alphabetically by the author's or editor's last names.

Books

1. **One author**

Blackmore, S. (1999). *The Meme Machine.* Oxford: Oxford University Press.

2. **Two or more authors**

Kesselman, A., McNair, L.D., & Schniedewind, N. (2008). *Women, Images and Realities: A Multicultural Anthology.* Boston: McGraw Hill.

3. **Organization as author**

Committee on Kindergarten Readiness, Massachusetts Early Childhood Council. (2004). *Preparing Our Children for Learning.* Boston: Boston University Press.

4. Editor

Brock, B.L. (Ed.). (1999). *Kenneth Burke and the 21st Century*. Albany: State University of New York Press.

5. Selection in a book with an editor

Hoffman, J. (2006). "Why blended learning hasn't (yet) fulfilled its promises. In C.J. Bonk & C.R. Graham (Eds.), *The Handbook of Blended Learning: Global Perspectives, Local Designs* (pp. 27–40). San Francisco: Pfeiffer.

6. Article in a reference work

Doe, J. (2000). How the brain works. In *The Human Body Illustrated Encyclopedia* (pp. 10-14). Princeton, N.J.: Medical Press.

Periodicals

7. Article in a journal paginated by volume

Heidensohn, F. (1986). Models of justice: Portia or Persephone? Some thoughts on equality, fairness and gender in the field of criminal justice. *International Journal of the Sociology of Law, 14,* 287–308.

8. Article in a journal paginated by issue

Jackson, S. (1997). Crossing borders and changing pedagogies: from Giroux and Freire to feminist theories of education. *Gender & Education, 9*(4), 457–469.

9. Article in a newspaper

Paulson, M. (2005, March 15). A natural devotion: Robert F. Kennedy Jr.'s faith inspired his children's book. *The Boston Globe,* p. C1.

10. Review

Haigh, J. (2005, March 13). [Review of the book *Paradise* by A.L. Kennedy]. *The Boston Globe*, D6.

Electronic Sources

Keep in mind that at times Internet sources do not include all the information you seek, such as title and copyright pages. As a guideline, include all the information you can, in the proper order, as you would for a print source. We've provided several examples here.

11. Chapter or a section of a website (Note author's name first if available.)

A Guide to Residential Services for Persons with Mental Retardation or Developmental Disabilities. (2002). American Health Care Association. Retrieved March 17, 2005, from http://www.ahca.org/news/index.html

12. **Article from an online database** (When referencing an article from an online database, do so just as you would a print article. According to APA, you include the database information only if the article may be difficult to locate.)

Welch, L. (2005). Disney characters soon to star on a dinner plate near you. *Alaska Journal of Commerce, 29*(4), A4.

13. **Article from an online newspaper**

Kurkjian, S. (2005, March 13) Secrets behind the largest art theft in history. *The Boston Globe.* Retrieved from http://www.boston.com

Other sources

1. **Government document**

Centers for Disease Control and Prevention. (2004). *State of the CDC: Protecting Health for Life.* Atlanta: Centers for Disease Control and Prevention.

YOUR TURN: Creating Your Ideas

Now it's your turn to demonstrate your researching and documentation skills. Choose a topic that is currently controversial, such as censorship of music, global warming, media violence, adult literacy, or gun control. Research your topic. What are the opposing viewpoints? After reading about these viewpoints, what do *you* think and why? Once you've answered those questions, write an essay that relies on your research to make your argument.

Have more questions about APA Style?
Go to: http://apastyle.apa.org

TECH TALK: Formatting Your Works Cited Page

There are several types of documentation formats used in academic disciplines:

- Modern Language Association (MLA)
- American Psychological Association (APA)
- Chicago Style
- Council of Science Editors (CSE)

Each format has its own rules about how the citations should be formatted. At times, you need to underline or italicize titles. Also, the different formats require indentations of lines. You need to always know what format your instructor requires, and then you need to use your handbook to ensure that you are following the correct format.

At the same time, it's useful to know how to create automatic indentations for your works cited pages. To do this, you need to use the **ruler** tool in your word processing program, which is pictured below:

Notice how the margin marker on the left highlighted above. By pointing your cursor over that marker, you can move it. If you move the bottom part of the margin marker to .5, you will set up an automatic indenting system for all lines after your first in citation. The ruler should look like this:

Notice how the margin marker is positioned differently now. Due to this positioning, your text will do the following automatically for you:

Welch, Laine. "Disney characters soon to star on a dinner plate near you." *Alaska Journal of Commerce* 29.4 (2005): A4. <u>ProQuest</u>. Web. 17 Mar. 2005.

The ruler tool is a great time saver and helps you follow the documentation formats more easily. You can use this tool to format indented quotations in your text as well if you move the margin marker fully to the number 1 on the ruler like this:

Chapter 8

Visual Rhetoric and Oral Communication

Visual Rhetoric

*A*ere is a common cliché: "A picture is worth a thousand words." Do you agree? Did you learn from picture books when you were younger? Do you remember things that you see better than things that you hear? If you do, you are not alone.

Active engagement and membership in our rhetorical culture require you to be able to interpret visual messages, as well as to effectively compose such messages. Whether composing graphs, writing email, constructing web pages, or developing a newsletter, attention to the visual features of your message will enhance your credibility, emphasize your points, and engage your audience.

Throughout this book, we have used many examples of visual rhetoric. The Uncle Sam poster, the Pocasset Mill poster, and even the Nike symbol all convey messages through image, symbol, and space.

Think Visually

How is the image above worth a thousand words? What story does that image tell? Make a list of all of the information contained in those images. Describe how the information is presented.

Using visual images effectively means you have to consider some of the basic elements of visual literacy, learn how to use visual information to expand your message, and finally, think about ways to arrange your message for the greatest impact and to best convey a visual story. This chapter discusses some of the basics you should think about when constructing messages visually and when interpreting the world around you. In addition to the obvious types of messages like web pages and PowerPoint presentations, the chapter also discusses how you can structure your writing assignments visually in order to support your message in varying ways.

The photographs of Arthur Mole and John Thomas, presented here, offer some interesting examples of the visual representation of citizenship and patriotism. These men attempted to "recover the old image of national identity at the very moment when the United States entered the Great War in 1917," according to author Louis Kaplan in *A Patriotic Mole: A Living Photograph* (2001, p. 107).

Mole and Thomas designed photographs of national icons like the Liberty Bell, President Wilson, the flag, and Uncle Sam using thousands of military service personnel. The Liberty Bell incorporated 25,000 troops at Camp Dix, New Jersey, and the profile of President Wilson, titled "Sincerely Yours, Woodrow Wilson," required 21,000 troops at Camp Sherman, Chillicothe, Ohio.

Although these images are interesting because they are "alive" (in the sense of using real people choreographed carefully into the patriotic designs), they are particularly evocative and powerful because of the icons they portray, their historical context in

Library of Congress, Prints and Photographs, LC-USZ62-70909
Library of Congress, Prints and Photographs, LC-USZ62-77278

terms of the United States entering World War I, and because the soldiers destined to fight that war form the material of the image.

The Mole and Thomas photographs were used by the government to promote the war effort—a form of propaganda. Many of the photographs entered public circulation at the time because Mole made copies of the images for all of the participants. Because of the connection between the image, the need for national support, and the people in the photographs, these pictures can be considered powerful representations of ideology and presentations of messages of national unity and pride. These images also help explain the concept of and need for visual literacy.

Visual Literacy

Interestingly, human beings have been communicating visually since prehistoric times. Just think about the cave paintings that have been preserved through time. Thus, the twenty-first-century focus on visual literacy is less of a phenomenon than it seems. Twenty-first-century technologies permit you to seamlessly integrate visual elements and allow you to appeal to multiple senses. For your purposes, visual literacy is the basic ability to interpret and understand visual imagery message components. In today's media and image-rich culture, you are bombarded by imagery.

On a basic level, visual literacy means understanding the composition of an advertisement we see in a magazine or on the Web. It also means being able to navigate forms, web pages, and other carriers of information. Visual texts include, but are not limited to:

- Photographs
- Films
- Diagrams
- Flow charts
- Storyboards
- Timelines
- Tables and graphs
- Maps
- Road signs

Can you read a map? Draw a map? Create a graph or table? Decipher a graph? If you can, you have many of the skills of visual literacy, whether you know it or not.

What information do you read in the following visual texts?

Image © Cloudia Newland, 2010. Used under license from Shutterstock, Inc.

Image © Tom Grundy, 2010. Used under license from Shutterstock, Inc.

Image © Vaju Ariel, 2010. Used under license from Shutterstock, Inc.

Even the graph pictured here tells us a story—in this case, a story about how different fertilizers have contributed to bean plant growth. Who would benefit from using this image? Who might be affected by the image? As with your writings, you need to consider an image's situation, purpose, and audience.

Images give you information. Some of the information will keep you safe (as in telling you when or where to cross the street or where not to drive). Other information visually represents facts. Information, in turn, helps you organize your world. Whether you notice a large group of people wearing the same T-shirt and infer that they're on a tour together, decide to buy the car you see advertised most frequently on billboards around your city, make your way around popular destinations like Walt Disney World, learn about political candidates from their campaign posters, or decide to fertilize your beans with a specific type of fertilizer, the visual messages you consume on a daily basis form an important part of your learning and your decision making.

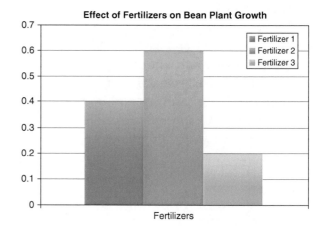

Have you ever played the game "Pictionary?" Pictionary is a game that requires players to draw messages, hoping that their team members will guess the message correctly and opponents will fail. It is similar to the age-old parlor game charades, which requires players to physically act out their messages with the same goals. These games both highlight the difficulties of visual communication. For example, how would you **draw** this sentence?

It was a dark and stormy night.

That would be a difficult task, wouldn't it? Luckily, we are more interested here in the combination of words and images in order to accomplish the goals of enhancing, clarifying, and improving our messages.

Because visual images are so important to what we know and how we operate in the world, it makes sense that you, as a citizen writer, should be aware of what makes a strong visual message. At the same time that you need to practice and perfect how you use language, you also need to practice your use of symbols and images.

Making Your Argument with Visual Information

Scenario: Julia is studying to be an architect. In order to complete her program, she must prepare a presentation of her final design project. Julia has designed a neighborhood child care center. Her presentation must target a variety of audiences in order to get her message across clearly: neighborhood parents, her professors, fellow students, and city officials who (in the "real world") would provide funding for the project. Julia's principal challenge is to condense her project into a presentation of five visual images. What kinds of products might she prepare?

As a student of writing, you may be thinking that you don't have anything in common with Julia, our graduating architect. However, you will also be faced with the challenge of presenting information in highly condensed forms such as images, charts, graphs, and diagrams. You may be asked to do something seemingly simple, like give someone directions to the campus library or the local post office. The skills of process analysis that we discussed in Chapter 4 might come in handy here. However, if you fail to explain the directions clearly and step by step, or if that person does not understand your verbal directions, you may need to draw a map. When you save for a big purchase like a car or a house, keeping track of your expenses may make more sense to you in the form of a graph that demonstrates where your money tends to go over time. Being skilled and creative in the presentation of information visually will make your written work more productive, efficient, and effective. Here, you will consider some of the most common means of condensing and presenting information in visual forms.

Charts and Graphs

Charts, graphs, and diagrams organize related information in a visual form. Such visual representations are very common. For example, consider the two images on the right.

Image © pichayasri, 2010. Used under license from Shutterstock, Inc.

Image © pichayasri, 2010. Used under license from Shutterstock, Inc.

When you were learning to read, you saw charts of the alphabet or pictures representing letters, probably in your schoolbooks and in the books you read at home with your family. The two images here present information designed to help teach the English alphabet and its sounds. So, we see the letter, an image of something familiar, and the word for that image. What kind of lesson would this information require if you didn't have access to the visual imagery? It would be difficult and time-consuming to convey.

Similarly, if you have taken chemistry, you have learned from the chart or table of the periodic elements, which organizes all of the essential chemical components. You've learned the multiplication tables. All of these examples illustrate the usefulness of collecting information into visual forms.

As far as graphing information, you can create

- Bar graphs
- Line graphs
- Pie charts
- Scatter graphs
- Tree diagrams
- Bubble graphs
- Histograms
- Combination graphs

Graphs can help you describe trends, progressions, and comparisons. Using dots, blocks, and lines may allow you to provide such information effectively and more persuasively than writing several paragraphs or pages. You will find computer programs that will help you transform numerical information or data into your preferred type of graph.

Imagine you are writing a paper about the economy for an economics class. Your paper's argument is about how the loss of manufacturing jobs in the United States is affecting the working class. To support your claim that manufacturing jobs are falling in number, you might consider adding a chart that visualizes the job loss, as pictured below:

"Overview: The Economy—Charts." *About.com*. 2010. Web. 10 March 2010.

This chart makes the job losses very real for your audience, as it illustrates the dip in manufacturing employment since the year 2000. However, remember that whatever graph you choose to use, you need to make sure you have considered how the graph helps you make your point to your audience. An effective writer knows when to add visual elements to his or her rhetorical acts depending on an analysis of the situation, purpose, and audience. Most importantly, an effective writer realizes that visual information helps you to reinforce and clarify our message, to gain and hold your audience's attention, and often to increase the effectiveness of our message. Clearly, visual information contains a great deal of rhetorical power.

Using Visual Information:
What kinds of visual information can you think of that might help you represent your campus community to high school students trying to decide where to attend college?

- **Images reinforce and clarify the message.**
  - Visual information plays an important role in reinforcing and clarifying messages. For example, the construction of an outline allows you to visually

---

Data from U.S. Bureau of Labor Statistics.

demonstrate the relationship between your ideas, supporting information, and subpoints. Thus, an outline can function as a form of visual information.

- Visual information is additionally useful when you use symbols or emblems to substitute for words. For example, a cookbook is much more interesting and easy to follow if you have pictures of what the recipe is supposed to look like when it is complete or what features a particular ingredient might have.

- Political campaign posters in the United States have much more of an impact on the public when they include symbols of patriotism or a political party, like an image of the flag, stars or stripes, or the colors red, white, and blue.

- A written report on an important issue in your community will contain more information if you subsidize your words with graphs, tables, pictures, and other visual representations.

- You can even think of how you present your work as a form of visual information. For example, your organization of a writing assignment also helps clarify your message. Imagine if you wrote a research paper and did not break it into paragraphs or sections. Imagine not using punctuation like commas or periods. The impact of your message would be very different.

- **Images help gain and hold the audience's attention.**

  - Visual images attract people's attention and give them something to focus on. Imagine that you want to write a compelling essay about your grandmother's garden. In addition to using vividly evocative language to paint a picture, including photographs or line drawings of flowers will draw your readers' attention to your work and help them to visualize the garden.

  - Creating posters or transparency slides to complement an oral presentation helps maintain the audience's attention, too. For example, if you are campaigning for a position in your student government on campus, or for a position on your local school board, there are many imaginative ways to incorporate visuals into a public presentation. You might show

Image © Hannamariah, 2010. Used under license from Shutterstock, Inc.

slides of campus or community problems you want to fix. You might project a picture of you with your family. You might simply provide a simple list of the reasons people should vote for you, revealing each reason visually as you emphasize that reason orally.

- Using visual elements like color or font changes and spacing on a page will draw the eye to your message, helping your audience attend to your message and remember it. You will learn more about these strategies in more detail later in the chapter.

- **Images increase the effectiveness of your message.**
  - Similar to adding clarity to your message, visual images can boost your effectiveness by being more comprehensive. For example, as noted earlier in this chapter, you can provide additional information with charts or graphs, helping your audience understand and believe your message more deeply.
  - Pictures often bring added pathos or emotion to a message, increasing its persuasiveness. Images and symbols can also add logos by providing evidence and further information, as well as ethos by enhancing the credibility of the author or rhetor. Imagine if the only information we received about Hurricane Katrina or 9/11 was through verbal reports or news stories. Then, think about the images that may have stayed with you of one of those events—the photographs, video accounts, and firsthand stories recorded in the moment. You didn't have to be present in New Orleans or New York in order to be swept into the stories because of the images.
  - Our retention of images from long ago is also a function of visual information. People, in general, are better able to recall or remember information that is reinforced visually. According to Cindy Griffin's book *Invitation to Public Speaking* (2008), studies have shown that when speeches do not include visual aids, an audience may hold onto 70 percent of the content after three hours; however, this recall rate decreases to 10 percent after three days. If a person uses visual aids only to present information, the recall rate increases significantly, as the audience remembers 72 percent of the content after three hours and 35 percent of the presentation after three days. And when a person uses both speech and visual aids, audience retention of information is even higher, as they remember 85 percent of the content after three hours and 65 percent after three days.

From that research, it is obvious that adding visual elements to your message will help your audience remember it. What kind of information do you tend to remember? Do you remember lectures in which the teacher simply talks to you (or at you!)? Do you remember most of what you read when it is straight text, only words? Most people benefit from some kind of visual reinforcement to help them remember information.

Visual Strategies

Many strategies exist for visually enhancing messages, such as the use of:

- Color
- Space
- Fonts
- Animation
- Content

You will be able to apply these strategies to just about any visual format you choose, whether you are using PowerPoint, posters, charts and graphs, or diagrams. There are some guidelines to consider when you use begin to explore, practice, and hone your visual communication skills.

Color

Color is key to effectively representing a visual message. You have probably heard that restaurants—especially fast food restaurants—design their space in bright, perky colors in order to stimulate appetite (red), engage children (orange), and generally keep the energy of the place high. Most fast food chains avoid cool colors like blue. Blue tends to be a relaxing, easy-on-the-eye kind of color. Fast food places do not want people hanging around for long periods of time, as their goal is to move customers in and quickly. A spa or therapist's office might be a better place for soothing colors.

As you know, color affects people's moods and how they are likely to react. Consequently, if you want to use color to communicate, it is important that you think various aspects of your message. For example:

- Who is your audience?
- What is the tone you want to set with your message?
- What is your purpose?
- What kind of energy do you wish to inspire in your audience?

Overall, it is probably good advice to say that you should avoid extremes of color—unless you have very good reasons for using them. For example, when composing PowerPoint slides, in most situations it will be better if you stay with a calm blue background instead of fancy patterns or blinking animations. Why? Simply because you want your information, your message to be what people focus on, not the background.

Consider these two slides. Which slide is more audience-friendly? Which slide is clearer for an audience to read?

Keep in mind that in addition to helping you set the mood for your message, the use of color can help keep your audience focused and directed. In other words, you can use color to show relationships and directions. Here's an example:

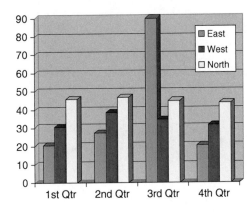

Notice how the colors indicate the differences between East, West, and North. The colors, in other words, show the relationship between the three categories in each quarter of the year.

Colors can emphasize lines on a graph, points on a diagram, or words on a poster or slide. Just remember that color should work with your use of space and content to emphasize, reinforce, and clarify your message.

Space

One of the most common mistakes made when designing visual messages is trying to include too much information. Whether it's putting together a transparency, writing a newsletter, making a poster, or designing a PowerPoint presentation, the writer must keep in mind that *space* helps your audience navigate your message, understand it, and remember your point. Crowding the presentational medium will not enhance your effectiveness. Look at the following two slides, for example:

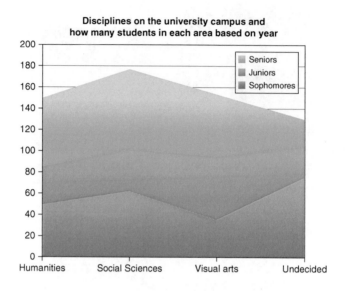

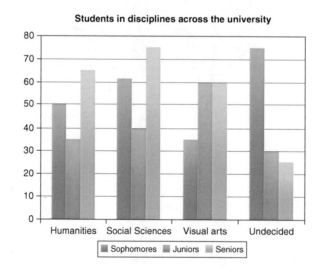

The second slide is easier to read. Why? First, the title contains fewer words and uses a larger font. This makes it easier to understand what you are supposed to see on the slide. In addition, the graphic itself is clearer, with delineated bars identifying the data and titles that are formatted properly and are thus simpler for a viewer to read. Overall, the viewer does not have to struggle to decipher the graph.

Writer Citizen

The first slide is not as **informational** as the second slide because the graphic is difficult to decipher and the titles are not well formatted; in addition, the title of the slide is in a font that is very small and not as direct in communicating what the slide is all about. When you are conveying a message, whether visually or with words, it is important to be sure you are doing so in the most productive manner possible. If your audience does not understand what you are conveying, your opportunity has been lost.

The lesson here is that you will sometimes have to forego the chance to use "interesting" visuals—whether colors, fonts, or images—in order to provide the information or overall message that you want your audience to receive.

Fonts

Note the fonts used in the slides above. The advantages of basic fonts are that they are easy to see, they are easy to read, and they don't distract from the message. Even if you're making up an invitation for a Halloween party, you don't want to use fonts that people can't read! How can they come to your party and be scared witless!? Compare the invitations on the right.

The first one is interesting, right? The second one is a little, well, boring. But the information presented is clearer for a viewer. There are a couple of strategies that could make the top invitation a little more consistent. First, you might want to just use one font and make sure that, although it keeps its interest and energy, your party-goers will be able to read it.

Are the "rules" for party invitations the same as for newsletters or PowerPoint slides? Probably not. Depending on your audience and your purpose, the party invitations may enjoy a lot more flexibility in terms of playfulness. When you're promoting something more serious than a Halloween party, some general rules of font use apply:

- Make sure your font is readable for the audience.
  - "Fancy" fonts like Black Adder are going to be difficult to read, particularly if you're projecting a PowerPoint slide, using it on a website, or including it in a newsletter. As an accent, a fancy or complicated font may provide visual interest, but it will not help your message overall.

- *Sans serif* fonts such as **Arial** work better than serif fonts on a projected image. *Serif* fonts, such as **Times Roman**, have thin lines that are harder to read across a distance.
- Be sure to size the font according to your medium.
  - A great general rule if your message is in a poster form is to tape it to the wall, step back eight feet, and determine how readable the poster is at a distance.
  - Use larger size fonts for titles and headings.
  - When projecting slides, your title font size should be about 44 points tall. Body text should be about 32 points.

Animation

Technology means that we have access to programs that make animations easy. When preparing PowerPoint slides, almost everyone has been tempted to use the animation features like flying text, rolling text, and checkerboards. Animated clip art is also fun for web pages. Though entertaining to play with and sometimes entertaining to watch, animations run the risk of detracting from your effective messages.

When tempted to include animated features, ask yourself what they bring to the message. If the features "look cool," add interest, or are just fun, you are probably better off focusing on effective design, word choice, and the overall structure of your message.

This is not to say, though, that just because you *can* use visual elements, that you *should* go crazy with them. Fun as it may be to play with font and color changes, too much of a good thing can be distracting. And, if you distract your audience visually, you run the risk of turning them off, confusing them, and ultimately losing your opportunity to share your message. You also may be turning off your viewers who cannot see variations in colors effectively.

Making Your Arguments Orally

Today's media-rich world means that it's increasingly common to receive audio messages through media such as podcasts sent via RSS feeds. Teachers are making use of audio recordings in classrooms and are even asking students to create oral presentations for a class website or for distribution over a class RSS feed where you share information and assignments with classmates. For example, last year Professor Houser (one of the writers of this textbook) taught a class titled "Women, Writing, and the Media." As one of the course projects, students learned about podcasting and then created their own podcasts on famous women in history. These audio files were then posted to the university website and shared with the campus community during women's history month. So, not only did the class learn how to use a new form of technology and about women's contributions to history, but they also used their assignments to educate their peers on campus.

Podcasts or audio messages recorded in MP3 formats or Flash formats require us to understand the elements of public speaking. After all, an audio presentation is calling upon your ability to communicate verbally with an audience, which is very different from communicating with them in writing. When writing, we have more space and time to explain our points; in addition, as discussed in this chapter, you have the ability to add visual information to support your arguments.

When speaking orally or creating a podcast, the following strategies are useful:

- **Take time to organize and prepare**.

Know what you want to say. What do you want your audience to know or believe when you're done speaking to them? Just as when considering what your next essay is going to be about, you need to consider your audience. Who are they? What do they know about your topic?

Then, decide on your goal for your public communication event. Perhaps you want to create a public service announcement, also known as a PSA. Or perhaps you need to demonstrate for a class your public speaking skills and ability to persuade an audience verbally. Knowing your goal is very important for it determine how you will:

- Talk to your audience (the kinds of language you'll choose)
- "Frame" your speech
- Select the types of examples and evidence you need
- Present yourself (how much emotion do you allow, what is your "persona")

- Finally, make an outline. Organize your thoughts so they make sense to you and your audience. Here's an example of what an outline might look like:

I. Introduction
   A. Response to welcome or give a greeting
   B. Opening (use one)
      1. Personal anecdote
      2. Startling statement or fact
      3. Appropriate quotation, poem, story
   C. Preview or purpose of what you plan to tell them
II. Body
   A. Main point no. 1 (past, present, future)
      1. Support material (story, incidents, exhibits, demonstrations, experiences, expert testimony or quotation)
      2. Support material

B. Main point no. 2 (problems, damage, solution)
      1. Support material (use at least two support statements or proofs for each point)
      2. Support material
   C. Main point no. 3 (cause, effect, action)
      1. Support material
      2. Support material
III. Conclusion
   A. Summary of points one by one
   B. Quotation, story, or poem that summarizes the importance of what you had to say
   C. Call for action or memorable closing line. **Do not end with "That's it."**

- **Practice.**

Practicing what you are going to say can help you relax and become comfortable with your presentation. In addition, you don't want your podcast to sound stilted or as if you are reading verbatim from a piece of paper. You need to talk in a way that engages your audience and that keeps them interested in what you are saying.

A Brief Review

Many times during your academic career, you will be asked to produce information that requires visualization and visual representation of information. For example, you may be asked to create a writing portfolio online. Your portfolio, in many ways, would be a visual representation of your academic career. How you organize and exemplify the required information says a great deal about what you have learned, as well as how you see yourself and want others to see you.

You will also often encounter the opportunity to include visual information in many forms of communication in everyday life, whether in the form of a map to your town hall, an invitation to a "meet the candidate" gathering, or a pamphlet informing new voters of the issues on the ballot. Your choices of symbols, fonts, colors, and usage of space will influence the success of your message and may, in fact, have a profound affect on your community.

Finally, as the world becomes more and more adept at using technology, you will find yourself creating audio files and sending MP3 files to friends and co-workers. Imagine working on a project and instead of typing an e-mail, you simply record a voice message and send it via e-mail to your colleague. Also, at times, you may find yourself creating presentations that are located on the Web for access by the entire world. For example, you could be responsible for setting up a Flash presentation that outlines how your company is a "green" workplace. This presentation is meant to showcase to the public the company's concern about the environment, and it's your job to present that message. Your audio file needs to consider the strategies we have outlined about length, clarity, and organization.

"On Photography"

Susan Sontag (1933-2004) was an American writer, filmmaker, and human rights activist. Her works include four novels, a collection of short stories, several works of non-fiction, and four feature-length films. During her lifetime, she received the National Book Award, the National Book Critics Circle Award, the 2003 Peace Prize of the German Book Trade, and more.

Prereading: What role does photography play in your life? Why do you take pictures? Why do you send pictures to your friends and family?

Recently, photography has become almost as widely practiced an amusement as sex and dancing—which means that, like every mass art form, photography is not practiced by most people as an art. It is mainly a social rite, a defense against anxiety, and a tool of power.

Memorializing the achievements of individuals considered as members of families (as well as of other groups) is the earliest popular use of photography. For at least a century, the wedding photograph has been as much a part of the ceremony as the prescribed verbal formulas. Cameras go with family life. According to a sociological study done in France, most households have a camera, but a household with children is twice as likely to have at least one camera as a household in which there are no children. Not to take pictures of one's children, particularly when they are small, is a sign of parental indifference, just as not turning up for one's graduation picture is a gesture of adolescent rebellion.

Through photographs, each family constructs a portrait-chronicle of itself—a portable kit of images that bears witness to its connectedness. It hardly matters what activities are photographed so long as photographs get taken and are cherished. Photography becomes a rite of family life just when, in the industrializing countries of Europe and America, the very institution of the family starts undergoing radical surgery. As that claustrophobic unit, the nuclear family, was being carved out of a much larger family aggregate, photography came along to memorialize, to restate symbolically, the imperiled continuity and vanishing extendedness of family life. Those ghostly traces, photographs, supply the token presence of the dispersed relatives. A family's photograph album is generally about the extended family—and, often, is all that remains of it.

As photographs give people an imaginary possession of a past that is unreal, they also help people to take possession of space in which they are insecure. Thus, photography develops in tandem with one of the most characteristic of modern activities: tourism. For the first time in history, large numbers of people regularly travel out of their habitual environments for short periods of time. It seems positively unnatural to travel for pleasure without taking a camera along. Photographs will offer indisputable evidence that the trip was made, that the program was carried out, that fun was had. Photographs document sequences of consumption carried on outside the view of family, friends, neighbors. But dependence on the camera, as the device that makes real what one is experiencing, doesn't fade when people travel more. Taking photographs fills the same need for the cosmopolitans accumulating photograph-trophies of their boat trip up the Albert Nile or their fourteen days in China as it does for lower-middle-class vacationers taking snapshots of the Eiffel Tower or Niagara Falls.

A way of certifying experience, taking photographs is also a way of refusing it—by limiting experience to a search for the photogenic, by converting experience into an image, a souvenir. Travel becomes a strategy for accumulating photographs. The very activity of taking pictures is soothing, and assuages general feelings of disorientation that are likely to be exacerbated by travel. Most tourists feel compelled to put the camera between themselves and whatever is remarkable that they encounter. Unsure of other responses, they take a picture. This gives shape to experience: Stop, take a photograph, and move on. The method especially appeals to people handicapped by a ruthless work ethic—Germans, Japanese, and Americans. Using a camera appeases the anxiety which the work-driven feel about not working when they are on vacation and supposed to be having fun. The have something to do that is like a friendly imitation of work: They can take pictures.

People robbed of their past seem to make the most fervent pictures-takers, at home and abroad. Everyone who lives in an industrialized society is obliged gradually to give up the past, but in certain countries, such as the United States and Japan, the break with the past has been particularly traumatic. In the early 1970s, the fable of the brash American tourist of the 1950s, and 1960s, rich with dollars and Babbittry[1], was replaced by the mystery of the group-minded Japanese tourist, newly released from his island prison by the miracle of overvalued yen, who is generally armed with two cameras, one on each hip.

Photography has become one of the principal devices for experiencing something, for giving an appearance of participation. One full-page ad shows a small group of people standing pressed together, peering out of the photograph, all but one looking stunned, excited, upset. The one who wears a different expression holds a camera to his eye; he seems self-possessed, is almost smiling. While the others are passive, clearly alarmed spectators, having a camera has transformed one person into something active, a voyeur: Only he has mastered the situation. What do these people see? We don't know. And it

---

[1]Babbittry is a term, based on Sinclair Lewis's novel *Babbit* (1925), for Americans who define themselves by ready-made products and opinions. [ed.]

doesn't matter. It is an Event: something worth seeing—and therefore worth photographing. The ad copy, white letters across the dark lower third of the photograph like news coming over a teletype machine, consists of just six words: "… Prague … Woodstock … Vietnam … Sapporo … Londonderry … LEICA." Crushed hopes, youth antics, colonial wars, and winter sports are alike—are equalized by the camera. Taking photographs has set up a chronic voyeuristic relation to the world which levels the meaning of all events.

A photograph is not just the result of an encounter between an event and a photographer; picture-taking is an event in itself, and one with ever more peremptory rights—to interfere with, to invade, or to ignore whatever is going one. Our very sense of situation is now articulated by the camera's interventions. The omnipresence of cameras persuasively suggests that time consists of interesting events, events worth photographing. This, in turn, makes it easy to feel that any event, once under way, and whatever its moral character, should be allowed to complete itself—so that something else can be brought into the world, the photograph. After the event has ended, the picture will still exist, conferring on the event a kind of immortality (and importance) it would never otherwise have enjoyed. While real people are out there killing themselves or other real people, the photographer stays behind his or her camera, creating a tiny element of another world: the image-world that bids to outlast us all.

Photographing is essentially an act of nonintervention. Part of the horror of such memorable coups of contemporary photojournalism as the pictures of a Vietnamese bonze[2] reaching for the gasoline can, of a Bengali guerrilla in the act of bayoneting a trussed-up collaborator, comes from the awareness of how plausible it has become, in situations where the photographer has the choice between a photograph and a life, to choose the photograph. The person who intervenes cannot record; the person who is recording cannot intervene. Dziga Vertov's great film, *Man with a Movie Camera* (1929), gives the ideal image of the photographer as someone in perpetual movement, someone moving through a panorama of disparate events with such agility and speed that any intervention is out of the question. Hitchcock's *Rear Window* (1954) gives the complementary image: The photographer played by James Stewart has an intensified relation to one event, through his camera, precisely because he has a broken leg and is confined to a wheelchair; being temporarily immobilized prevents him from acting on what he sees, and makes it even more important to take pictures. Even if incompatible with intervention in a physical sense, using a camera is still a form of participation. Although the camera is an observation station, the act of photographing is more than passive observing. Like sexual voyeurism, it is a way of at least tacitly, often explicitly, encouraging whatever is going on to keep on happening. To take a picture is to have an interest in things as they are, in the status quo remaining unchanged (at least for as long as it takes to get a "good" picture), to be in complicity with whatever makes

---

[2]A *bonze* is a Buddhist monk.

a subject interesting, worth photographing—including, when that is the interest, another person's pain or misfortune. 🐟

Comprehending the Text:

1. What does Sontag say about one's relationship to the past and the need to take photographs?

2. What does Sontag mean by saying "Photography is essentially an act of nonintervention"?

3. According to Sontag, how does taking photographs change how one experiences travel?

Analyzing the Text:

1. What is Sontag's argument? Are you persuaded by her argument? Why or why not?

2. Sontag writes about the role of photography in weddings, travel, and tragedies. What kind of appeal is she making to her audience?

3. Research how the Navajo Indians feel about photography and compare those ideas to Sontag's argument in this essay.

"Border Town"

Reynaldo Leal. Leal is a photographer who was born and raised in Texas. He is the son of Mexican immigrants and a corporal in the United States Marine Corps.

Hooded Child, Las Flores, Mexico, 2002.

Prereading: In venturing to new places, whether foreign countries or simply places outside of your community, do you take photographs? Why?

Since the moment a foreign foot first touched American soil, there has been a constant inward flow of immigrants; each for their own reason but most to escape hardships and oppressions and to search for a better way of life. All have made their indelible imprint and unique contributions to the American way of life. How today's Americans so quickly forget that they are the children of those who journeyed, endured and sacrificed to remake themselves as Americans. For some it was two hundred years ago, while for others it was just yesterday. The question remains: what are the criteria to be considered American?

As a first-generation American, the son of Mexican immigrants, the sacrifices my parents endured to come to this country are at the forefront of my mind. Their intention was not to take from or be a burden to society but simply to escape hopelessness and provide their children a fighting chance to flourish and grow as Americans.

"Jente de la Calle," a series I began before I joined the Marine Corps in 2004, are photos of those who live and work on the streets of Las Flores, Mexico. But as the issue of illegal immigration grew in importance, I decided to extend my portrayal to border towns stretching from Tijuana to Matamoros, and that is how "Border Town" was born. For the selection here, I have chosen to focus particularly on the lives of children. Ultimately, my goal is to produce images of who these "aliens" really are; not just faceless demons but humans whose daily struggle takes place just south of a man-made line. ⟿

Antonio, 2007. Antonio, a young boy living in the Casas de Carton (a village outside Tijuana, where the houses are literally made from cardboard). He is a regular at the weekly donation site in the village. During the week he works on the streets of Tijuana to bring in some money for his family; he does not go to school.

The Border, 2007. The child of a volunteer stands inside the gates of the church that weekly gives donations to the community called Casas de Carton, while the other children stand outside waiting to be let in. This gate is just another border waiting to be crossed in Tijuana.

Bridge over Troubled Waters, 2007. The inhabitants of Casas de Carton have constructed bridges with whatever materials they can find to cross a river of human waste.

Comprehending the Text

1. In his introduction, Leal notes his history as part of an immigrant family. What do you think his message is in these photographs?

2. What story can you tell just by looking at these photographs, without the information in the cutlines?

3. What do all of these photographs all have in common?

Analyzing the Text

1. Describe what is different about the night shot from all of the other photos. Why is this shot a part of this photo narrative?

2. Compare and contrast the first two images—the boy behind bars and the blonde child.

3. Why do these photos of children depict adult activities?

"Vivian, Fort Barnwell"

Ethan Canin (b. 1960). American author, physician, and educator. Canin has published four novels and short story collections, along with articles in *Atlantic Monthly, Esquire, The New Yorker*, and *Granta*.

Prereading: What do you think is more reliable, your memory of a moment or a photograph of that same moment?

I tell my wife, I'll always remember this photograph of my mother. She's out in back, hanging the blankets to dry on our backyard lines after one of our picnics, and she looks so young, the way I remember her before we moved to California. I was ten, I think. We used to have picnics out there under the water tower when my father got home from work, out in back on the grass on a set of big gray movers' blankets. My father and the man next door had built a pool from a truck tire set in concrete, and they filled it with water for my brother and me to splash in. I remember the day this picture was taken, because my mother had to hang the blankets to dry after we'd soaked them from the pool, my father was mad but she wasn't. She was never mad at us. I haven't seen that picture in years, I tell my wife. But I remember it.

And then one day, for no reason I can fathom, my wife is looking through the old cardboard-sided valise where my mother had kept her pictures, and she says, Here? Is this the one you're always talking about? And I say, Yes, I can't believe you found it. And she says. Those aren't movers' blankets, those are some kind of leaves up in the foreground.

They look like something tropical, maybe rubber leaves. She's not hanging laundry at all. I say, Wait a minute—let me see. And I laugh and say, You're right. How can that be? My whole life I've remembered that picture of her hanging those blankets after we'd soaked them. I can even remember the picnic. She says, That's funny, isn't it? I say, My mother was so beautiful.

Our own children are out back in our own yard. It's too cool here for a pool, but I've built them a swing set from redwood, and I take a look out the window at them climbing it the way I've told them not to.

And then a few minutes later my wife says, Look at this, and she hands me the picture again, turned over. On the back it says, Vivian, Fort Barnwell, 1931. That's not your mother at all, she says. That's your grandmother. I say, Let me see that. I say, My God, you're right. How could that have happened? ❧

Comprehending the Text

1. What is Canin's point in this brief essay?

2. What does he tell us about his father and why is that important to the story?

3. What is Canin saying about the value of memory vs. the value of an old photograph?

Analyzing the Text

1. Why does he tell us about his children?

2. How would this essay be different with the photograph included? How would seeing the actual photograph change your understanding of the essay?

3. The essay is called, "Vivian, Fort Barnwell," yet it is not about her at all. Why does Canin give the essay that title?

YOUR TURN: Analyzing Images

1. Below are the bumper stickers for the leading presidential candidates in the 2008 race for the presidency. Now that we've discussed different strategies for visual images, look at each image individually and write down a brief descriptive series of words that come to your mind when looking at them.

Image © John Henkel, 2010. Used under license from Shutterstock, Inc.

Image © John Henkel, 2010. Used under license from Shutterstock, Inc.

Try not to react from a political point of view, but instead jot down what the *visual rhetoric* of the image evokes. Look at the fonts, the use of color, the use of first name vs. last name, the movement in the image or the lack thereof. What feelings are the colors and fonts and layout—the visual rhetoric—trying to evoke in the viewer? Write an essay that argues for the most effective image. Which one works most effectively and why?

2. By the mid-1920s, smoking had become commonplace in the United States and cigarette tobacco was the most popular form of tobacco consumption. At the same time, women had just won the right to vote, widows were succeeding their husbands as governors of such states as Texas and Wyoming, and more were attending college and entering the workforce. Although women seemed to be making great strides in certain areas, socially they still were not able to achieve the same equality as their male counterparts. Women were permitted to smoke only in the privacy of their own homes. Public opinion and certain legislation at the time did not permit women to smoke in public, and in 1922 a woman from New York City was arrested for lighting a cigarette on the street.

Mrs. Taylor-Scott Hardin parades down New York's Fifth Avenue with her husband while smoking "torches of freedom," a gesture of protest for absolute equality with men.

Cigarette sales would soar if [they] could entice women to smoke in public.

Photos courtesy of prmuseum.com.

George Washington Hill, president of the American Tobacco Company and an eccentric businessman, recognized that an important part of his market was not being tapped into. Hill believed that cigarette sales would soar if he could entice more women to smoke in public. In 1928 Hill hired Edward Bernays, an early pioneer of public relations, to expand the sales of his Lucky Strike cigarettes. Recognizing that women were still riding high on the suffrage movement, Bernays used this as the basis for his new campaign. He consulted Dr. A. A. Brill, a psychoanalyst, to find the psychological basis for women's smoking. Dr. Brill determined that cigarettes, which were usually equated with men, represented torches of freedom for women. The event caused a national stir and stories appeared in newspapers throughout the country. Though not doing away with the taboo completely, Bernays's efforts had a lasting effect on women smoking.

Consider your current environment and the persuasive messages you've been subjected to throughout your life. Can you give examples of this same sort of visual persuasion used to change the attitude of the people across the country? Does your campus put a wrecked car in front of the campus to make the point about drunken driving? Can you recall the visuals used in anti-drug campaigns? How effective are these visuals in persuading you? Is there an issue you feel strongly about and would like to changes other people's attitude about? Write a brief essay incorporating images to persuade your audience of your views and get them to change their behavior.

3. After reading Leal's photo essay "Border Town," create your own photo essay. Your essay should, like Leal's, engage your audience in a current cultural or political issue. It could be a local issue for your community, or it could be a national or global issue. Your goal is to create an essay that presents an argument to your audience about your chosen issue.

4. Pick a favorite photograph. Following the example set by Ethan Canin in "Vivian, Fort Barnwell," tell the story of the photo. You will need to rely on your powers of description and exposition here, as well as narration. You may want to review these writing strategies before embarking on your writing.

TECH TALK: Inserting Images and Creating Audio Files

Inserting Images

How do you add images to your papers? First, you need to locate images that you want to use or to create your own charts (you can use the Microsoft Excel program to do this work). When you locate an image, if you are copying it from the Internet, you need to make sure to cite your source, just as you would a quote you take from an article or

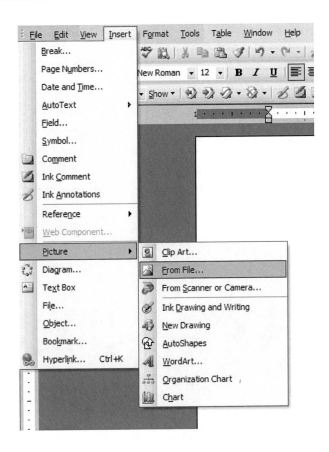

book. It's also important to know when you can use an image and when you cannot. For example, the Library of Congress offers many images for free use without copyright restrictions.

Once you have your image downloaded, you need to insert the image into your paper. To do so in a Microsoft program, click Insert > Picture > From File, as illustrated.

Position the image on the page by clicking on it and dragging it with your mouse.

Creating Audio

Believe it or not, creating an audio file in WAV or MP3 format is easier than it seems, especially if you go to the Internet and download a free open source program called Audacity (http://audacity.sourceforge.net). Audacity is a free program that enables you to record and edit sounds.

First, you need to purchase a microphone. Microphones that look like headsets can be found at office and electronics stores. You can purchase a good one for under $20 these days.

Next, you need to download Audacity and install it on your computer. Once you've installed the program, open it. You will see the following:

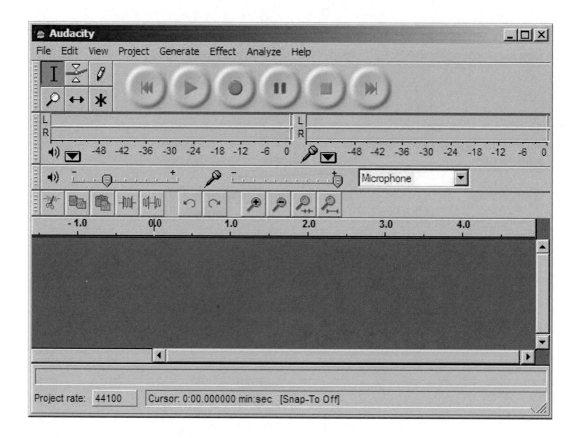

This program is relatively simple to use; it mimics a tape recording machine or the buttons on a CD player.

REWIND PLAY RECORD PAUSE STOP FORWARD

Plug your microphone into your computer and get to work. Once you've recorded your presentation, save the file as an MP3 or WAV file. This way, the audio file can easily be opened using the Windows Media Player, Real Player, or QuickTime. You save the file by exporting it as illustrated:

Writer Citizen

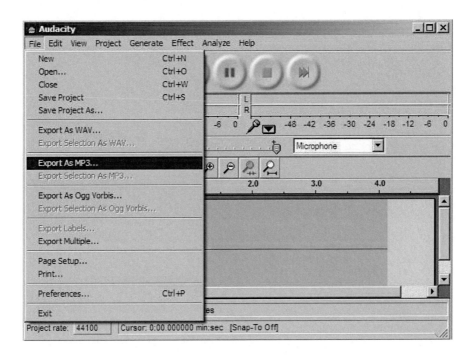

A "save" box will open, prompting you to label your file and click Save. The audio file is now ready for use. You can send it someone via e-mail, post it to your class website, or even download it to your MP3 player.

Chapter 9

The Art of Revision

*S*ome writers view revision as they do exercise; resisting it even though they know it's good for them. Their deliverance from the struggle within lies in the simple phrase, "Just do it!" because eventually all careful thinkers and true writers must embrace the opportunity to rewrite. Once a writer sees his or her work take shape to powerfully and effectively deliver the message, then he or she will understand what the seasoned writer knows: successful writing lies in rewriting. As noted in the opening chapters, writing is a recursive process—a process that repeats itself—so you have to go back to the beginning and work through the writing process again to see where and how you can improve your writing and the finished product.

In this chapter, you will learn about the act of revision as an inherent part of the process that includes strategies for content revision and sentence revision. You will also discover how you can learn to evaluate your own writing as you seek to improve your drafts to create finely tuned final products. Finally, you will explore how you can work with your peers to engage in the revision process. Getting feedback from others is always a useful revision strategy; after all, writing is all about how the audience receives your message.

Why Revise?

It is a very rare writer who can stop writing after the first draft and submit their work. If your goal is effective communication, you will need to think through what you have written and evaluate its success, regardless of the form in which you are writing. All good writers take time to review what they've written and find ways to improve it. This process is called **revision**, or better yet, **re-vision**: the act of re-visioning and re-seeing your written work, from the first word forward. Revision is actually a fairly straightforward process.

Here are some strategies for reconsidering your rhetorical decisions.

Create Distance

When revising your writing, you want to set aside what you think you know about your essay, and remove the defenses that will prevent you from really seeing it. Ideally, you should try to meet your work as you would someone you don't know—without preconceptions. To do this, you must create as much distance as possible between yourself and your work. Distance allows you to see your essay as others would. It allows for objectivity, which you need to evaluate your essay's effectiveness.

The passage of time can help you establish that distance. If you put your draft away for a week or two or three and then read it, you'll see its flaws and miscommunications far more clearly than you can immediately upon its completion. Sometimes, impatience and/or deadlines make waiting to revise your work unfeasible or undesirable. If that's the case, the next best thing to your own objectivity is an outside reader—someone who is a stranger to your essay. But before you take that first bold step of exposure, revise your work as best as you can. Try to step back from your essay to scrutinize it and ask yourself, "What's wrong with this picture?" Several strategies can help you understand and evaluate your work with an eye to its improvement.

Reconsider Your Situation

Review the situation to which your work is responding. For example, in Chapter 1 we imagined that your state legislature had determined that high school sports are too expensive. They decided that all high school sport programs should be eliminated. You decided to write an essay in response to this situation in an effort to reinstate school sport programs. So your essay should be guided by your desire to create change in the state legislative policy. You should also take time to review the *occasion* for your writing. In-class writing assignments look for you to express yourself clearly and quickly; out-of-class assignments look for more detail, more explanation, and fewer mechanical errors.

Reconsider Your Purpose

Remember, as we discussed in Chapter 1, good writing has a purpose. Your purpose sets the limits for what you say and also helps you decide how to say it. For example, you may be writing a **reflective** essay. In that case, your writing can use personal information and experiences. You may be writing an **informative** or presentation essay. In that case, you provide all the relevant information necessary to present your point or controlling idea. Much college writing is informative or **persuasive/argumentative**. In persuasive/argumentative writing, you want to persuade the reader to agree with your point of view. Such an essay typically relies on outside support and skillful use of ethos, pathos, and logos.

Reconsider Your Thesis

It's important to evaluate the organizing principle behind your draft and that is captured by your thesis. Ask yourself the following questions:

- What is the overall claim that you are trying to make in your essay?
- How well have you established that thesis in the opening paragraph of your essay?
- Have you organized your essay so that it supports your thesis?

What's the Difference Between Purpose and Thesis?

Your **purpose** is your reason for writing. That writing can be anything from a "to do" list, to a letter home to your parents, an email inviting people to a party, a comparison/contrast essay for your biology class, or a letter to the editor of your local paper protesting tax hikes. Being clear about your purpose will help you choose the right form for your writing, that is, list, letter, e-mail, website, essay, research paper, and so on.

Your **thesis** is your point (or argument) you're trying to make with your writing. Of course, you normally wouldn't have a thesis for a to do list: not everything you write will have a thesis. However, most of what you write will have a thesis; otherwise, what's the point?

Reconsider Your Audience

You should always keep your audience in mind because you want to make sure you are communicating clearly and effectively with that audience. Above all, remember that writings often have a rhetorical purpose. Thus, you want to make sure your writing is reaching and affecting your selected audience—the people who are reading your work and thinking about it. To influence this audience, your writing needs to employ strategies that affect readers in the way that you, the writer, desire. So take time to remind yourself of who your audience is.

Once you have reviewed the broad rhetorical decisions you've made, you'll want to begin focusing on the specifics of your writing. Here are some **strategies for revising** your own writing:

- Evaluate your essay's **organization** and **paragraph development.** If you have created a visual presentation, evaluate your work's **visual appeal**, such as the use of space and evidence. It is important to move from global revision, the larger pieces of your essay or visual work such as the thesis, audience, purpose, and situation, to more local revisions of organization, paragraph development, sentence construction, style, use of images, and more. First, read your work from beginning to end, then come back and read your introduction again to see if your ideas connect from beginning to end. Here are some questions that might help you focus on this process:

- **How well do the introduction and conclusion work in your paper?**
  - How well does your introduction grab the reader's attention and express your objectives or articulate your thesis?
  - Do you bring up unrelated points in your conclusion that direct your reader to tangential ideas?
- **How well have you developed the body paragraphs of your paper?**
  - Is the information that you provide detailed enough? You need to keep in mind that your reader may not be as informed on the topic as you are. Here, again, is where an accurate assessment of your audience will help you focus your writing in that direction.
  - Does each body paragraph set up a main idea in a topic sentence that opens the paragraph? Are all of the elements of a paragraph connected to that main idea? Are the main ideas related to your paper's argument?
  - Identify your main point in each paragraph and ask yourself how and why you have made that point.
  - How well do your ideas build toward a cohesive argument? Have you made conscious and obvious transitions and connections from paragraph to paragraph? Sentence to sentence? Have you made a general statement anywhere without adequate explanations?
  - How does your evidence and other support prove your thesis?
  - Have you built your argument logically? To see if you have, annotate your paragraphs on the left side margin and see if your points build coherently.
  - If you have used images, how well do the images support the text and contribute to your argument?

Using Peer Review Groups Effectively

The next best step to improve your writing is engaging in the **peer review** process. Most experienced writers find trusted readers whose opinions they respect, readers who won't tell them they are brilliant, but will respond honestly with constructive criticism. Many writers belong to a writers' group where they find the support and feedback they need. Often, peer review groups provide valuable insight into how you can further develop your writing.

There is some bad news and good news when engaging in peer review. It can be painful and discouraging to share new work for the first time. As writers, we are so certain of what we intend to be on that page that we often cannot see the missing pieces or faulty logic. Honest readers will tell us. The good news is that the reader's honest response will eventually benefit you and your writing because it will help you to refashion it. Fixing a piece of writing can sometimes be as simple as adding or deleting a few words or sentences.

Strategies for Effective Peer Review

Effective peer review requires your commitment and a great deal of critical thought. Just as you would like your paper reviewed thoughtfully, you need to review your fellow writer's work, whether you are in a class or a writing group. Here are some basic ground rules to keep in mind when peer reviewing:

1. *Have your draft ready.* In order to benefit from the peer review process, you need to meet the draft deadlines. Sounds like a silly reminder, but everyone knows how deadlines can creep up. Plan ahead and make sure you bring the appropriate number of copies that your instructor requests to class. Keep in mind that a "draft" is a thoroughly thought out, finished piece of work, not just a collection of ideas.

2. *Read closely and carefully.* Read your peer's paper through more than once so you can provide thoughtful feedback. Don't rush the review process or think you can do it in one quick reading. Consider audience and purpose as you read the essay.

3. *Analyze and criticize carefully.* Think about how you offer your review to your classmate. Avoid statements like "I don't like your thesis." Say instead, "I found your thesis a bit confusing because it doesn't seem to be supported by the rest of your paper. You might want to consider writing a new thesis that better summarizes and supports the evidence in your paper."

4. *Ask questions.* One of the most effective ways to help with the revision process is to ask questions in the margins where you, the reviewer, get confused. Think of it as annotating the text. Those questions can help a writer figure out what information needs to be added or clarified. Also, when you have questions for a writer, you need to remember that simple statements like "What do you mean?" are not enough. You need to be specific about what confused you as a reader and why.

5. *Make suggestions.* Don't just say what is wrong with a paper. Offer suggestions for revisions that will help the writer.

6. *Review honestly.* Review the paper like you would like to have your own paper reviewed.

7. *Consider your tone.* This point is important. You want to be tactful and respectful when reviewing someone else's work. Use an appropriate tone.

8. *Edit and proofread.* Make suggestions for editing at the sentence level. If you read something that's awkward or you see grammar, punctuation, or usage

errors, be sure to point them out. When a writer is using a documentation format for his or her evidence, don't forget to consider the accuracy of that documentation.

9. *Offer positive feedback.* Don't forget to point out what's good about a paper as well! Everyone needs positive feedback as writers.

Writer to Writer: Questions to Guide Your Peer Review

- Has the writer clearly set up his or her controlling idea early enough for you as a reader of the paper? Do you know where the writer is going with his argument?

- Does the writer have a complex argument taking place? For example, it's not enough to simply argue that rhetoric is a part of one's life, which is a self-evident fact. The writer needs to be able to explain how and why rhetoric plays a role in his or her life. What impact does rhetoric have on the writer?

- How well does each paragraph work? A paragraph needs to have a central point, an example supporting that point, and analysis explaining how the point supports the main thesis of the paper.

- How well do the introduction and conclusion work? Does the introduction set the context of the topic well enough for you as a reader? Does the conclusion adequately wrap up the argument presented in the paper?

- Has the writer effectively addressed his audience and fulfilled his purpose?

- Are there many sentence-level errors that affect your ability to easily read the paper? What one issue does the writer need to concentrate on before he or she turns the paper in for a grade?

- When you finish reading the paper, do you find yourself agreeing or disagreeing with the writer's argument? Why or why not? Remember, each writer is trying to convince the audience to see his or her point of view on a particular topic. If the writer hasn't persuaded you to see that point of view, he or she needs to revise and add in information that will persuade the reader. What suggestions can you make that will help the writer achieve that?

Developing Your Skills: Peer Review Exercise #1

In Class: Please respond to the following questions about the response papers of two or your colleagues. Read each response once without worrying about these questions. Then, answer the questions below, referring to the response and rereading when necessary. It should take you approximately 50 minutes to complete two reviews (30 minutes each). When done, return your review to the writer. The writer should then turn in his or her response and two reviews.

Author's name: _____

Reader's name: _____

1. **Summarizing:** What is the main point of the response? (Summarize in approximately three sentences.)
2. **Read with the grain:** Accept the writer's point of view and try to extend the writer's argument. Provide additional examples, suggest questions that might provoke further thought, and discuss other common ideas from the other readings.
3. **Read against the grain:** Provide counter-evidence and counter-arguments for the author. If you did not accept this argument, what objections might you raise? Are there other interpretations for this problem? Suggest several concerns briefly.
4. **Offer suggestions:** What suggestions can you offer the writer for improvement/ revision of this response? Tell the author if s/he merely repeats what the essay(s) say(s). Offer possibilities and questions for places where the author can develop his/her ideas more fully. Also, take time to suggest editing revisions (correct comma errors, suggest stronger verbs, fix pronoun-agreement errors, and more).

Developing Your Skills: Peer Review Exercise #2 for the Computer Lab

Please follow these steps:

1. Complete the top of the form with your name and three to five sentences that explain your essay's objective.
2. List any questions you have for your reviewers.
3. Send the form to each of your reviewers so they can use it for the peer review conference process.

The reviewer should complete the form. In addition, each reviewer should use the Microsoft track changes and commenting tools to ask questions in the margins and point to places that the reviewer thinks need improvement and revision.

Writer's name: _____

Objective of paper: _____

Questions I have for my reviewer: _____
_____

Reviewing Directions:

1. Add your name to the paper and complete questions 1–7 from the following list.
2. Make sure to add comments to the actual essay using the Microsoft commenting feature. This tool is a good way to help identify key areas that need revision or that raise questions for a reader. Also, it's helpful to address sentence-level issues that the writer might be having.
3. Send the reviewing sheet with the essay back to the writer.

Reviewer's Name:

1. What exactly is the writer's controlling idea/argument? How is the controlling idea maintained and fully developed throughout the paper (for example, does the writer use quotes effectively to provide evidence)? What about the argument is interesting and worth knowing? *If you cannot follow the argument, this spot is a good place to tell the writer why not.*

2. Look at the essay as a whole. How is it organized? What elements of persuasion work particularly effectively? Using the Microsoft commenting tool, add comments to places that need revision.

3. Choose one section of the essay that works really well and explain why. Writers can learn from how a reader "sees" one's paper.

4. Choose one section in particular that doesn't work well and explain why. *Suggest a possible revision.*

5. Does this essay meet the writer's stated objective? If so, explain why. If not, suggest what you would do if you were going to rewrite the essay so that it would meet the writer's objective.

6. Answer the questions the reader asked at the beginning of this review sheet (if you have not done so already in questions 1–5).

7. Provide an end comment for the writer here with your suggestions on how to go about the revision process. What tips can you provide for assistance?

Editing Your Work

You have completed your writing; you have read it and revised it on your own; you have had one of your peers read it and offer suggestions for how to improve the essay. What's next? In a word: style.

Style is your own distinctive manner of expression. Everyone has it. You have it in the way you dress and you have it, naturally, in the way you write, as style emerges in the *way* you put words together to create sentences. Just as you would dress for certain occasions—put on a suit and tie to go to work on Wall Street—so too would you want to consider the rhetorical situation you are dealing with for each piece of writing you do. The rhetorical situation—your purpose, audience, and argument—will largely determine the language you use and how you use it.

Often, college students think they need to "sound intelligent" when they write for college classes and usually that misunderstanding of the rhetorical situation leads to ineffective writing. Your purpose is not to "sound intelligent" but rather to clearly communicate your ideas. Keep in mind that no matter what the rhetorical situation, there are some basic elements common to all good writing.

Sentence-Level Revision Strategies

1. *Delete meaningless words.* Don't use words that add nothing to a sentence.

EXAMPLE:

I was wondering how to figure out how to improve my writing.

vs.

I wonder how to improve my writing.

Notice how the second sentence is more direct and concise. As a result, the meaning of the sentence is clearer and the writing is tighter.

2. *Delete doubled words.* Don't use a pair of adjectives, nouns, or verbs (i.e., full and complete, each and every), when your readers only need one of them.

EXAMPLE:

Terry Tempest Williams writes about how humans need to bend and yield to the teachings of nature.

vs.

Terry Tempest Williams examines how humans need to yield to nature's teachings.

Notice how the second sentence drops the verb "bend" because the verb "yield" does the same work. Also, notice how the second sentence replaces "writes about how" with "examines," which creates a tighter sentence (also see strategies 5 and 10).

3. *Delete what readers can infer.* Consider eliminating redundant modifiers. These are words that repeat what the first word implies. For example: "completely finish," "past history," "each individual." The most common redundancy happens when a preposition is implied by a verb, as in these examples: "continue on," "return back to," "circle around."

EXAMPLE:

During that period ~~of time,~~ the membrane ~~area~~ became pink in color and shiny in appearance.

4. *Spend less time on things your reader will know and more time on developing your own ideas.*

EXAMPLE:

In his classic novel *Moby Dick,* Herman Melville tells the tale of Captain Ahab and his hunt for the great whale Moby Dick.

vs.

Moby Dick stands as a powerful metaphor for man's powerlessness in the face of the forces of nature.

Assuming you're writing this essay in a literature class and you're answering a question about Melville's novel *Moby Dick*, it is less important to repeat obvious facts about the book than it is to say something significant about it.

5. *Replace a phrase with a word.* Often times, in writing, we use more words than we need. Strong writing is often tight, meaning that there's no excess word baggage in sentences. Ask yourself, "How can I say this simply, directly, and concisely?"

EXAMPLE:

The reason for the snow day is due to the fact that the weather made travel difficult.

vs.

The snow day occurred **because** weather made travel difficult.

> **Often, these substitutions can be made:**
>
> the reason for = because
>
> due to the fact that = since, because
>
> despite the fact that = although, even though

6. *Be direct whenever possible; choose the affirmative voice.* Using the affirmative voice creates stronger sentences and a forceful tone. Also, your point will be much clearer to your readers.

EXAMPLE:

Do not submit payments if you have not notified this office, unless you are paying less than $100.

vs.

Submit payments to this office only if you are paying less than $100.

Notice how the second sentence gets to the point more quickly.

7. *Eliminate "metadiscourse."* In other words, don't write about the act of writing.

EXAMPLE:

In this essay, I will discuss Robert Frost's bird imagery.

vs.

Robert Frost uses bird imagery.

See how the statement became a claim or what we call an **objective**? The same principle should be followed after quotations. Don't write, "In this quote, the author means..."

8. *Be confident!* You want to express your ideas with confidence. Even when you are not 100 percent sure, a word like "suggests" is much stronger than "seems." Consider your verb choices carefully. Also consider whether you might be better off rewriting a sentence completely.

EXAMPLE:

It seems like Lorde is saying that the categories of age, class, race, and sex affect all of us.

vs.

Lorde suggests that the categories of age, class, race, and sex affect all of us.

vs.

Lorde argues that age, class, race, and sex, all social constructs, affect us.

Notice how the second sentence is more assertive, and the third sentence became more direct.

9. *Summarize concisely.* Yes, you need to provide information to your reader, but your focus in papers should always be on your argument and analysis of the argument. Summary should be used, but concisely.

10. *Try to use active verbs.* Many writers fall into the bad habit of overusing forms of the verb "to be" (am, is, are, was, were, be, being, been). Writers also tend to use passive sentence constructions that decrease the power of their sentences.

EXAMPLE:

Catherine MacKinnon's article "Sexuality" is about how our culture's view of sexuality is based on how men view women as objects.

vs.

Catherine MacKinnon's article "Sexuality" argues that our culture's view of sexuality stems from men's objectification of women.

Notice how "argues" and "stems" replaces "is" in the sentence. Notice, as well, how the second sentence asserts a point more forcefully.

Proofreading Strategies

- Always read your paper out loud. Reading your paper out loud helps you identify sentence fragments and run-on sentences. Also, listen for grammar and punctuation. For example, when reading out loud, you'll often hear where a sentence needs or doesn't need a comma. Our natural breathing as we read out loud helps to point out where we need punctuation. Ask yourself these questions as well: Can you eliminate choppiness by varying sentence length?

Can you combine sentences to promote flow? Did you develop your argument confidently?

- Read your paper backward. Forcing yourself to make sense of your sentences can help you see typos and spelling errors. Remember that you can't rely on the spellchecker to do all your work.

- Have someone else read your paper just for sentence-level errors. You want your paper to have as few mechanical errors as possible.

Finally, take a deep breath, save your paper to your computer one more time, and print it out for class. You're done, at least for now—remember, writing is a recursive process, and you'll go through the process hundreds of times.

Rhetoric in Action

"The Maker's Eye: Revising Your Own Manuscripts"

Donald Murray (1923–2006). Pulitzer Prize–winning writer and teacher. Murray authored several books on the practice of writing and revision, as well as a column on writing for the *Boston Globe*.

Prereading What do you think Murray means by the "maker's eye"?

THE MAKER'S EYE: REVISING YOUR OWN
MANUSCRIPTS* by DONALD M. MURRAY

When ~~the beginning writer~~ completes ~~his~~ first draft, ~~he~~
a- students   a   they

~~usually reads it through to correct typographical errors and~~
-- And their teachers too often agree.

~~considers~~ the job of writing done ∧ When ~~the~~ professional
the

writer complete ~~his~~ first draft, ~~he~~ usually feel ~~he is~~ at the
they   they are

start of the writing process. ~~Now that he has~~ a draft, ~~he can~~
When

~~begin~~ writing / can begin.   is completed, the job of

Donald M. Murray, "The Maker's Eye: Revising Your Own Manuscripts," Used by permission of The Poynter Institute.

Writer Citizen

That difference in attitude is the difference between amateur and professional, inexperience and experience, journeyman and craftsman. Peter F. Druc~~k~~er, the prolific business writer, for example, calls his first draft "the zero draft"--after that he can start cou~~r~~ting. Most ~~productive~~ writers share the feeling ~~that~~ the first draft all~~and~~ ~~most of those~~ which follow~~s is an~~ are opportunity its ~~opportunity~~ to discover what they have to say and how they can best say it.

~~Detachment and easing~~

To produce a progression of drafts, each of which says more and says it better, the writer has to develop a special kind of reading skill. In school we are taught to decode ~~read~~ what ~~is~~ appears on the page as finished writing. ~~We try to comprehend what the author has said, what he meant, and what are the implications of his words.~~

Writers however face a different category of possibility and responsibility. To them, the words are never finished on the page. Each can be changed, rearranged, set off a chain reaction of confusion or clarified meaning. This is a different kind of reading, possibly more difficult and certainly more exciting.

---

* A different version of this article was published in *The Writer*, October 1973.

110

learn to their   Writers
5   ~~The writer~~of ~~each draft~~ must ~~be his~~ own best enemy. ~~He~~
    E   --especially teachers--   they
    must accept the criticism of others, and be suspicious of it; ~~he~~ must
        --especially teachers--   Writers
    accept the praise of others, and be even more suspicious of it. ~~He~~
                    they   themselves   their
    cannot depend on others. ~~He~~ must detach ~~himself~~ from ~~his~~ own pages
        they   their   their   their
    so that ~~he~~ can apply both ~~his~~ caring and ~~his~~ craft to ~~his~~ own work.

6   Detachment is not easy. Science fiction writer Ray Bradbury
    supposedly puts each manuscript away for a year and then rereads
    it as a stranger. Not many writers can afford the time to do
    this. We must read when our judgment may be at its worst, when
    we are close to the euphoric moment of creation. The writer
    "should be critical of everything that seems to him most delight-
    ful in his style," advises novelist Nancy Hale. "He should excise
    what he most admires, because he wouldn't thus admire it if he
    weren't . . . in a sense protecting it from criticism."

7   ~~The writer must learn to protect himself from his own ego,~~
    ~~when it takes the form of uncritical pride or uncritical~~
    ~~self-destruction.~~ A ~~As~~ poet John Ciardi points out, ". . . the
    E
    last act of the writing must be to become one's own reader.
    It is, I suppose, a schizophrenic process, to begin passionately
    and to end critically, to begin hot and to end cold; and, more
    important, to be passion-hot and critic-cold at the same time."
                    unproductive
    ~~Just as dangerous as the protective writer is the despairing~~
    ~~one, who thinks everything he does is terrible, dreadful, awful.~~
    ~~If he is to publish, he must save what is effective on his page~~
    ~~while he cuts away what doesn't work. The writer must hear and~~
    ~~respect his own voice.~~

Remember ~~how each~~ how the craftsman*e* you have seen--the carpenter   9

~~eyeing the level~~ looking at the lie of a shelf, the mechanic listening to the motor--

takes the instinctive step back. This is what ~~the writer has to~~ have to

do when ~~he~~ they ~~reads~~ ~~his~~ their own work. "The writer must survey his work

critically, coolly, and as though he were a stranger to it,"

says children's book writer Eleanor Estes. "He must be willing

to prune, expertly and hard-heartedly. At the end of each

revision, a manuscript may look like a battered old hive, worked

over, torn apart, pinned together, added to, deleted from, words

changed and words changed back. Yet the book must maintain its

original freshness and spontaneity."   8

If we are aware of ~~the~~ writers who think everything they have written is literature but a more ~~serious~~ frequent and serious problem ~~is the~~ are writers ~~is~~ who are ~~overly~~ overly critical of each page, tears up each page and never completes a draft. The ~~cut~~ writer must cut what is bad to ~~save~~ reveal what is good.

~~It is far easier for most beginning writers to understand   10~~

~~the need for rereading and rewriting than it is to understand~~

~~how to go about it. The publishing writer doesn't necessarily~~

~~break down the various stages of rewriting and editing; he~~

~~just goes ahead and does it.~~ *H* One of our most prolific ~~fiction~~

in the English-speaking world,

writers, (Anthony Burgess,) says, "I might revise a page twenty

times." Short story and children's writer Roald Dahl states,

"By the time I'm nearing the end of a story, the first part

will have been reread and altered and corrected at least 150

times. . . . Good writing is essentially rewriting. I am

positive of this."

11   ~~There is nothing virtuous~~ *isn't virtuous itself about* in the rewriting process.   It is

simply an essential condition of life for most writers.   There

are *a few* writers who do very little rewriting, mostly because they

have the capacity and experience to create and review a large

number of invisible drafts in their minds before they get to

the page.   And *some* writers ~~perform~~ *who slowly produce finished pages, performing* all ~~of~~ the tasks of revision

simultaneously, page by page, rather than draft by draft.   But

it is still possible to break down the process of rereading

one's own work into the sequence most published writers follow

most of the time.

~~as he studies his own page.~~

~~Seven elements—~~

12   Many writers ~~at first just~~ scan their manuscript, reading *to catch the larger* as quickly as possible ~~for~~ problems of subject and form.   *They take the craftsman's step back.* ~~In this way, they stand back~~ from the more ~~technical~~ *superficial* details of language *the larger problems in writing.* ~~so they can spot any weaknesses in content or in organization.~~ *Then as they reread — and reread and ~~the reader~~ reread — they* ~~When the writer reads his manuscript, he is usually looking~~ *move in closer in a logical sequence which usually ~~most~~ involves* ~~for seven elements.~~

As a worrier

The first is ~~subject~~.   ~~Do you have anything to say?   If~~ *Sometimes writers are lucky, they* *Writers look first to discover if they have —* ~~you are lucky, you will find that indeed you do have something to~~ *that they* ~~say,~~ *said anything* ~~perhaps a little more than you expected.   It the subject~~ *writers know they can't write nothing* ~~is not clear, or if it is not yet limited or defined enough~~ ~~for you to handle, don't go on.   What you have to say is~~ *SAVE* ~~always more important than how you say it.~~

Novelist Elizabeth Janeway says, "I think there's a nice cooking word ~~which~~ that explains a little of what happens while (the manuscript is) standing. It clarifies like a consommé perhaps."

"The Maker's Eye: Revising Your Own Manuscripts"

When students complete a first draft, they consider the job of writing done—and their teachers too often agree. When professional writers complete the first draft, they usually feel they are at the start of the writing process. When a draft is completed, the job of writing can being.

That difference in attitude is the difference between amateur and professional, inexperience and experience, journeyman and craftsman. Peter F. Drucker, the prolific business writer, calls his first draft "the zero draft"—after that he can start counting. Most writers share the feeling the first draft, and all which follow, are opportunities to discover what they have to say and how they can best say it.

To produce a progression of drafts, each of which says more and says it more clearly, the writer has to develop a special kind of reading skill. In school we are taught to decode what appears on the page as finished writing. Writers, however, face a different category of possibility and responsibility when they read their own drafts. To them the words on the page are never finished. Each can be changed and rearranged, can set off a chain reaction of confusion or clarified meaning. This is a different kind of reading which is possibly more difficult and certainly more exciting.

Writers must learn to be their own best enemy. They must accept the criticism of others and be suspicious of it; they must accept the praise of others and be even more suspicious of it. Writers cannot depend on others. They must detach themselves from their own pages so that they can apply both their caring and their craft to their own work.

Such detachment is not easy. Science fiction writer Ray Bradbury supposedly puts each manuscript away for a year to the day and then rereads it as a stranger. Not many writers have the discipline or the time to do this. We must read when our judgment may be at its worst, when we are close to the euphoric moment of creation.

Then the writer, counsels novelist Nancy Hale, "should be critical of everything that seems to him most delightful in his style. "He should excise what he most admires, because he wouldn't thus admire it if he weren't … in a sense protecting it from criticism." John Ciardi, the poet, adds, "The last act of the writing must be to become one's own reader. It is, I suppose, a schizophrenic process, to begin passionately and to end critically, to begin hot and to end cold; and, more important, to be passion-hot and critic-cold at the same time."

Most people think that the principal problem is that writers are too proud of what they have written. Actually, a greater problem for most professional writers is one shared by the majority of students. They are overly critical, think everything is dreadful, tear up page after page, never complete a draft, see the task as hopeless.

The writer must learn to read critically but constructively, to cut what is bad, to reveal what is good. Eleanor Estes, the children's book author, explains: "The writer must survey his work critically, coolly, as though he were a stranger to it. He must be willing to prune, expertly and hard-heartedly. At the end of each revision, a manuscript may look … worked over, torn apart, pinned together, added to, deleted from, words changed and words changed back. Yet the book must maintain its original freshness and spontaneity."

Most readers underestimate the amount of rewriting it usually takes to produce spontaneous reading. This is a great disadvantage to the student writer, who sees only a finished product and never watches the craftsman who takes the necessary step back, studies the work carefully, returns to the task, steps back, returns, steps back, again and again. Anthony Burgess, one of the most prolific writers in the English-speaking world, admits, "I might revise a page twenty times." Roald Dahl, the popular children's writer, states, "By the time I'm nearing the end of a story, the first part will have been reread and altered and corrected at least 150 times.... Good writing is essentially rewriting. I am positive of this."

Rewriting isn't virtuous. It isn't something that ought to be done. It is simply something that most writers find they have to do to discover what they have to say and how to say it. It is a condition of the writer's life.

There are, however, a few writers who do little formal rewriting, primarily because they have the capacity and experience to create and review a large number of invisible drafts in their minds before they approach the page. And some writers slowly produce finished pages, performing all the tasks of revision simultaneously, page by page, rather than draft by draft. But it is still possible to see the sequence followed by most writers most of the time in rereading their own work.

Most writers scan their drafts first, reading as quickly as possible to catch the larger problems of subject and form, then move in closer and closer as they read and write, reread and rewrite.

The first thing writers look for in their drafts is *information*. They know that a good piece of writing is built from specific, accurate, and interesting information. The writer must have an abundance of information from which to construct a readable piece of writing.

Next writers look for *meaning* in the information. The specifics must build to a pattern of significance. Each piece of specific information must carry the reader toward meaning.

Writers reading their own drafts are aware of *audience*. They put themselves in the reader's situation and make sure that they deliver information which a reader wants to know or needs to know in a manner which is easily digested. Writers try to be sure that they anticipate and answer the questions a critical reader will ask when reading the piece of writing.

Writers make sure that the *form* is appropriate to the subject and the audience. Form, or genre, is the vehicle which carries meaning to the reader, but form cannot be selected until the writer has adequate information to discover its significance and an audience which needs or wants that meaning.

Once writers are sure the form is appropriate, they must then look at the *structure*, the order of what they have written. Good writing is built on a solid framework of logic, argument, narrative, or motivation which runs through the entire piece of writing and holds it together. This is the time when many writers find it most effective to outline as a way of visualizing the hidden spine by which the piece of writing is supported.

The element on which writers may spend a majority of their time is *development*. Each section of a piece of writing must be adequately developed. It must give readers enough information so that they are satisfied. How much information is enough? That's as difficult as asking how much garlic belongs in a salad. It must be done to taste, but most beginning writers underdevelop, underestimating the reader's hunger for information.

As writers solve development problems, they often have to consider questions of *dimension*. There must be a pleasing and effective proportion among all the parts of the piece of writing. There is a continual process of subtracting and adding to keep the piece of writing in balance.

Finally, writers have to listen to their own voices. *Voice* is the force which drives a piece of writing forward. It is an expression of the writer's authority and concern. It is what is between the words on the page, what glues the piece of writing together. A good piece of writing is always marked by a consistent, individual voice.

As writers read and reread, write and rewrite, they move closer and closer to the page until they are doing line-by-line editing. Writers read their own pages with infinite care. Each sentence, each line, each clause, each phrase, each word, each mark of punctuation, each section of white space between the type has to contribute to the clarification of meaning.

Slowly the writer moves from word to word, looking through language to see the subject. As a word is changed, cut, or added, as a construction is rearranged, all the words used before that moment and all those that follow that moment must be considered and reconsidered.

Writers often read aloud at this stage of the editing process, muttering or whispering to themselves, calling on the ear's experience with language. Does this sound right—or that? Writers edit, shifting back and forth from eye to page to ear to page. I find I must do this careful editing in short runs, no more than fifteen to twenty minutes at a stretch, or I become too kind with myself. I begin to see what I hope is on the page, not what actually is on the page.

This sounds tedious if you haven't done it, but actually it is fun. Making something right is immensely satisfying, for writers begin to learn what they are writing about by writing. Language leads them to meaning, and there is the joy of discovery, of understanding, of making meaning clear as the writer employs the technical skills of language.

Words have double meanings, even triple and quadruple meanings. Each word has its own potential for connotation and denotation. And when writers rub one word against the other, they are often rewarded with a sudden insight, an unexpected clarification.

The maker's eye moves back and forth from word to phrase to sentence to paragraph to sentence to phrase to word. The maker's eye sees the need for variety and balance, for a firmer structure, for a more appropriate form. It peers into the interior of the paragraph, looking for coherence, unity, and emphasis, which make meaning clear.

I learned something about this process when my first bifocals were prescribed. I had ordered a larger section of the reading portion of the glass because of my work, but even so, I could not contain my eyes with this new limit of vision. And I still find myself taking off my glasses and bending my nose towards the page, for my eyes unconsciously flick back and forth across the page, back to another page, forward to still another, as I try to see each evolving line in relation to every other line.

When does this process end? Most writers agree with the great Russian writer Tolstoy, who said, "I scarcely ever reread my published writings, if by chance I come across a page, it always strikes me: all this must be rewritten; this is how I should have written it."

The maker's eye is never satisfied, for each word has the potential to ignite the new meaning. This article has been twice written all the way through the writing process, and it was published four years ago. Now it is to be republished in a book. The editors made a few small suggestions, and then I read it with my maker's eye. Now it has been re-edited, re-revised, re-read, re-re-edited, for each piece of writing to the writer is full of potential and alternatives.

A piece of writing is never finished. It is delivered to a deadline, torn out of the typewriter on demand, sent off with a sense of accomplishment and shame and pride and frustration. If only there were a couple more days, time for just another run at it, perhaps then.... ❧

Comprehending the Text

1. What is Murray's main argument about the art of revision?

2. What role does the "maker's eye" play in the revision process?

3. What strategies does Murray offer for revising your writing?

Analyzing the Text

1. Who is Murray's audience, and how do you know this?

2. What rhetorical strategies does Murray employ in his essay?

3. If you were to offer Murray suggestions for revising his essay, what would you suggest? Why?

Developing Your Skills: The Art of Revision

It's your turn to focus on the act of revision. Using a draft of one of your assignments, annotate and revise the essay on paper. Just like Murray, you want to engage actively in the revision process at the content and sentence level.

YOUR TURN: Engaging in Revision

1. Before turning in a formal writing assignment, do the following:
   - In one or two sentences, articulate your paper's thesis on the top of the first page.
   - Annotate your essay by adding comments in the left-hand margin that explain to your reader how you developed your paper. Your goal here is to identify your writing strategies and how you built your content to create a persuasive piece of rhetorical communication.
   - At the end of your paper, do a self-analysis. Write down three things you think you did effectively in your paper. Then write down three things you think you could still improve in the paper with further time for revision and editing.

TECH TALK: Computer Tools for Writing and Revising

We use computers increasingly often as we write. There are tools in word processing programs that can help you hone your revision skills and writings. The reviewing tools in Microsoft Word are very useful. Here are directions for using the Microsoft reviewing tools:

1. To turn on the reviewing feature, select View > Toolbars > Reviewing from the main toolbar. A new toolbar with little sticky note symbols will appear.

2. Once the reviewing toolbar is available, you need to turn on the change tracking. To do so, click the "Track Changes" icon (it is picture of a piece of paper with a pencil over it). Now, when you write in the text, any changes you make will be "tracked" so that you can visually see what you are revising.

3. One effective way to engage in peer review with your classmates in a computer classroom, or via e-mail, is to use the commenting tool, which is available from the reviewing toolbar. This tool allows you to insert comment boxes in the right-hand margin of the text. As you move through the text, put your cursor next to the line you would like to make a comment about. Click the yellow note with the words "new comment" next to it. A comment box will open on the right-hand side of the page. Type your comments in the box.

Chapter 10

Writing into Citizenship:
The Environment

In 1962, environmentalist Rachel Carson published *Silent Spring*, a book that is thought to have started the environmental movement of the twentieth century. The work developed from Carson's focus on the increasing use of pesticides after World War II in the United States. With *Silent Spring*, Carson created a metaphor for environmental loss that continues to resonate for the conservation and environmental movement:

> There was once a town in the heart of America where all life seemed to live in harmony with its surroundings... . Then a strange blight crept over the area and everything began to change... . There was a strange stillness... . The few birds seen anywhere were moribund; they trembled violently and could not fly. It was a spring without voices. On the mornings that had once throbbed with the dawn chorus of scores of bird voices there was now no sound; only silence lay over the fields and woods and marsh. (Carson)

Here, Carson equates the use of pesticides with the loss of plant and bird life, creating an environment where birds cannot fly or thrive, thus silencing the harbingers of spring. The argument Carson made asked key questions: Who is in charge of the environment, man or nature? For what purpose does the environment exist—is its bounty purely for human use and gain? Carson's book became a bestseller, and many environmentalists still draw upon her work and ideas as the foundation of the current environmental movement.

In recent years, people across the world have grown increasingly concerned with the environment, especially with regard to climate change and global warming. Some believe that things like global warming do not exist or that the human influences on the

Rachel Carson, *Silent Spring*, Boston: Houghton Mifflin, 1962.

environment are the price we must pay for development and prosperity. It's also important to recognize that concerns regarding the environment today revolve around more than just pesticide use and global warming. If you turn to the news, you will find the following topics constantly debated by the public:

- Organic foods vs. genetically modified foods
- Landfills and the need for recycling
- Mining and clear cutting
- Land use to store nuclear waste and test nuclear weapons
- Air pollution
- Conservation of wildlife and wilderness

Recent years have seen many heated controversies around these and other issues: drilling for oil in the Arctic National Wildlife Refuge, building wind farms in Nantucket Sound and other places, deregulating industrial emissions into the air, the causes and effects of Hurricane Katrina, and tap water vs. bottled water, to name only a very few.

- Where do you stand in relation to some of these environmental dilemmas?
- What problems do you see in your communities related to environmental issues?
- What are people talking about on your campus, in your town, and in your state?

"Eating is an agricultural act," as Wendell Berry famously said. It is also an ecological act, and a political act, too. Though much has been done to obscure this simple fact, how and what we eat determines to a great extent the use we make of the world—and what is to become of it. To eat with a fuller consciousness of all that is at stake might sound like a burden, but in practice few things in life can afford quite as much satisfaction. By comparison, the pleasures of eating industrially, which is to say eating in ignorance, are fleeting. Many people today seem perfectly content eating at the end of an industrial food chain, without a thought in the world; this book is probably not for them. There are things in it that will ruin their appetites...

–Michael Pollan, *The Omnivore's Dilemma*

Out of these various topics, the environmental movement has focused on the concept of **sustainability**. According to the U.S. Environmental Protection Agency, "The 1970 National Environmental Policy Act (NEPA) formally established as a national goal the creation and maintenance of conditions under which humans and nature "can exist in productive harmony, and fulfill the social, economic and other requirements of *present and future generations of Americans*" (www.epa.gov). In other words, the goal of sustainability centers on equalizing our use of natural resources, including space, with efforts to replace or sustain those resources. The statement implies that we need to find a balance—economically, politically, and socially—with the environment. A key question to ask for those interested in creating sustainable communities is: *are we using resources faster than they can be replaced?* People who want sustainable communities believe that we need to balance our use of resources so that we do not deplete them for future generations.

The readings here offer you the opportunity to contextualize the environmental movement. Here are some questions to guide your reading:

- What problems do people across the globe face environmentally?
- What do people believe about the environment?
- How do politics affect environmental issues?
- How do environmental policies affect your life? Your community?

Readings (in order of appearance):

- "Global Warming: A Divide on Causes and Solutions," Pew Research Center for the People & the Press
- Cartoon: "Gore-bal Warming," Larry Wright
- Cartoon: "On a Clear Cut Day, You Can See Forever," Steve Greenburg
- Cartoon: Dilbert cartoon on environmental attitudes
- "Conservatives Are Liberal and Liberals Are Conservative—On the Environment," Stephen M. Colarelli
- "We Can't Wish Away Climate Change," Al Gore
- Excerpt from *The Omnivore's Dilemma: A Natural History of Four Meals,* Michael Pollan

Global Warming: A Divide on Causes and Solutions

Public Views Unchanged by Unusual Weather

Pew Research Center for the People & the Press (January 24, 2007). The Pew Research Center is a independent, non-partisan public research organization. The Pew Research Center administers polls and studies how people feel about public policy issues, the press, politics, and more.

Prereading Have you heard of the Pew Research Center? What does the center do?

President Bush's mention in his State of the Union Message of the "serious challenge of global climate change" was directed at an American public, many of whom remain

"Global Warming: A Divide on Causes and Solutions; *Public Views Unchanged by Unusual Weather,*" January 24, 2007, Pew Research Center for the People of the Press, a project of the Pew Research Center. Used by permission.

Stable views of globle warming				
	June	July	Aug	Jan
Solid evidence that	2006	2006	2006	2007
the earth is warming?	%	%	%	%
Yes,solid evidence	70	79	77	77
Due to human activity	41	50	47	47
Due to natural patterns	21	23	20	20
No, no solid evidence	20	17	17	16
Mixed/Don't know	10	4	6	7
	100	100	100	100

lukewarm about the importance of the issue. The unusual weather affecting the nation this winter may have reinforced the widely held view that the phenomenon of rising temperatures is real (77% of Americans believe that), but the public continues to be deeply divided over both its cause and what to do about it. But there is considerably less agreement over its cause, with about half (47%) saying that human activity, such as the burning of fossil fuels, is mostly to blame for the earth getting warmer.

Moreover, there are indications that most Americans do not regard global warming as a top-tier issue. In Pew's annual list of policy priorities for the president and Congress, global warming ranked fourth-lowest of 23 items tested, with only about four in ten (38%) rating it a top priority. A survey last year by the Pew Global Attitudes Project showed that the public's relatively low level of concern about global warming sets the U.S. apart from other countries. That survey found that only 19% of Americans who had heard of global warming expressed a great deal of personal concern about the issue. Among the 15 coun-tries surveyed, only the Chinese expressed a comparably low level of concern (20%).

The latest national survey by the Pew Research Center for the People & the Press, conducted January 10–15 among 1,708 Americans, finds a majority (55%) saying that global warming is a problem that requires immediate government action. But the per-centage of Americans expressing this view has declined a bit since August, when 61% felt global warming was a problem that required an immediate government response.

The survey finds deep differences between Republicans and Democrats—and within both political parties—over virtually every issue related to global warming. These disagreements extend even to the question of whether the earth is getting warmer. Just 54% of conservative Republicans say there is solid evidence that average temperatures have been getting warmer over the past few decades; by contrast, more than three-quarters of both moderate and liberal Republicans and independents (78% each), and even higher percentages of Democrats, believe the earth has been getting warmer.

The political divisions are still greater over the issue of whether global warming is a problem that requires immediate government action. About half of moderate and liberal Republicans (51%) express this view, compared with just 22% of conservative

Writer Citizen

Global warming a polarizing issue						
	Total	Mod/ Cons Rep	Lib Rep	Ind	Cons/ Mod Dem	Lib Dem
Believe that...	%	%	%	%	%	%
Earth is getting warmer	77	54	78	78	83	92
Due to human activity	47	20	46	47	54	71
How serious a problem is global warming?						
Very serious	45	18	35	46	52	73
Somewhat serious	32	33	39	35	31	20
Not too serious	12	29	15	9	10	5
Not a problem	8	17	10	8	4	2
DK/refused	3	3	1	2	3	*
	100	100	100	100	100	100
*Global warming requires immediate govt. action?**						
Yes	55	22	51	58	61	81
No	31	54	37	29	29	14
Not a problem^	11	20	12	10	7	1
DK/refused	3	4	*	3	3	4
	100	100	100	100	100	100

* Asked of those who said global warming is a problem.
^Includes those who answered don't know on whether global warming is a problem.

Republicans. The differences among Democrats are somewhat smaller; 81% of liberal Democrats, and 61% of moderate and conservative Democrats, say global warming is a problem that requires immediate government action.

Education and Party

There also are striking educational differences in partisans' views of global warming. Among Republicans, higher education is linked to greater skepticism about global warming – fully 43% of Republicans with a college degree say that there is no evidence of global warming, compared with 24% of Republicans with less education.

But among Democrats, the pattern is the reverse. Fully 75% of Democrats with college degrees say that there is solid evidence of global warming and that it is caused by human activities. This is far higher than among Democrats with less education among whom 52% say the same. Independents, regardless of education levels, fall in between these partisan extremes.

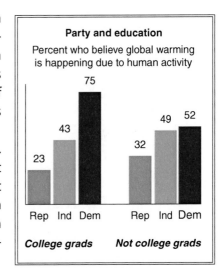

Party and education

Percent who believe global warming is happening due to human activity

College grads: Rep 23, Ind 43, Dem 75
Not college grads: Rep 32, Ind 49, Dem 52

College grads　　*Not college grads*

Global Warming Not a High Priority

Roughly twice as many Democrats as Republicans say that dealing with global warming should be a top priority for the president and Congress this year (48% vs. 23%). However, the issue is a relatively low priority for members of both parties, as well as for independents.

The issue of dealing with global warming rates near the bottom of the priorities list for both Democrats and independents, and is the lowest priority for Republicans. Notably, there is much greater support, across the political spectrum, for the broader goal of protecting the environment. Two-thirds of Democrats (67%) view protecting the environment as a top priority, and it ranks near the middle of their policy priorities list. Many more independents and Republicans also rate protecting the environment an important priority than say the same about dealing with global warming.

Global warming lags as a policy priority

Percent rating each as a 'top priority'

Republicans		Democrats		Independents	
Terrorism	93	Health care costs	77	Terrorism	77
Education	65	Economy	77	Education	66
Economy	65	Terrorism	74	Health care costs	66
Illegal immigration	63	Education	74	Medicare	61
Social security	62	Social security	72	Economy	60
Health care costs	58	Minimum wage	71	Social security	60
Stronger military	56	Medicare	70	Job situation	60
Crime	56	Health insurance	70	**Environment**	**59**
Morality	54	Crime	69	Energy	58
Medicare	53	**Environment**	**67**	Crime	57
Tax Cuts	49	Poverty	67	Budget deficit	53
Poverty	48	Job situation	67	Health insurance	52
Energy	45	Energy	64	Minimum wage	50
Health insurance	44	Budget deficit	57	Illegal immigration	49
Budget deficit	42	Tax cuts	54	Poverty	46
Environment	**41**	Illegal immigration	48	Stronger military	45
Job situation	39	**Global warming**	**48**	Morality	42
Int'l trade	33	Morality	45	Tax cuts	41
Minimum wage	28	Govt. ethics*	44	**Global warming**	**40**
Govt. ethics*	28	Stronger military	42	Govt. ethics*	35
Global warming	**23**	Int'l trade	35	Int'l trade	31

* Reducing the influence of lobbyists and special interests in Washington

---

About this Survey

Results for this survey are based on telephone interviews conducted under the direction of Princeton Survey Research Associates International among a nationwide sample of 1,708 adults, 18 years of age or older, from January 10–15, 2007. For results based on the total sample, one can say with 95% confidence that the error attributable to sampling is plus or minus 3 percentage points. For results based on January 11–15, 2007 (N=1,384), the sampling error is plus or minus 3.5 percentage points.

In addition to sampling error, one should bear in mind that question wording and practical difficulties in conducting surveys can introduce error or bias into the findings of opinion polls. ⮞

Comprehending the Text

1. What story does the data in this document tell?
2. What are the differences between Republicans and Democrats regarding global warming?
3. How would you answer the survey questions, and why?

Analyzing the Text

1. What purpose does the data in this survey serve? How do the charts and graphs affect you as a reader?
2. Does this document present an argument? Why or why not?

Gore-Bal Warming, *Detroit News*, Larry Wright, 2004

Steve Greenberg for the Seattle Post-Intelligencer, 1991

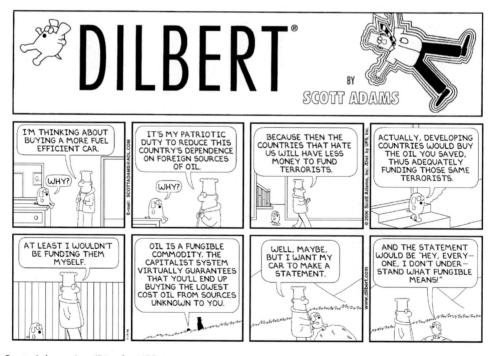

© Scott Adams, Inc./Dist. by UFS, Inc.

Developing Your Skills: Entering the Debate

Consider the cartoons included here. Choose one to write a short essay about. In your essay:

- Describe the cartoon.
- Describe the argument or point being made in the cartoon.
- Explain how the argument is being made.
- Take a position on that argument. Is it funny? Why or why not? Is it persuasive? Why or why not?

"Conservatives Are Liberal and Liberals Are Conservative—On the Environment"

Stephen M. Colarelli is a psychologist, writer, and teacher. Colarelli currently teaches at Central Michigan University.

Prereading Make a list of your views about the environment. Are you views liberal or conservative?

Conservatives and liberals differ on a host of issues: abortion, the death penalty, welfare, school choice, and gun control, among others. Yet beneath these particular differences are two *fundamental* differences: beliefs about tradition and human nature. Most of conservatives' and liberals' positions stem from their differences on these basic beliefs—except for their positions on the environment. The environment presents a paradox. When it comes to the environment, conservatives are liberals, and liberals are conservatives.*

Conservatives seek to preserve the past; they proceed cautiously and slowly with change; they are suspicious of social engineering and social reformers. They believe that society evolved organically and is therefore a seamless web of interconnected parts. A change in one part of the social fabric affects other parts of society—parts that initially may appear unrelated to the change. Conservatives also believe that society is

---

Stepen M. Colarelli is a professor of psychology at Central Michigan University.

* *Editor's note*: In this article, the term *liberals* refers to those who are liberal in the contemporary American sense (that is, social democrats), not to the classical liberals, who are sometimes called *conservatives* in the present-day United States. *The Independent Review, v, VII, n, 1, Summer 2002, ISBN 1086–1653, Copyright © 2002, pp. 103–107.*

---

unfathomably complex. Isaiah Berlin writes that classical conservatives, such as Burke and Chateaubriand, spoke of the unique power and value of the infinitely complex and unanalyzable network—as in Burke's myriad strands of social and spiritual relationships by which the successive generations of mankind were shaped from birth and to which they owed most of what they possessed and were.

Because society is organic and complex, people should have a deep respect for tradition, according to conservatives. The structures that exist in society (the family, government, religion) do so because they emerged and proved successful over hundreds of years of social evolution. Therefore, social change and social reform should be viewed with suspicion. Humankind does not understand the complexity and interconnectedness of society well enough to predict the outcome of social reforms. In fact, social reforms may make things worse because they often result in unanticipated consequences. Therefore, if social change must be undertaken, it must be undertaken cautiously, slowly, and incrementally.

Liberals look askance at tradition. They view it as oppressive, as often hindering the advancement and reducing the well-being of those who have not benefited from traditional social structures. They take a positive view of social engineering and social reforms. Beginning with the philosophers of the French Enlightenment, liberals believed—and continue to believe—that humankind should not be shackled by tradition and ignorance, and society should be molded into something better than what exists. They believe that science and rational analysis will permit us to understand how society and the economy work and will enable us to manipulate society to attain desired ends. Liberals are impatient. Rather than take an incremental approach, they prefer rapid change. As John Maynard Keynes is said to have quipped when asked about the long-term, go-slow approach: "in the long run, we are all dead." "Change" was the rallying cry of the Clinton presidency.

Conservatives and liberals also have different views of human nature. Conservatives believe that human nature, though good in many ways, has an inherently base side. Although humans have the capacity for doing good (former president George H. W. Bush's "thousand points of light"), the capacity for doing evil is also an inherent part of human nature. Therefore, conservatives support programs that keep evil actions in check. They favor tough sentences for criminals, more prisons, and a strong national defense. We need traditional authorities and the iron fist to keep the evil side of our natures in check. Liberals, on the other hand, believe that people are basically good. They believe that human nature is not inherently bad and that human nature can be progressively improved. When people break the law or act immorally, they do so not because of their inherent baseness (except for political enemies, such as Adolf Hitler, who are inherently evil); rather, they do so because of their circumstances. Improve the circumstances, and you improve the people. To bring out the best in people, provide education and equal opportunity.

When it comes to the environment, however, liberals are conservative, and conservatives are liberal. Conservatives oppose preservation of the environment. They believe that the environment should be exploited for economic ends. Developers—usually Republicans—complain about regulations that slow their drainage of wetlands to develop golf courses and build condominiums. Logging executives and workers—usually political conservatives—complain that they should be able to "harvest" forests as they see fit. Western ranchers and mining executives complain that new regulations requiring them to pay market rates to lease federal land will drive them out of business. Conservatives favor "management" of the natural environment. They speak about "wise use" or "multiple use." The environment exists for humankind to dominate and to bend to its will.

Because the social world is complex and contains an endless web of interconnections, conservatives are hesitant to tamper with it. Yet when it comes to the natural environment, they are blind to the interconnectedness of natural ecosystems; they cannot see how alterations in one part of the natural environment affect other parts of it and thus feel that it can withstand trauma, change, and exploitation. Conservatives refused to recognize the relationships between chlorofluorocarbons (CFCs) and the depletion of the ozone layer; and when they finally did, they minimized its seriousness and urged a go-slow approach. They were slow to recognize the relationships among industrial pollution in Lake Michigan, contaminated fish, and cancer in humans. Conservative farmers and chemical manufacturers were reluctant to recognize the relationship between agricultural pesticides and fertilizers and contaminated water. It is as though nature exists in isolated compartments delineated by private property. What one does on one's own private property—or on property leased from the government—affects nothing outside of it.

Liberals acknowledge that damage to one part of the environment may have negative consequences in another part. Although they are eager to move forward with social programs—ignoring traditions, continuity, and the interconnected fabric of society—they revere the tradition in nature. Unlike conservatives, who are slow to stop polluters and developers, liberals demand quick action to halt practices that harm the environment or are likely to harm it. Whereas conservatives want more research and conclusive proof about the effects of industrial practices on the environment, liberals take a conservative approach and urge hands off when there is a suggestion of environmental damage. Conservatives have a history of waiting too long to stop pollution and the destruction of wilderness. They usually move to action at the behest (through lawsuits and legislation) of liberals.

Conservatives' assumptions about *human* nature lead to another paradox. Conservatives believe that strong laws, stiff sentences, tough judges, and well-funded police departments are necessary to keep human nature's base and irrational side in check—except when it comes to the environment. Left to their own devices, guided only by rational self-interest and the invisible hand of the marketplace, people will do what is good regarding environmental matters. Society and the environment will benefit from each person's pursuit of self-interest, and the only problem is getting rid of laws and regulations that restrict people's pursuit of self-interest. That pursuit may involve destroying wildlife habitat in order to develop mining, ranching, or logging operations, or destroying the integrity of ecosystems in order to develop shopping malls, motels, condos, and wilderness retreats for the rich and famous. The principal purpose of the Council on Competitiveness, which began operation in 1986 and continued full-steam during the George H. W. Bush presidency with Dan Quayle at its helm, was to help the business community skirt regulations. Two liberals, Bill Clinton and Al Gore, disbanded the Council on Competitiveness.

Although liberals normally have a sanguine view of human nature, they take a conservative turn when it comes to humans and the environment. They believe that the masses are "environmentally illiterate." Because the public does not know its own best interests and the best interests of the planet, it cannot be allowed to pursue unbridled free enterprise and self-interest. Unless restricted by law and regulation, businesspersons, drivers of four-wheel-drive vehicles, hunters, farmers, ranchers, miners, and developers will run roughshod over the delicate fabric of the environment.

National symbols also present a paradox of conservative ideology. Conservatives have a strong affinity for national symbols—in particular those symbols constructed by humans. These symbols are cultural icons that preserve the social order, so conservatives support strict laws against defacing national symbols. For example, George H. W. Bush and other conservatives supported a constitutional amendment prohibiting flag burning. Liberals tend not to take such an extreme view. Though most do not condone flag burning, they believe that the issue does not merit a constitutional amendment.

Yet when it comes to the environment, conservatives are the first to permit the desecration of our national symbols in the natural world. Acre after acre of wilderness and wetland, mile after mile of beach and riverfront have fallen prey to conservative politicians and businesspersons. Yet our wilderness areas, wildlife, mountains, lakes, and rivers are as much national symbols of America as the flag. Like cities, flags, and monuments, a nation's natural treasures symbolize its uniqueness. What would Australia be without the Koala bear, America without the bald eagle, Switzerland without the Alps, Germany without its rivers, England without its countryside? In America, the wilderness holds an even more special place as a national symbol. It is the symbol of all that is good and all that is possible in the New World. As historian Leo Marx wrote in his classic book *The Machine in the Garden: Technology and the Pastoral Ideal in America* (New York: Oxford University Press, 1964), "The pastoral ideal has been used to define the meaning of America ever since the age of discovery" (3).

Although it is difficult to deny these paradoxes, some might say that I have missed an obvious reason why conservatives take a laissez-faire approach toward the environment: money. Conservatives view the environment as an economic entity, and they favor maximum individual liberty in the economic sphere. Yet how can this preference account for the most curious paradox of all: that communists, the conservatives' archenemies, embraced this very same disrespectful view of nature? Reports from the former Soviet Union and former East Bloc countries reveal that the communist regimes permitted environmental degradation on a scale unprecedented in the West.

How can conservatives, who value tradition in the social world, be blind to the tradition in the environment? How can they respect the integrity of social ecosystems, yet disrespect the integrity of natural ecosystems? What accounts for these paradoxes? I am not sure. Perhaps they believe that humankind is separate from nature rather than part of it, as many liberals believe. Perhaps out of a respect for religious tradition they believe that humans are predestined to dominate the earth and mold it to human will. Or perhaps their attitude has to do with the belief that we are in a tooth-and-claw Darwinian struggle for existence, competing not only with other humans but also with nature. Perhaps it has to do with individual liberty and self-interest. Just as Adam Smith's "invisible hand" works with respect to the market, so too should it work with respect to the environment.

We are only beginning to understand the complex nature of ecosystems and their interaction with humans. Environmentalism and political ideology are more likely to raise paradoxes than to expose clear ideological divisions. There are no easy answers or clearly acceptable solutions. The problem is (as vanishing wildlife know all too well) that our solutions, based on self-interest and ignorance, so far are often too little and too late. ❧

Comprehending the Text

1. In what ways are liberals conservative and conservatives liberal on the environment?

2. Why do liberals believe the public is "environmentally illiterate"?

3. What conclusion does the author come to in his essay? Explain if you agree or disagree with that conclusion.

Analyzing the Text

1. How does Colarelli use the strategies of comparison-contrast and definition together to shape his discussion?

2. As a reader, how do you respond to Colarelli's discussion and why?

3. Do you find the essay's argument to be effective? Why or why not?

"We Can't Wish Away Climate Change"

Al Gore is the former vice president of the United States (1993–2001), founder of the Alliance of Climate Protection, and author of *An Inconvenient Truth* and *Our Choice: A Plan to Solve the Climate Crisis*. Gore has long been involved in environmental issues in the United States. This op-ed piece was published in *The New York Times* on February 27, 2010.

Prereading: What is your reaction to the title of Gore's essay? What does it make you think and why?

It would be an enormous relief if the recent attacks on the science of global warming actually indicated that we do not face an unimaginable calamity requiring large-scale, preventive measures to protect human civilization as we know it.

Of course, we would still need to deal with the national security risks of our growing dependence on a global oil market dominated by dwindling reserves in the most unstable region of the world, and the economic risks of sending hundreds of billions of dollars a year overseas in return for that oil. And we would still trail China in the race to develop smart grids, fast trains, solar power, wind, geothermal and other renewable sources of energy—the most important sources of new jobs in the 21st century.

But what a burden would be lifted! We would no longer have to worry that our grandchildren would one day look back on us as a criminal generation that had selfishly and blithely ignored clear warnings that their fate was in our hands. We could instead celebrate the naysayers who had doggedly persisted in proving that every major National Academy of Sciences report on climate change had simply made a huge mistake.

I, for one, genuinely wish that the climate crisis were an illusion. But unfortunately, the reality of the danger we are courting has not been changed by the discovery of at least two mistakes in the thousands of pages of careful scientific work over the last 22 years by the Intergovernmental Panel on Climate Change. In fact, the crisis is still growing because we are continuing to dump 90 million tons of global-warming pollution every 24 hours into the atmosphere—as if it were an open sewer.

It is true that the climate panel published a flawed overestimate of the melting rate of debris-covered glaciers in the Himalayas, and used information about the Netherlands provided to it by the government, which was later found to be partly inaccurate. In addition, e-mail messages stolen from the University of East Anglia in Britain showed that scientists besieged by an onslaught of hostile, make-work demands from climate skeptics may not have adequately followed the requirements of the British freedom of information law.

But the scientific enterprise will never be completely free of mistakes. What is important is that the overwhelming consensus on global warming remains unchanged. It is also worth noting that the panel's scientists—acting in good faith on the best information then available to them—probably underestimated the range of sea-level rise¹ in this century, the speed with which the Arctic ice cap is disappearing and the speed with which some of the large glacial flows in Antarctica and Greenland are melting and racing to the sea.

Because these and other effects of global warming are distributed globally, they are difficult to identify and interpret in any particular location. For example, January was seen as unusually cold in much of the United States. Yet from a global perspective, it was the second-hottest January since surface temperatures were first measured 130 years ago.

Similarly, even though climate deniers have speciously argued for several years that there has been no warming in the last decade, scientists confirmed last month that the last 10 years were the hottest decade since modern records have been kept.

The heavy snowfalls this month have been used as fodder for ridicule by those who argue that global warming is a myth, yet scientists have long pointed out that warmer global temperatures have been increasing the rate of evaporation from the oceans, putting significantly more moisture into the atmosphere—thus causing heavier downfalls of both rain and snow in particular regions, including the Northeastern United States. Just as it's important not to miss the forest for the trees, neither should we miss the climate for the snowstorm.

Here is what scientists have found is happening to our climate: man-made global-warming pollution traps heat from the sun and increases atmospheric temperatures. These pollutants—especially carbon dioxide—have been increasing rapidly with the growth in the burning of coal, oil, natural gas and forests, and temperatures have increased over the same period. Almost all of the ice-covered regions of the Earth are melting—and seas are rising. Hurricanes are predicted to grow stronger and more destructive, though their number is expected to decrease. Droughts are getting longer and deeper in many mid-continent regions, even as the severity of flooding increases. The seasonal predictability of rainfall and temperatures is being disrupted, posing serious threats to agriculture. The rate of species extinction is accelerating to dangerous levels.

Though there have been impressive efforts by many business leaders, hundreds of millions of individuals and families throughout the world and many national, regional and local governments, our civilization is still failing miserably to slow the rate at which these emissions are increasing—much less reduce them.

And in spite of President Obama's efforts at the Copenhagen climate summit meeting in December, global leaders failed to muster anything more than a decision to "take note" of an intention to act.

Because the world still relies on leadership from the United States, the failure by the Senate to pass legislation intended to cap American emissions before the Copenhagen meeting guaranteed that the outcome would fall far short of even the minimum needed to build momentum toward a meaningful solution.

The political paralysis that is now so painfully evident in Washington has thus far prevented action by the Senate—not only on climate and energy legislation, but also on health care reform, financial regulatory reform and a host of other pressing issues.

This comes with painful costs. China, now the world's largest and fastest-growing source of global-warming pollution, had privately signaled early last year that if the United States passed meaningful legislation, it would join in serious efforts to produce an effective treaty. When the Senate failed to follow the lead of the House of Representatives, forcing the president to go to Copenhagen without a new law in hand, the Chinese balked. With the two largest polluters refusing to act, the world community was paralyzed.

Some analysts attribute the failure to an inherent flaw in the design of the chosen solution—arguing that a cap-and-trade approach is too unwieldy and difficult to put in place. Moreover, these critics add, the financial crisis that began in 2008 shook the world's confidence in the use of any market-based solution.

But there are two big problems with this critique: First, there is no readily apparent alternative that would be any easier politically. It is difficult to imagine a globally harmonized carbon tax or a coordinated multilateral regulatory effort. The flexibility of a global market-based policy—supplemented by regulation and revenue-neutral tax policies—is the option that has by far the best chance of success. The fact that it is extremely difficult does not mean that we should simply give up.

Second, we should have no illusions about the difficulty and the time needed to convince the rest of the world to adopt a completely new approach. The lags in the global climate system, including the buildup of heat in the oceans from which it is slowly reintroduced into the atmosphere, means that we can create conditions that make large and destructive consequences inevitable long before their awful manifestations become apparent: the displacement of hundreds of millions of climate refugees, civil unrest, chaos and the collapse of governance in many developing countries, large-scale crop failures and the spread of deadly diseases.

It's important to point out that the United States is not alone in its inaction. Global political paralysis has thus far stymied work not only on climate, but on trade and other pressing issues that require coordinated international action.

The reasons for this are primarily economic. The globalization of the economy, coupled with the outsourcing of jobs from industrial countries, has simultaneously heightened fears of further job losses in the industrial world and encouraged rising expectations in emerging economies. The result? Heightened opposition, in both the industrial and developing worlds, to any constraints on the use of carbon-based fuels, which remain our principal source of energy.

The decisive victory of democratic capitalism over communism in the 1990s led to a period of philosophical dominance for market economics worldwide and the illusion of a unipolar world. It also led, in the United States, to a hubristic "bubble" of market fundamentalism that encouraged opponents of regulatory constraints to mount an aggressive effort to shift the internal boundary between the democracy sphere and the market sphere. Over time, markets would most efficiently solve most problems, they argued. Laws and regulations interfering with the operations of the market carried a faint odor of the discredited statist adversary we had just defeated.

This period of market triumphalism coincided with confirmation by scientists that earlier fears about global warming had been grossly understated. But by then, the political context in which this debate took form was tilted heavily toward the views of market fundamentalists, who fought to weaken existing constraints and scoffed at the possibility that global constraints would be needed to halt the dangerous dumping of global-warming pollution into the atmosphere.

Over the years, as the science has become clearer and clearer, some industries and companies whose business plans are dependent on unrestrained pollution of the atmospheric commons have become ever more entrenched. They are ferociously fighting against the mildest regulation—just as tobacco companies blocked constraints on the marketing of cigarettes for four decades after science confirmed the link of cigarettes to diseases of the lung and the heart.

Simultaneously, changes in America's political system—including the replacement of newspapers and magazines by television as the dominant medium of communication—conferred powerful advantages on wealthy advocates of unrestrained markets and weakened advocates of legal and regulatory reforms. Some news media organizations now present showmen masquerading as political thinkers who package hatred and divisiveness as entertainment. And as in times past, that has proved to be a potent drug in the veins of the body politic. Their most consistent theme is to label as "socialist" any proposal to reform exploitive behavior in the marketplace.

From the standpoint of governance, what is at stake is our ability to use the rule of law as an instrument of human redemption. After all has been said and so little done, the truth about the climate crisis—inconvenient as ever—must still be faced.

The pathway to success is still open, though it tracks the outer boundary of what we are capable of doing. It begins with a choice by the United States to pass a law establishing a cost for global warming pollution. The House of Representatives has already passed legislation, with some Republican support, to take the first halting steps for pricing greenhouse gas emissions.

Later this week, Senators John Kerry, Lindsey Graham and Joe Lieberman are expected to present for consideration similar cap-and-trade legislation.

I hope that it will place a true cap on carbon emissions and stimulate the rapid development of low-carbon sources of energy.

We have overcome existential threats before. Winston Churchill is widely quoted as having said, "Sometimes doing your best is not good enough. Sometimes, you must do what is required." Now is that time. Public officials must rise to this challenge by doing what is required; and the public must demand that they do so—or must replace them. ❧

Comprehending the Text

1. What burden would be lifted, according to Gore, if we turned to alternative sources of energy?

2. Outline Gore's argument. How does he shape his argument for readers?

3. What steps does Gore think we need to take to solve climate change issues?

Analyzing the Text

1. Does Gore persuade you that global climate change is an important issue? Why or why not?

2. How does Gore employ ethos, logos, and pathos in his essay?

3. Who do you think is Gore's audience? How do you know?

The Omnivore's Dilemma: A Natural History of Four Meals (excerpt)

Michael Pollan is a journalist and author of *In Defense of Food: An Eater's Manifesto* and *The Omnivore's Dilemma: A Natural History of Four Meals,* which was named by the *New York Times* and the *Washington Post* as one of the ten best books of 2006.

Prereading Think about your eating habits. What types of food do you eat? Are you a vegetarian? Do you buy organic foods? What factors influence what you eat?

What should we have for dinner?

This book is a long and fairly involved answer to this seemingly simple question. Along the way, it also tries to figure out how such a simple question could ever have gotten so complicated. As a culture we seem to have arrived at a place where whatever native wisdom we may once have possessed about eating has been replaced by confusion and anxiety. Somehow this most elemental of activities—figuring out what to eat—has come to require a remarkable amount of expert help. How did we ever get to a point where we need investigative journalists to tell us where our food comes from and nutritionists to determine the dinner menu?

For me the absurdity of the situation became inescapable in the fall of 2002, when one of the most ancient and venerable staples of human life abruptly disappeared from the American dinner table. I'm talking of course about bread. Virtually overnight, Americans changed the way they eat. A collective spasm of what can only be described as carbophobia seized the country, supplanting an era of national lipophobia dating to the Carter administration. That was when, in 1977, a Senate committee had issued a set of "dietary goals" warning beef-loving Americans to lay off the red meat. And so we dutifully had done, until now.

What set off the sea change? It appears to have been a perfect media storm of diet books, scientific studies, and one timely magazine article. The new diet books, many of them inspired by the formerly discredited Dr. Robert C. Atkins, brought Americans the welcome news that they could eat more meat and lose weight just so long as they laid off the bread and pasta. These high-protein, low-carb diets found support in a handful of new epidemiological studies suggesting that the nutritional orthodoxy that had held sway in America since the 1970s might be wrong. It was not, as official opinion claimed, fat that made us fat, but the carbohydrates we'd been eating precisely in order to stay slim. So conditions were ripe for a swing of the dietary pendulum when, in the summer of 2002, the *New York Times Magazine* published a cover story on the new research entitled "What if Fat Doesn't Make You Fat?" Within months, supermarket shelves were restocked and restaurant menus rewritten to reflect the new nutritional wisdom. The blamelessness of steak restored, two of the most wholesome and uncontroversial foods known to man—bread and pasta—acquired a moral stain that promptly bankrupted dozens of bakeries and noodle firms and ruined an untold number of perfectly good meals.

So violent a change in a culture's eating habits is surely the sign of a national eating disorder. Certainly it would never have happened in a culture in possession of deeply rooted traditions surrounding food and eating. But then, such a culture would not feel the need for its most august legislative body to ever deliberate the nation's "dietary goals"—or, for that matter, to wage political battle every few years over the precise design of an official government graphic called the "food pyramid." A country with a stable culture of food would not shell out millions for the quackery (or common sense) of a new diet book every January. It would not be susceptible to the pendulum swings of food scares or fads, to the apotheosis every few years of one newly discovered nutrient and the demonization of another. It would not be apt to confuse protein bars and food supplements with meals or breakfast cereals with medicines. It probably would not eat a fifth of its meals in cars or feed fully a third of its children at a fast-food outlet every day. And it surely would not be nearly so fat.

Nor would such a culture be shocked to discover that there are other countries, such as Italy and France, that decide their dinner questions on the basis of such quaint and unscientific criteria as pleasure and tradition, eat all manner of "unhealthy" foods, and, lo and behold, wind up actually healthier and happier in their eating than we are. We show our surprise at this by speaking of something called the "French paradox," for how could a people who eat such demonstrably toxic substances as foie gras and triple crème cheese actually be slimmer and healthier than we are? Yet I wonder if it doesn't make more sense to speak in terms of an American paradox—that is, a notably unhealthy people obsessed by the idea of eating healthily.

To one degree or another, the question of what to have for dinner assails every omnivore, and always has. When you can eat just about anything nature has to offer, deciding what you should eat will inevitably stir anxiety, especially when some of the potential foods on offer are liable to sicken or kill you. This is the omnivore's dilemma, noted long ago by writers like Rousseau and Brillat-Savarin and first given that name thirty years ago by a University of Pennsylvania research psychologist named Paul Rozin. I've borrowed his phrase for the title of this book because the omnivore's dilemma turns out to be a particularly sharp tool for understanding our present predicaments surrounding food.

In a 1976 paper called "The Selection of Foods by Rats, Humans, and Other Animals" Rozin contrasted the omnivore's existential situation with that of the specialized eater, for whom the dinner question could not be simpler. The koala bear doesn't worry about what to eat: If it looks and smells and tastes like a eucalyptus leaf, it must be dinner. The koala's culinary preferences are hardwired in its genes. But for omnivores like us (and the rat) a vast amount of brain space and time must be devoted to figuring out which of all the many potential dishes nature lays on are safe to eat. We rely on our prodigious powers of recognition and memory to guide us away from poisons (Isn't that the mushroom that made me sick last week?) and toward nutritious plants (The red berries are the juicier, sweeter ones). Our taste buds help too, predisposing us toward sweetness, which signals carbohydrate energy in nature, and away from bitterness, which is how many of the toxic alkaloids produced by plants taste. Our inborn sense of disgust keeps us from ingesting things that might infect us, such as rotten meat. Many anthropologists believe that the reason we evolved such big and intricate brains was precisely to help us deal with the omnivore's dilemma.

Being a generalist is of course a great boon as well as a challenge; it is what allows humans to successfully inhabit virtually every terrestrial environment on the planet. Omnivory offers the pleasures of variety, too. But the surfeit of choice brings with it a lot of stress and leads to a kind of Manichaean view of food, a division of nature into The Good Things to Eat, and The Bad.

The rat must make this all-important distinction more or less on its own, each individual figuring out for itself—and then remembering—which things will nourish and which will poison. The human omnivore has, in addition to his senses and memory, the incalculable advantage of a culture, which stores the experience and accumulated wisdom of countless human tasters before us. I don't need to experiment with the mushroom now called, rather helpfully, the "death cap," and it is common knowledge that that first intrepid lobster eater was on to something very good. Our culture codifies the rules of wise eating in an elaborate structure of taboos, rituals, recipes, manners, and culinary traditions that keep us from having to reenact the omnivore's dilemma at every meal.

One way to think about America's national eating disorder is as the return, with an almost atavistic vengeance, of the omnivore's dilemma. The cornucopia of the American supermarket has thrown us back on a bewildering food landscape where we once again have to worry that some of those tasty-looking morsels might kill us. (Perhaps not as quickly as a poisonous mushroom, but just as surely.) Certainly the extraordinary abundance of food in America complicates the whole problem of choice. At the same time, many of the tools with which people historically managed the omnivore's dilemma have lost their sharpness here—or simply failed. As a relatively new nation drawn from many different immigrant populations, each with its own culture of food, Americans have never had a single, strong, stable culinary tradition to guide us.

The lack of a steadying culture of food leaves us especially vulnerable to the blandishments of the food scientist and the marketer, for whom the omnivore's dilemma is not so much a dilemma as an opportunity. It is very much in the interest of the food industry to exacerbate our anxieties about what to eat, the better to then assuage them with new products. Our bewilderment in the supermarket is no accident; the return of the omnivore's dilemma has deep roots in the modern food industry, roots that, I found, reach all the way back to fields of corn growing in places like Iowa.

And so we find ourselves where we do, confronting in the supermarket or at the dinner table the dilemmas of omnivorousness, some of them ancient and others never before imagined. The organic apple or the conventional? And if the organic, the local one or the imported? The wild fish or the farmed? The transfats or the butter or the "not butter"? Shall I be a carnivore or a vegetarian? And if a vegetarian, a lacto-vegetarian or a vegan? Like the hunter-gatherer picking a novel mushroom off the forest floor and consulting his sense memory to determine its edibility, we pick up the package in the supermarket and, no longer so confident of our senses, scrutinize the label, scratching our heads over the meaning of phrases like "heart healthy," "no transfats," "cage-free," or "range-fed." What is "natural grill flavor" or TBHQ or xanthan gum? What is all this stuff, anyway, and where in the world did it come from?

My wager in writing The Omnivore's Dilemma was that the best way to answer the questions we face about what to eat was to go back to the very beginning, to follow the food chains that sustain us, all the way from the earth to the plate—to a small number of actual meals. I wanted to look at the getting and eating of food at its most fundamental, which is to say, as a transaction between species in nature, eaters and eaten. ("The whole of nature," wrote the English author William Ralph Inge, "is a conjugation of the verb to eat, in the active and passive.") What I try to do in this book is approach the dinner question as a naturalist might, using the long lenses of ecology and anthropology, as well as the shorter, more intimate lens of personal experience.

My premise is that like every other creature on earth, humans take part in a food chain, and our place in that food chain, or web, determines to a considerable extent what kind of creature we are. The face of our omnivorousness has done much to shape our nature, both body (we possess the omnicompetent teeth and jaws of the omnivore, equally well suited to tearing meat and grinding seeds) and soul. Our prodigious powers of observation and memory, as well as our curious and experimental stance toward the natural world, owe much to the biological fact of omnivorousness. So do the various adaptations we've evolved to defeat the defenses of other creatures so that we might eat them, including our skills at hunting and cooking with fire. Some philosophers have argued that the very open-endedness of human appetite is responsible for both our savagery and civility, since a creature that could conceive of eating anything (including, notably, other humans) stands in particular need of ethical rules, manners, and rituals. We are not only what we eat, but how we eat, too.

Yet we are also different from most of nature's other eaters—markedly so. For one thing, we've acquired the ability to substantially modify the food chains we depend on, by means of such revolutionary technologies as cooking with fire, hunting with tools, farming, and food preservation. Cooking opened up whole new vistas of edibility by rendering various plants and animals more digestible, and overcoming many of the chemical defenses other species deploy against being eaten. Agriculture allowed us to vastly multiply the populations of a few favored food species, and therefore in turn our own. And, most recently, industry has allowed us to reinvent the human food chain, from the synthetic fertility of the soil to the microwaveable can of soup designed to fit into a car's cup holder. The implications of this last revolution, for our health and the health of the natural world, we are still struggling to grasp.

The Omnivore's Dilemma is about the three principal food chains that sustain us today: the industrial, the organic, and the hunter-gatherer. Different as they are, all three food chains are systems for doing more or less the same thing: linking us, through what we eat, to the fertility of the earth and the energy of the sun. It might be hard to see how, but even a Twinkie does this—constitutes an engagement with the natural world. As ecology teaches, and this book tries to show, it's all connected, even the Twinkie.

Ecology also teaches that all life on earth can be viewed as a competition among species for the solar energy captured by green plants and stored in the form of complex

Writer Citizen

carbon molecules. A food chain is a system for passing those calories on to species that lack the plant's unique ability to synthesize them from sunlight. One of the themes of this book is that the industrial revolution of the food chain, dating to the close of World War II, has actually changed the fundamental rules of this game. Industrial agriculture has supplanted a complete reliance on the sun for our calories with something new under the sun: a food chain that draws much of its energy from fossil fuels instead. (Of course, even that energy originally came from the sun, but unlike sunlight it is finite and irreplaceable.) The result of this innovation has been a vast increase in the amount of food energy available to our species; this has been a boon to humanity (allowing us to multiply our numbers), but not an unalloyed one. We've discovered that an abundance of food does not render the omnivore's dilemma obsolete. To the contrary, abundance seems only to deepen it, giving us all sorts of new problems and things to worry about.

Each of this book's three parts follows one of the principal human food chains from beginning to end: from a plant, or group of plants, photosynthesizing calories in the sun, all the way to a meal at the din-way we ate then. In order to make this meal I had to learn how to do some unfamiliar things, including hunting game and foraging for wild mushrooms and urban tree fruit. In doing so I was forced to confront some of the most elemental questions—and dilemmas—faced by the human omnivore: What are the moral and psychological implications of killing, preparing, and eating a wild animal? How does one distinguish between the delicious and the deadly when foraging in the woods? How do the alchemies of the kitchen transform the raw stuffs of nature into some of the great delights of human culture?

The end result of this adventure was what I came to think of as the Perfect Meal, not because it turned out so well (though in my humble opinion it did), but because this labor- and thought-intensive dinner, enjoyed in the company of fellow foragers, gave me the opportunity, so rare in modern life, to eat in full consciousness of everything involved in feeding myself: For once, I was able to pay the full karmic price of a meal.

Yet as different as these three journeys (and four meals) turned out to be, a few themes kept cropping up. One is that there exists a fundamental tension between the logic of nature and the logic of human industry, at least as it is presently organized. Our ingenuity in feeding ourselves is prodigious, but at various points our technologies come into conflict with nature's ways of doing things, as when we seek to maximize efficiency by planting crops or raising animals in vast mono-cultures. This is something nature never does, always and for good reasons practicing diversity instead. A great many of the health and environmental problems created by our food system owe to our attempts to oversimplify nature's complexities, at both the growing and the eating ends of our food chain. At either end of any food chain you find a biological system—a patch of soil, a human body—and the health of one is connected—literally—to the health of the other. Many of the problems of health and nutrition we face today trace back to things that happen on the farm, and behind those things stand specific government policies few of us know anything about.

I don't mean to suggest that human food chains have only recently come into conflict with the logic of biology; early agriculture and, long before that, human hunting proved enormously destructive. Indeed, we might never have needed agriculture had earlier generations of hunters not eliminated the species they depended upon. Folly in the getting of our food is nothing new. And yet the new follies we are perpetrating in our industrial food chain today are of a different order. By replacing solar energy with fossil fuel, by raising millions of food animals in close confinement, by feeding those animals foods they never evolved to eat, and by feeding ourselves foods far more novel than we even realize, we are taking risks with our health and the health of the natural world that are unprecedented.

Another theme, or premise really, is that the way we eat represents our most profound engagement with the natural world. Daily, our eating turns nature into culture, transforming the body of the world into our bodies and minds. Agriculture has done more to reshape the natural world than anything else we humans do, both its landscapes and the composition of its flora and fauna. Our eating also constitutes a relationship with dozens of other species—plants, animals, and fungi—with which we have coevolved to the point where our fates are deeply entwined. Many of these species have evolved expressly to gratify our desires, in the intricate dance of domestication that has allowed us and them to prosper together as we could never have prospered apart. But our relationships with the wild species we eat—from the mushrooms we pick in the forest to the yeasts that leaven our bread—are no less compelling, and far more mysterious. Eating puts us in touch with all that we share with the other animals, and all that sets us apart. It defines us.

What is perhaps most troubling, and sad, about industrial eating is how thoroughly it obscures all these relationships and connections. To go from the chicken (Gallus gallus) to the Chicken McNugget is to leave this world in a journey of forgetting that could hardly be more costly, not only in terms of the animal's pain but in our pleasure, too. But forgetting, or not knowing in the first place, is what the industrial food chain is all about, the principal reason it is so opaque, for if we could see what lies on the far side of the increasingly high walls of our industrial agriculture, we would surely change the way we eat.

"Eating is an agricultural act," as Wendell Berry famously said. It is also an ecological act, and a political act, too. Though much has been done to obscure this simple fact, how and what we eat determines to a great extent the use we make of the world—and what is to become of it. To eat with a fuller consciousness of all that is at stake might sound like a burden, but in practice few things in life can afford quite as much satisfaction. By comparison, the pleasures of eating industrially, which is to say eating in ignorance, are fleeting. Many people today seem perfectly content eating at the end of an industrial food chain, without a thought in the world; this book is probably not for them. There are things in it that will ruin their appetites. But in the end this is a book about the pleasures of eating, the kinds of pleasure that are only deepened by knowing. ⤙

Comprehending the Text

1. What are the signs of the "national eating disorder" Pollan writes about?
2. How does Pollan define the "omnivore's dilemma"?
3. Explain the premise that Pollan bases his book upon.

Analyzing the Text

1. Though this essay is an introduction to Pollan's book length work, it still presents an argument. What is that argument?
2. Do you encounter the omnivore's dilemma in your own life? In what ways?
3. How is this essay organized? What writing strategies are at work? Are they effective? Why or why not?

Developing Your Skills: Entering the Debate

Read the excerpt from Michael Pollan's introduction to *The Omnivore's Dilemma* carefully. He argues that eating is a "political act," indicating our relationship to the land and the industries that produce the food we need. Think about the food you like to eat. Where does it come from? From what sorts of ingredients is it made? In a short essay, explore your most recent meal and discuss the "politics" of the food you ate. Be creative and reference at least one of the readings in this casebook.

YOUR TURN: Creating Your Ideas

1. Choose one of the readings provided in this casebook to analyze. In a short essay, respond to the following prompts.
   - Identify the reading you have selected, and explain why you chose it.
   - What is the main argument (the thesis) of the reading?
   - What is the perspective taken regarding the environment and environmental issues?
   - What is *your* position on the issues discussed in the reading? Do you agree or disagree?
2. It seems there is general agreement among people, including politicians, that we should take care of the environment because it provides so many basic requirements for our lives. However, there are several ways to approach this

issue given the breadth of the environmental issues that exist. As an educated citizen, what do *you* think we should do about the environment? What is our responsibility? Your task here is to explore and articulate your position on environmental issues.

This task is complex. As we've discussed, a central step to any project in which you need to present your ideas is to narrow your focus. Will you discuss, as Terry Tempest Williams did in her essay "The Clan of the One Breasted Woman" in Chapter 4, the ways in which the land has been damaged by our actions and how we need to take action? Or will you discuss how we need to create sustainable practices? Or will you discuss the need for organic and sustainable farming practices so that we can grow healthy food across the globe? Whatever your interests and viewpoints, you need to narrow in on a specific aspect of the environment.

The following assignment sequence asks you, the citizen writer, to consider this question and demonstrate your ability to use multiple writing strategies to craft your response.

1. Once you decide how *you* feel about environmental issues, select one aspect of the debate for this assignment. Identify a problem that you feel needs to be solved, keeping in mind that you should be true to your values and convictions. You may think this is all hogwash and that government has no responsibility to address any of these issues. You may argue that too much attention is being paid to environmental issues, or that government needs to stop putting so many environmental regulations on business and industry, or that your community needs to use alternative energy-powered vehicles for public transportation, for example.

Then, create a policy argument, including an **action plan** that will be submitted to your state council for approval. *(Be clear about your audience!)* How do you think the community should create change? What steps are needed? Your goal is to outline a realistic plan that the state will adopt and fund. You may not believe that what's happening with the environment is just a natural part of the evolutionary process. Or, maybe you believe that if there is something wrong in the environment, we should just allow the free market and individual entrepreneurial enterprises to deal with the issues. You can develop an argument and a plan of action (or recommended inaction) on the part of the government.

Make sure to use outside sources (including the readings here) to support your analysis of the problem and the plan you propose.

2. Let's assume that the state has decided that your plan will work. As a result, you have received funding to implement this plan on a test basis in your local community. The next important step is to gain the support of the community to follow your plan. How will you convince your fellow citizens to implement your plan?

Some options you might consider include a public service campaign that includes radio announcements, posters, and other forms of advertisement; a newsletter; newspaper articles or a website.

- Choose your method of delivering your persuasive argument.
- Describe the campaign you will create.
- Include one example of the writing you will include in the campaign. For example, write a newsletter announcement inviting public participation; write an op-ed piece for your local paper; design the homepage of the website.
- Explain, in careful detail, the decisions you have to make in order to effectively reach your audience.

3. Good news! Your plan has been adopted by your fellow citizens and is successful. Now, develop at least two promotional items, such as a brochure, poster, blog, podcast, and/or email message, for the rest of the state in order to encourage other towns to take steps to address your environmental issue and adopt your plan. These materials need to educate your audience about your issue, explain why the issue is important, and **persuade** your audience to implement the plan.

Works Cited

American Council on Science and Health. *The Scoop on Smoking*. 2010. Web. 17 June 2010.

Burke, Kenneth. *A Rhetoric of Motives*. Berkeley: University of California Press, 1969. Print.

Burke, Kenneth. *The Philosophy of Literary Form*. Berkeley: University of California Press, 1974. Print.

Carson, Rachel. *Silent Spring*. New York: Houghton Mifflin Harcourt, 2002. Print.

Dewey, John. *Education and Democracy*. Norwood, MA: Norwood Press, 1916. Print.

Didion, Joan. "Why I Write." *The New York Times Book Review* December 5, 1976.: 276. Print.

Dillard, Annie. "Write Till You Drop. The New York Times. May 28, 1989. Web. 19 June 2010.

Ehrenreich, Barbara. *Nickel and Dimed: On (Not) Getting By in America*. New York: Holt Publishers, 2001. Print.

Fremon, Celeste. "Of Girls and Crime and Desks." *WitnessLA*. 6 April 2007. Web. 7 April 2007.

Griffin, Cindy. *Invitation to Public Speaking*. Florence, KY: Cengage/Wadsworth Publishing, 2008. Print.

Hauser, Gerard. *Introduction to Rhetorical Theory*. Longrove, IL: Waveland Press, 2002. Print.

Kaplan, Louis. "A Patriotic Mole: A Living Photograph." *CR: The New Centennial Review* 1. 1 (Spring 2001): 107–139.

Kennedy, George. *Classical Rhetoric and Its Christian and Secular Tradition*. Chapel Hill, NC: University of North Carolina Press, 1999. Print.

Kingston, Maxine Hong. *The Woman Warrior: Memoirs of a Girlhood Among Ghosts,* London: Vintage, 1998. Print.

Lauter, Paul. *Canons and Contexts*. New York: Oxford University Press, 1991. Print.

Levitt, Steven D. and Stephen J. Dubner. *Freakonomics*. New York: Harper Collins, 2009. Print.

Mann, Thomas. *Confessions of Felix Krull, Confidence Man: The Early Years*. London: Vintage Books, 1992. Print.

Marsh, Bill. "A Battle Between the Bottle and the Faucet." *New York Times* July 15, 2007. Web. 19 June 2010.

Morreal, John. *Taking Laughter Seriously.* Albany, NY: SUNY Press, 1983. Print.

"Overview: The Economy—Charts." *About.com.* 2010. Web. 10 March 2010.

Poulakos, Takis. *Speaking for the Polis: Isocrates' Rhetorical Education.* Columbia, SC: University of South Carolina Press, 1997. Print.

Sagan, Carl. *The Dragons of Eden: Speculations on the Evolution of Human Intelligence.* New York: Ballantine Books, 1977. Print.

"Sustainability: Basic Information." *United States Environmental Protection Agency.* 2010. Web. 20 June 2010.